Psychoanalysis Comparable and Incomparable

Psychoanalysis Comparable and Incomparable describes the rationale and ongoing development of a six year programme of highly original meetings conducted by the European Psychoanalytic Federation Working Party on Comparative Clinical Methods. The project comprises over seventy cases discussed by more than five hundred experienced psychoanalysts over the course of sixty workshops.

Authored by a group of leading European psychoanalysts, this book explores ways for psychoanalysts using different approaches to learn from each other when they present their work to fellow psychoanalysts, and provides tools for the individual practitioner to examine and improve his or her own approach. As described in detail in its pages, sticking to the task led to some surprising experiences, raising fundamental questions about the way clinical discussion and supervision are conducted in psychoanalysis.

Well known by many in the psychoanalytic community and the object of much interest and debate, this project is described by those who have had the closest contact with it and will satisfy a widely held curiosity in psychoanalysts and psychotherapists throughout the world.

David Tuckett, Roberto Basile, Dana Birksted-Breen, Tomas Böhm, Paul Denis, Antonino Ferro, Helmut Hinz, Arne Jemstedt, Paola Mariotti, Johan Schubert. The authors of this book are a group of leading European Psychoanalysts asked by the European Psychoanalytic Federation (EPF) to form a working party devoted to understanding and comparing the different ways psychoanalysts work. They include among their number the current and former Editor of the *International Journal of Psychoanalysis* and the former editor of the *Revue Française de Psychoanalyse*. Between them they have contributed numerous books and scientific articles in English and other languages

Perhaps the most critical task for psychoanalysis today is to distinguish a pluralism of valuable ideas from a state of sloppy disarray. Psychoanalysts of different regions and schools have increasing difficulty distinguishing a diversity of valid ideas from mere babel. This extraordinary volume describes the enormous progress made by an ongoing international scientific effort to help analysts identify a core of the psychoanalytic process that is compatible with the variety of theories and techniques that now exists in the international community. By implication, this effort will also draw limits to what is properly considered psychoanalysis. A key element in this project has been the education of groups of analysts to listen to clinical material without the usual supervisory stance; rather, the effort is to understand the implicit analytic concepts of the presenter.

I know of no project more important than this one for the future of psychoanalysis. Each chapter is filled with ideas, and every working analyst will come away from this book stimulated to think in new and interesting ways about his or her own clinical activity.

Arnold M. Cooper, Professor Emeritus in Consultation–Liaison psychiatry at the Weill Cornell Medical College and the Payne Whitney Psychiatric Clinic

THE NEW LIBRARY OF PSYCHOANALYSIS
General Editor   Dana Birksted-Breen

The New Library of Psychoanalysis was launched in 1987 in association with the Institute of Psychoanalysis, London. It took over from the International Psychoanalytical Library which published many of the early translations of the works of Freud and the writings of most of the leading British and Continental psychoanalysts.

The purpose of the New Library of Psychoanalysis is to facilitate a greater and more widespread appreciation of psychoanalysis and to provide a forum for increasing mutual understanding between psychoanalysts and those working in other disciplines such as the social sciences, medicine, philosophy, history, linguistics, literature and the arts. It aims to represent different trends both in British psychoanalysis and in psychoanalysis generally. The New Library of Psychoanalysis is well placed to make available to the English-speaking world psychoanalytic writings from other European countries and to increase the interchange of ideas between British and American psychoanalysts.

The Institute, together with the British Psychoanalytical Society, runs a low-fee psychoanalytic clinic, organizes lectures and scientific events concerned with psychoanalysis and publishes the *International Journal of Psychoanalysis*. It also runs the only UK training course in psychoanalysis which leads to membership of the International Psychoanalytical Association – the body which preserves internationally agreed standards of training, of professional entry, and of professional ethics and practice for psychoanalysis as initiated and developed by Sigmund Freud. Distinguished members of the Institute have included Michael Balint, Wilfred Bion, Ronald Fairbairn, Anna Freud, Ernest Jones, Melanie Klein, John Rickman and Donald Winnicott.

Previous General Editors include David Tuckett, Elizabeth Spillius and Susan Budd. Previous and current Members of the Advisory Board include Christopher Bollas, Ronald Britton, Catalina Bronstein, Donald Campbell, Sara Flanders, Stephen Grosz, John Keene, Eglé Laufer, Juliet Mitchell, Michael Parsons, Rosine Jozef Perelberg, David Taylor and Mary Target, and Richard Rusbridger, who is now Assistant Editor.

ALSO IN THIS SERIES

TITLES IN THE NEW LIBRARY OF PSYCHOANALYSIS TEACHING SERIES

THE NEW LIBRARY OF PSYCHOANALYSIS

General Editor: Dana Birksted–Breen

Psychoanalysis Comparable and Incomparable

The Evolution of a Method to Describe and Compare Psychoanalytic Approaches

David Tuckett, Roberto Basile,
Dana Birksted–Breen, Tomas Böhm,
Paul Denis, Antonino Ferro, Helmut Hinz,
Arne Jemstedt, Paola Mariotti and
Johan Schubert

Routledge
Taylor & Francis Group

LONDON AND NEW YORK

First published 2008
by Routledge
27 Church Road, Hove, East Sussex BN3 2FA

Simultaneously published in the USA and Canada
by Routledge
270 Madison Avenue, New York, NY 10016

Routledge is an imprint of the Taylor & Francis Group, an Informa business

Typeset in Bembo by RefineCatch Limited, Bungay, Suffolk
Printed and bound in Great Britain by
TJ International Ltd, Padstow, Cornwall
Cover design by Sandra Heath

British Library Cataloguing in Publication Data
A catalogue record for this book is available from the British Library

Library of Congress Cataloging-in-Publication Data
Psychoanalysis comparable and incomparable : the evolution of a method to
describe and compare psychoanalytic approaches / [edited by] David Tuckett.
p. ; cm.—(New library of psychoanalysis)
Includes bibliographical references and index.
ISBN 978–0–415–45142–0 (hardback) – ISBN 978–0–415–45143–7 (pbk.)
1. Psychoanalysis. I. Tuckett, David. II. Series: New library of psychoanalysis
(Unnumbered)
[DNLM: 1. Psychoanalysis—methods. 2. Evaluation Studies.
3. Interprofessional Relations. 4. Psychoanalysis—standards.
WM 460 P97439 2008]
RC504.P755 2008
616.89′17—dc22

2007029653

ISBN 978–0–415–45142–0 (Hbk)
ISBN 978–0–415–45143–7 (Pbk)

Contents

Contents

Illustrations

Figures

Tables

About the authors

Roberto Basile is a full member of the International Psychoanalytical Association, an associate member of the Italian Psychoanalytic Society, a guest member of the British Psychoanalytical Association and a member of the European Editorial Board of the *International Journal of Psychoanalysis*. Dr Basile's main research interests include the psychoanalytic field, child psychoanalysis, intersubjectivism and the work of Bion. His recent publications include articles for the *International Journal of Psychoanalysis* and *Psychoanalytic Quarterly*.

Dana Birksted-Breen is a training and supervising psychoanalyst of the British Psychoanalytic Society. She is the general editor of the New Library of Psychoanalysis and the joint editor-in-chief of the *International Journal of Psychoanalysis*. Dr Birksted-Breen has given lectures and taught internationally. She won an international prize for her paper 'Phallus, Penis and Mental Space' (1996, *International Journal of Psychoanalysis*, 77, 4: 649–657). She maintains a full-time private practice in London.

Tomas Böhm is a training analyst and supervisor member of the Swedish Psychoanalytical Society and Swedish Psychoanalytical Association. He also has a private practice. His main research interests include psychoanalytic techniques, love relations, xenophobia, racism, orthodoxy, fundamentalism and revenge phenomena. Dr Böhm's recent publications include articles for the *International Journal of Psychoanalysis* and the *Scandinavian Psychoanalytic Review*. Books in Swedish include (with Suzanne Kaplan) *Revenge – and*

Refraining from Retaliation (2006), *The Love Relation* (2001), *To be Right: About Conviction, Tolerance and Fundamentalism* (1996) and novels, including *The Vienna Jazz Trio* (2000).

Paul Denis is a psychiatrist and psychoanalyst. He is a member of the Paris Psychoanalytical Society and was on the editorial board of *La Psychiatrie de L'Enfant* for many years as well as the *Revue Française de Psychanalyse*. He has worked in the field of child psychoanalysis with Serge Lebovici and Rene Diatkine. Dr Denis was the winner of the Prix Maurice Bouvet in 1991 and is now a permanent member of the prize jury. He is also the author of *Eloge de la Bêtise* (2001).

Antonino Ferro is a training analyst of the SPI (Italian Psychoanalytical Society) and a full member of the International Psychoanalytical Association. He is a 2007 winner of the Sigourney award for Psychoanalysis and also editor for Europe of the *International Journal of Psychoanalysis*. His main research interests include child analysis and severe pathologies. Dr Ferro's recent publications include *Seeds of Illness and Seeds of Recovery: The Genesis of Suffering and the Role of Psychoanalysis* (2004) and *Psychoanalysis as Therapy and Storytelling* (2006).

Helmut Hinz is a psychiatrist, neurologist, psychoanalyst and training analyst of the German Psychoanalytical Association and the International Psychoanalytical Association. He has worked in the University Department for Psychoanalysis, Psychotherapy and Psychosomatics in Tübingen. Dr Hinz has had a private practice for many years as well as being supervisor in two mental hospitals and leader of a Balint-Group. He has also been co-editor of the *Jahrbuch der Psychoanalyse*. He has mainly published in the area of clinical problems including projective identification, involvement, psychotic mechanisms in neurotic patients, suspended attention, preconditions of psychic change, constructions in psychoanalysis and repetition compulsion.

Arne Jemstedt is a psychoanalyst with a private practice in Stockholm. He is a member and training analyst of the Swedish Psychoanalytical Association and director of its Institute. Dr Jemstedt is also a member of the International Editorial Panel for the *Complete Works of D.W. Winnicott* and editor of Swedish translations of Winnicott's work. He is a member of the 'nomenclature group' for the Swedish translation of Freud's *Standard Edition*. He has also published articles and chapters in both Swedish and international psychoanalytic journals and books.

Paola Mariotti is a member of the British Psychoanalytic Society. Dr Mariotti is interested in the criteria of suitability for psychoanalysis as a treatment of choice and has published work on mothering and reproduction.

Johan Schubert is a training analyst of the Swedish Psychoanalytic Society. He is a former member of the board of the Swedish Psychoanalytic Institute and is responsible for the clinical part of the training. After the Swedish Psychoanalytic Institute's training programme was elevated to a college programme in 2001, he was appointed as its first examiner and still holds that role. Dr Schubert is also an Associate Professor at the Karolinska Institute. For many years he was the director of the Institute of Psychotherapy in Stockholm, an institute for treatment, training and research in psychodynamic psychotherapy. He has written on time and termination in psychoanalysis, on outcomes in psychotherapy and on psychotherapy and antidepressant medication.

David Tuckett is a 2007 winner of the Sigourney award for Psychoanalysis, a 2006 Leverhulme Research Fellow and visiting professor at the Psychoanalysis Unit, University College London. He is a training and supervising analyst in the British Psychoanalytical Society and chair of the European Psychoanalytic Federation (EPF) Working Party on comparative clinical methods. Professor Tuckett is a former editor-in-chief of the *International Journal of Psychoanalysis* and has previously authored three books and numerous scientific articles.

Acknowledgements

This book is the fruit of a great deal of labour by many people, starting with my nine co-authors, who have responded magnificently to the challenge of an international writing project, in most cases in a second language. I am very grateful to them for a rewarding and enjoyable experience. Meetings we have had over the years have been the most incredible source of stimulation. As labourers we have also received a great deal of support without which the entire enterprise would have failed long ago and which I now want to acknowledge.

I would like to begin by thanking all the participants in the workshops and especially those who volunteered to present their work and report on the group discussions. About 500 people have taken part in at least one of the six workshop series by now and about 200 have attended three or more; 70 of them have presented their work. I am especially grateful to those recent participants and presenters who filled in the questionnaire we sent them in 2006 asking them to tell us about their experience. I contacted about 120 people once in May 2006 but received over 70 detailed and thoughtful replies. Without all this help we would have little or nothing to report.

A number of colleagues played a significant role in the intellectual development of the project. Haydée Faimberg initiated it and selected the initial moderators – also kindly encouraging them to carry on with the project subsequently, when she went her own way to develop a parallel interest. Haydée also attended and made contributions to several of the main Paris meetings in 2003 and 2004, as did Roger Perron, Evelyne Sechaud and Iréne Matthis. Julia Fabricius and Manuel Fernández Criado were part of the moderator's team before having to leave to keep other commitments and Jorge Canestri,

Werner Bohleber, Paul Denis and Peter Fonagy – as members of the EPF Working Party on Theoretical Issues – frequently provided incisive assistance; on two occasions we formally held joint meetings. Antonino Ferro and Helmut Hinz have attended just about every meeting since Brussels in 2001 and have been continuously imaginative and supportive. Antonino has become an accomplished English speaker over the period and has worked tirelessly to bridge the gap between more Anglo-Saxon and Francophile approaches. I am grateful to all of them.

Next, I would like to thank all the members of the European Psychoanalytic Federation's Executive and Council since 1999. They helped me to devise both the new scientific policy and the idea of working parties as well as supporting the 'new style' conferences. Among them Guillermo Bodner, Vincenzo Bonaminio, Donald Campbell, Domenico Chianese, Shmuel Erlich, Julia Fabricius, Gabor Flaskay, Andreas Giannakoulas, Maria Teresa Hooke, Arne Jemstedt, Gabriele Junkers, Sven Lagerlof, Aira Laine, Timmo Niemi, Frederico Pereira, Emma Piccioli, Eike Wolf, Jordi Sala, Michael Sebek, Evelyne Sechaud, Imre Szecödy and Anders Zachrisson many times went out of their way to help. It was the EPF and the financial success of the new style conferences we introduced which provided the funding for the working party – for tape-recording and transcription but principally for travel to the Paris meetings. The two treasurers over the period, Henk Jan Dalewijk and Duveken Engels, deserve special mention for their support and appropriately imaginative ingenuity.

We have also been helped a great deal by our colleagues from the International Psychoanalytic Association (IPA). The earliest meetings (along with the activities of the other working parties) were funded from a small IPA regional grant, negotiated with Piers Pendred, Robert Tyson and Otto Kernberg of the IPA. The research undertaken by Naama Ben Yehoyada was then financed with a grant from the IPA Research Advisory Board. I am grateful to Marianne Leuzinger Bohleber, Peter Fonagy, Robert Wallerstein and the anonymous referees for that help. Then since 2004 all the EPF working parties have been funded by the EPF's ten-year scientific initiative and the IPA's Developing Psychoanalytic Practice and Training programme. This support, and all the efforts of Daniel Widlocher, Donald Campbell, Nadine Levinson, Claudio Eizirik and Peter Blos to go on making it possible, have been important. I am very grateful. They have made it possible for me to assist several research-orientated colleagues to attend the workshops and work hard on the transcription and conceptualization of the workshop discussions. Charu Mangla Goel, Mary Heller, Maria Parissis, Annsi Perakyla, Alejandra Perez and Anne Ward have done this work and continue to do so. I am grateful to them and to Naama Ben Yehoyada for their dedication.

I am also very grateful to Olivier Bonard, Michael Diercks, Dimitri James Jackson, Anssi Perakyla, Bernard Reith and Anne Ward for their careful comments on reading various sections of the manuscript. The completion of the book would also not have been possible without the very skilful help of Elizabeth Allison and William Brown at the UCL Psychoanalysis Unit. Liz and William are gifted scholars and editors and I am deeply indebted to them and to Peter Fonagy, who very kindly lent them to us, for all their work in putting an otherwise incomprehensible manuscript into something much nearer readable English than before.

Dana Birksted-Breen, the editor of the New Library of Psychoanalysis (NLP) and also a moderator and co-author, has throughout the project been a highly committed source of initiative, strength and encouragement. I am very grateful to her. The NLP is peer reviewed so this book was assessed by Dana's deputy, Richard Rusbridger, as well as three anonymous readers. We are grateful to them for the care they took with their comments.

Finally, I should like to thank my family. Writing a book is a considerable intrusion into family time and especially in this case as my wife (Paola Mariotti) was both a moderator and co-author. I am very grateful to her for her many creative and incisive ideas and for her ongoing advice and support. My youngest daughter, Miranda, has the final mention. She has produced numerous PowerPoint slides for presentations and helped to design all the tables and figures in the book.

David Tuckett
July 2007

Time chart

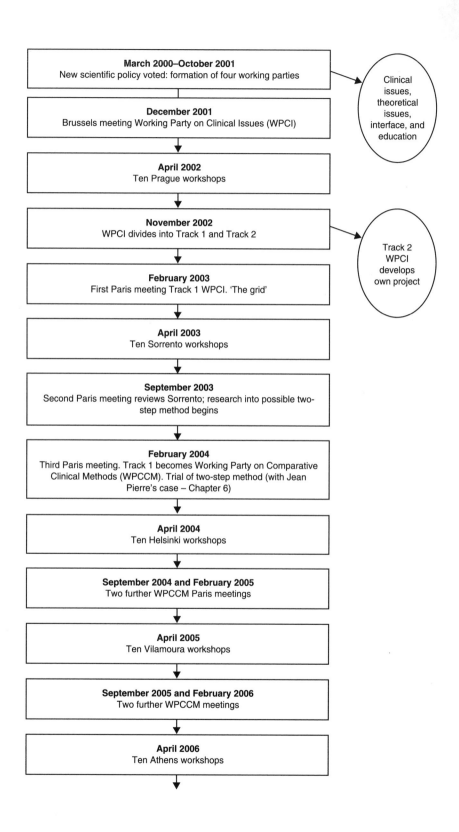

Introductory foreword

Dana Birksted-Breen (UK)

The project described in this book started off as a desire to increase communication between psychoanalysts working in different traditions, using the annual conferences of the European Federation as the point of contact. It was also an attempt, in a world of ever-increasing psychotherapeutic approaches and a blurring of boundaries between psychoanalysis and psychotherapy, to define what psychoanalysis is.

To be meaningful, this would not be approached from a theoretical angle or from the angle of the setting (frequency of sessions, etc). Instead we would start from the observation of what happens in practice when a psychoanalyst is 'doing psychoanalysis'. Only once we had recorded and abstracted the multiplicity of ways of working would we begin to be able to address the question: what is and what is not psychoanalysis? It was important not to confuse plurality with the idea that 'anything goes' (Tuckett, 2005). This meant finding a way of abstracting the models that lay, usually implicitly, behind the different ways of working, eventually describing various 'types'. Such an approach meant recognizing that psychoanalysis cannot be psychoanalysis without the structure of a theoretical model, even if models vary. In my view, this is the recognition of the importance of 'the third' – that is, of the oedipal structure at the heart of psychoanalysis. To be psychoanalysis the two person situation must include a theory as its 'third object'. Psychoanalysis is not just two people talking; the setting itself implies a theoretical structure which comes from outside and is essential to it. This is why the theory, which may vary with practitioners, is an

1

inherently necessary feature. Respecting difference is the other essential element of the oedipal structure, which is based upon differences of sex and generation.

The project did not start with a hypothesis to be tested, but with an open-ended investigation, which, in its trajectory, developed a lens for observing phenomena. During the project, what came as a surprise was that in itself the development of a new method of looking at the various implicit theoretical models and the differences between them proved interesting – both in terms of the evolution of that method and the collecting of the data. The way of looking became as interesting as the findings. In this sense, the project paralleled psychoanalysis itself, with the process being the aim (Donnet, 2001). The new method is also like psychoanalysis in that by its nature it is constantly evolving. Furthermore, it can also be said that we were all 'participant observers' (Malinowski, 1922) in the workshops at the annual conferences, just as the psychoanalyst is simultaneously inside and outside the analytic situation, objective and subjective, and influencing and influenced.

What also came as a surprise was that what had started out as an investigation into different models turned out to be a new way of facilitating a new and fascinating clinical discussion among colleagues from different 'schools' and cultures. This was reflected in the enthusiasm of many participants, who joined the workshops in increasing numbers and who took a version of our comparative method back to their own country to use with their colleagues. This is not to say that the new method of comparing models and the project as a whole were without opposition, in particular from those who have an 'allergic' reaction to anything that involves systematic investigation. Nevertheless, as it became clear that the new approach was psychoanalytic in its spirit, these negative reactions subsided.

The novelty of this comparative method lies in a dual shift in perspective: from the patient to the analyst and from emphasizing a single 'truth' to valuing difference. Instead of the traditional discussion of a 'case' in which the leader and participants suggest a better or deeper understanding of the clinical material, there is a radical shift of focus towards understanding the analyst herself, what she is doing in the psychoanalytic encounter, and for what reason. The attempt to elucidate the implicit model of the presenter/analyst shifts attention away from evaluation and towards understanding. This is the hallmark of psychoanalysis in the consulting room: the psychoanalyst's role is to

2

understand rather than to judge the patient's way of thinking and the beliefs that it rests on. Furthermore, the new comparative method involves a shift in perspective, in that it involves trying to transcend, or at the very least question, one's own point of view and to place an interest specifically in difference and different points of view. This is made possible by the very lengthy and very detailed discussions of material, which is an integral aspect of the method.

In my view this comparative, clinical method does not *replace* the more traditional clinical discussion or supervision (each still has its place in certain settings), but it does add to the possibilities of exchange and of a new kind of discussion, a discussion in which perspectives shift in an interesting and valuable way, and, perhaps, given the multi-cultural nature of our psychoanalytic world nowadays, even in an essential way. We believe that this shift in perspective is helped and enhanced by a formal method. It is always easy, when coming from a different tradition, to offer alternative, 'deeper' (and, in some analysts' eyes, even 'better') interpretations; but, when the model is different, and/or when the 'third' position/object is a different one, the new interpretation often makes little sense and cannot help the analyst whose work is being presented. I believe that a current analytic situation can be fully understood only if the 'third object', the psycho-analyst's theory, is understood. Only once that model and its effect in shaping the current analytic situation are taken into account can an alternative interpretation be meaningful and useful to the analyst. Only then can there be a productive intercourse between two different minds. Otherwise we are in the territory of 'wild analysis'.

This book serves several different purposes: to find out about a method for enabling a new kind of clinical discussion and for en-abling a discussion about psychoanalysis; to find out about a way of enabling an exchange between different psychoanalytic cultures; to further a discussion about epistemological issues; and to find out about a method that can be developed further for research and/or for educational purposes.

The chapters themselves reflect a multiplicity of styles and perspec-tives. In Chapter 1, David Tuckett introduces the aims, early efforts, and the difficulties and surprises that have arisen from this project. Three theoretical chapters, by Paul Denis (Chapter 2), Helmut Hinz (Chapter 5) and David Tuckett (Chapter 6), underpin the book from different angles. Interwoven with these are descriptions of the stages of development of the method, by Tomas Böhm (Chapter 3), Arne

Jemstedt (Chapter 4) and Dana Birksted-Breen, Antonino Ferro and Paola Mariotti (Chapter 7). These developments are then revisited by Johan Schubert (Chapter 8) from the perspective of group processes and with the benefit of participants' own comments. Next, Roberto Basile and Antonino Ferro (Chapter 9) provide their thoughts and those of some participants and presenters on the value of our proposed comparative method, particularly in the light of traditional super-vision or what we might term 'over-vision', to use the phrase that David Tuckett coins in the concluding comments (Chapter 10). This kaleidoscope of perspectives is in the spirit of the method and of the project as a whole. Each of the contributors has his or her own per-spective, but feels able to collaborate in an interchange of ideas that has proved fruitful and rewarding.

On difference, discussing differences and comparison

An introduction

David Tuckett (UK)

- How do we know when what is happening between two people should be called psychoanalysis?
- What is a psychoanalytic process?
- How do we know when one is taking place?

Recognizing difference provides scope for thought. Comparison aids reflection. Difference, differentiation and comparison allow articulated thought and are at the heart of much creative development in many fields. But difference is also a potential fault line at the heart of the human psyche – and one along which prejudice, stigma, projection and xenocidal impulses can flow.

This book is about developing ways to describe and compare different methods of practising as a psychoanalyst. The aspiration behind the project is to develop ways of learning from each other, and to provide tools for individual practitioners to examine and improve their own approach. As we will be describing, this task has led us to some surprising experiences and has raised fundamental questions about the way clinical discussion and supervision are conducted in psychoanalysis.

This chapter will describe the background to the project's inception, the early enthusiasm, the somewhat unexpected emotional and conceptual difficulties we encountered, and the outlines of the way we came to approach them. Each of the subsequent chapters will add details and further reflection, with a final chapter looking at wider uses of the method of clinical discussion that eventually evolved. We will argue that although psychoanalysis is unique and, therefore, incomparable, methods of practising can usefully be compared.

The growth of pluralism and its difficulties

Different conceptions of the psychoanalytic project have existed since its beginning (see, for example, Bergmann, 2004). Before now, however, these differences have not provided the basis for a creative and sustained process of elaboration, in which the common ground of psychoanalysis has become deeper, more secure or consensual.

In Freud's lifetime, differences over technique and practice were largely held in check by the use of his authority to silence dissent (Bergmann, 2004; see also Tuckett, 2000). The tendency to invoke Freud as a silencing authority persisted even after his death, while individual psychoanalysts were similarly able to command authority in particular geographical or social contexts. In such contexts, deviants were controlled by a significant element of self-censorship, actual censorship and, in the last resort, by exclusion. Divergent individuals and their ideas could be and were deprived of influential positions in professional organizations or they were expelled completely. Others just walked out, together with key followers, before starting their own training institutions – a tendency shared by 'scientific' journals, meaning that there have been an increasing number of them over the years. Such methods of 'resolving' differences (i.e. by isolating and removing deviance) have been highly problematic – with a tendency at times for orthodoxy to enjoy an 'intellectual reign of terror' (Cooper, 2003).

All psychoanalytic groups have experienced charismatic authority, with the problem intensified by the integral role of training analyses, which have inevitable emotional and social consequences within societal life. Some groups were more affected than others and some developed ways of institutionalizing differences within subgroups rather than removing them to different groups (see, for example, King and Steiner, 1991). Nonetheless, insofar as it existed, the reign of terror is now largely over, and the imposition of orthodoxy by authority has failed. This can, at least partially, be explained by anti-authoritarian changes in cultural and political ideology in the latter part of the twentieth century. It may also follow from the fact that psychoanalysts in many places find a faltering demand for their services, as well as a declining supply of trainees, thus forcing them to work in more innovative ways (see, for example, Ahmed, 1994; Allison, 2000; Jaffe and Pulver, 1978; Rothstein, 1992; Wurmser, 1989, 1994). Most groups now have a wide range of different ways of practising within their membership.

It has seemed to me that to survive and to compete, adjustments have been made, for example in the criteria for analysability (now encompassing the more 'difficult' patient), and in the demands psychoanalysis has made on both the patient's and the analyst's time. Psychoanalysis has tried to become less elitist and more friendly, as well as less medical – whether these changes developed as a result of innovation within established societies moving towards a less authoritarian stance, or through the development of new ideas by those once excluded by but now embraced in new institutions. A further factor has been the greater accessibility of analysts' own analysis for critical discussion and appraisal.

From the beginning of the discipline, training analyses have left a residue of unconscious ambivalent feelings about the process, including a lack of conviction about its efficacy, prompting both conscious doubt and unconscious hostility, the latter evident not so much directly but through observable defences such as the idealization or denigration of institutions, analytic methods and colleagues (see, for example, Bergmann, 2004; Kernberg, 1986, 1993, 2006, 2007). Such residues have also sparked changes – be they progressive or regressive.

The main argument in this book is that in the absence of open discussion about differences in psychoanalytic technique, the debate about opposing ideas and practices has been very difficult to maintain – with what I consider many negative consequences for psychoanalysis' creative development as a secure and specific discipline. The usual way of proceeding in academia is by the critical scrutiny and debate of new approaches and ideas, leading to a consensus about the evidence for and usefulness of a particular argument. In the field of psychoanalysis, however, this approach has mostly been eschewed on account of the unease and dissatisfaction that many psychoanalysts seem to feel about the value of using evidence from their consulting rooms to support points to each other.

On the one hand, most reports of psychoanalytic sessions are thought of as inadequate to convey the subtlety of the unique experience of human individuality. On the other hand, they are dismissed as flawed because they are too subjective to 'prove' anything. In short, the task of convincingly conveying ways of understanding one person's unconscious to another person has been considered too great for many to undertake. As a result, empirical study in psychoanalysis has often been overwhelmed by attempts to impose authority through theoretical and oratorical rhetoric – despite Freud's undoubted commitment to some form of 'facts'. Paul Denis discusses this at greater length in Chapter 2.

A consequence of the reliance on authority and exclusion is that psychoanalytic differences have tended to become politicized as well as personalized, something that Chapter 2 also demonstrates. Since about 1970 (and particularly in North and South America) this has to me seemed rather clear: struggles over differences in theory, practice and transmission have largely become the history of politics and personalities (see, for example, Richards (2003) and the following commentaries). As mentioned, the context of psychoanalytic politics has altered so that the capacity to impose authority seems to have become greatly weakened in recent times. However, one of the untoward consequences of this has been a plethora of ideas and techniques described in different languages, often using the same concepts to describe entirely different ideas (see, for example, Canestri, 2002; Hinz, 2002; Spillius, 2002).

It must be granted that a clear formulation of psychoanalytic ideas is inherently difficult. Concepts are elastic and practice is implicit (Sandler, 1983). Moreover, the discipline deals with subjective experience beyond consciousness and reason. At its heart it is and must be individualistic, emotional and highly personal. The unconscious processes codified by Freud are condensation, displacement and absence of contradiction. They involve symmetrical (rather than Aristotelian) logic – in which ordinarily divergent propositions are equally true, space is multi-dimensional and time is bi-directional or even 'shattered' (Faimberg, 2005; Green, 2000; Matte Blanco, 1988). Practice necessarily involves sensibility and intuition as well as cognition.

To add to all this, psychoanalytic data are hard to transmit between persons. 'Misunderstandings between psychoanalysts from different schools or different countries are not common – they are the norm', writes Denis in Chapter 2 (p. 38). Fundamental to psychoanalysis is that understanding is inherently personal and emotional, dependent on the feelings and phantasies that a particular set of ideas or practices evoke in the subject, and many of which influence comprehension in ways of which the subject is not conscious. This is one reason why the transmission of psychoanalysis from one generation to another has not been easy; insofar as there is a gap between experience and theory, this is especially true in the area of technique. Further exacerbating this gap between experience and theory is the tendency for such lacunae to have been filled using 'authority' and 'deference' – perhaps leading to an unconscious, sadomasochistic and unnecessary submission to said authority, and to the unstable and ambivalent relationship to knowledge and teachers that such a submission would imply.

Since the early 1980s, it has seemed to me that the difficulties in transmitting psychoanalysis have accumulated, becoming fused with the problems of evaluating individual differences in practice. Together with the various efforts to treat more disturbed patients, these trends have led to gradual but significant shifts in views about what psychoanalysis 'really' is about, as well as many alterations in the understood meaning of important concepts. A situation has arisen whereby there are multiple viewpoints concerning both the practice and the theory of psychoanalysis, and it this multiplicity that we term as 'pluralism'.[1]

It has also seemed to me inevitable that once pluralism was finally accepted – as it needed to be – the pace of 'pluralistic' tolerance of new and varied approaches would accelerate. Nothing really exists to contain or discipline it. In fact, the pace of change that has characterized the period since the early 1980s has been so rapid that it is now seriously difficult to know what does and does not constitute psychoanalytic work, and so it is difficult to distinguish when it is being practised creatively and competently.

Moreover, to the extent that this is an accurate observation, significant difficulties within the profession are compounded at the interface with other professions. In the absence of operational clarity, it is inevitable that boundary relationships with psychoanalytical psychotherapy have become marred either by confusion or by the arbitrary politics of exclusion. If there is no reliable and definitive difference in definition and practice between psychoanalysis and psychoanalytical

---

[1] I am indebted to Robert Wallerstein for a conversation in 1990, in which he explained to me the crucial role played by Heinz Kohut in American psychoanalysis: Kohut and self psychology were the first major deviations from orthodoxy that did not lead to exclusion. Kohut himself was President of the American Psychoanalytic Association before becoming the 'inventor of self psychology and the revered and excoriated leader of this new movement within psychoanalysis that claimed to raise psychoanalytic theory and technique to a new conceptual level' (Cooper, 1988: 175).

psychotherapy, then boundaries inevitably get determined by bureaucratic decisions with potentially harmful consequences to all.

Throughout the course of this book many accounts will support the idea of a very wide range of contradictory practices calling themselves 'psychoanalysis', as well as much confusion in current psychoanalytic theory and technique – particularly at the level of its specific implementation. Such confusion may be highlighted for the reader if he or she takes a moment to consider the challenge of trying to give clear exemplified answers to questions like the following:

- What is a *psychoanalytic* interpretation and when and for what purpose can it be said to be a transference interpretation?
- Is all practice by a psychoanalyst psychoanalysis? What is the difference between psychoanalysis and psychotherapy – especially if practised by the same person?
- What does it mean when a psychoanalyst advocates attending to a patient's unconscious and (if we describe it in traditional terms) how exactly can we recognize when free association and free-floating attention are taking place?
- When and for what purpose might an analyst 'construct' hitherto unconscious traces of a patient's history or infantile sexual wishes and phantasies; how does the analyst know when such wishes and phantasies are there?
- What is the meaning and value in the clinical situation of recognizing or not such phenomena as transference, resistance, empathy, psychic conflict, etc?
- Most crucially: how does psychoanalysis 'work' and for whom? And, if it does work, do some ways of 'working' 'work' better than others?

Beginning a Pan–European Project to compare differences

The evolution of a method to explore and compare differences in psychoanalytic work, which will be described in the chapters of this book, is not intended to answer the above questions in a definitive way. Rather, we will explain how we tried to find a psychoanalytic method that allowed us to make secure comparisons, with the eventual aim being to generate a clear and comparable description of the range of answers that different psychoanalysts might give to the above questions – focusing not on abstract 'official' answers, but on examples from their practice. The context in which we have tried to do this follows on from the idea of inviting European (and later North and South American) psychoanalysts to meet at annual workshops and to try to see if they could describe and compare their work more rigorously than hitherto. It started, therefore, from the wish to be *empirical*: to base our study on experience of descriptions of analytic work.

The project began with what had seemed a simple strategy: to mobilize European colleagues to become interested in tackling the problems just mentioned and to create the conditions in which they could do so in an ongoing way.[2] What we did one year would be reflected on during the succeeding months and then be fed back into the plan for the following year – and so on for several years. (A ten-year initiative was agreed, as a further part of the institutional structure: see Appendix.) The project as a whole had four aims:

- To increase the possibility for all of us to reflect on what we were doing and to learn from each other and to debate with each other much more precisely.
- To identify when we thought two colleagues were or were not, in their detailed practice, using the same or a different psychoanalytic method.
- To give us the future possibility of recognizing the competence of a candidate or a colleague who aspires to use a particular psychoanalytic method.
- To recognize a pseudo-application of any particular psycho-analytic method/model.

A preliminary meeting involving some of the analysts most closely involved in the project took place in Brussels three months before the first workshops. (Further details of this meeting are in the Appendix.) The idea was to try to anticipate some of the issues that we would face in these workshops, which were to be the core setting for exploring the different ways in which psychoanalysts work. It was also our intention in Brussels to test the usefulness of the proposed strategy

---

[2] These workshops were part of the implementation of the EPF's 'new' scientific policy agreed in 2000. The Appendix 'Setting out' provides a description of this and other institutional changes which were the background to the project.

of workshops followed by working party reflection on the work, followed by more workshops, and so on.

The workshops would be held at the annual European Psychoanalytic Federation (EPF) Conference, which brings together experienced psychoanalysts from more than twenty societies working in twenty or so languages. The first took place in Prague in 2002, followed by Sorrento in 2003, Helsinki in 2004, Vilamoura in 2005, Athens in 2006 and Barcelona in 2007 – although this chapter will concentrate almost exclusively on the work done in Prague, Sorrento and Helsinki.

In Prague, 120 clinicians from about twenty countries were divided up as evenly as possible and invited to sit in small groups of twelve. Each group listened to a clinical presentation from two colleagues apparently working in different psychoanalytic cultures. The workshop sessions lasted for five or six hours, and towards the end the group would try to compare the two analysts' methods of working.

The presenting analysts for these workshop groups were chosen via recommendations. They were to be colleagues thought of as gifted clinicians (rather than theorists or society leaders) based on word-of-mouth reputation in their society. The cases they were to present should be from a treatment that the clinician defined as 'a' psychoanalysis.

To maximize the range of viewpoints in each group, workshops were in English and, in a few cases, French. Each group would have at least one bilingual person to moderate the discussion, and members of the groups were all asked to adhere to the defined task: to make the assumption that the colleague presenting in their workshop *was* a psychoanalyst with an established way of working and to use the time to try to describe what this way of working was – with a view to comparing the essentials of the work of the two presenting analysts.

Enthusiasm and excitement were an immediate response both at the preliminary meeting and at the workshops themselves; it was felt that, however ill-defined, something novel was happening. In the preliminary meeting in Brussels and then in the first two workshops in Prague and Sorrento (see Chapters 3 and 4), the vast majority of participants became enthusiastically committed to the project, and in many cases – including my own – felt they had participated in a new and rich kind of clinical meeting. I think this success was largely attributable to the very high quality of thinking by those who accepted their invitations, as well as to the enjoyment gained from taking

in-depth clinical material seriously and from hearing other experienced and thoughtful colleagues reflect on it. Significantly, the time
allocated for discussion was longer than usual.[3] Furthermore, thanks
to the range of experienced colleagues present, the usual 'star system'
of conference-based discussion was significantly abated, and in most
cases, people ended the meetings wanting more.

Nonetheless, there were significant problems, which took a long
time to understand and to address, a process that is the main theme of
this book. Initially, these problems took the form of a series of obstacles and difficulties: participants were aware of the extent of their
differences and it was necessary emotionally to manage those differences when they arose; some had emotional and intellectual problems
in making comparisons; there were also problems with the emotional
experience and structure of a discussion between a presenter and an
audience with psychoanalytic material; a tendency to judge (or even
to attack) rather than to seek to understand the presenter; various
enactments by presenters who could more or less unconsciously
select inappropriate material; problems with shared assumptions as to
the nature of comparison as an epistemological activity; problems of
regressive or basic assumption group functioning (and in particular
the difficulty some groups had in establishing themselves as work
groups); a general lack of tools for the comparative task and confusion
about the meaning of psychoanalytic terms. In retrospect we might
say that these were all inevitable difficulties – but at the time we were
surprised at just how difficult things were.

Combined, the difficulties expressed themselves through anxiety
and sometimes even hostility – some of which came from people
whose relationship to the project was established only through hearsay.
The extent to which this was an emotional as well as an intellectual
issue is illustrated by the fact that at one stage anxieties were actually
expressed about the project as being an attempt either to 'kill' psychoanalysis or to kill all forms of psychoanalysis not associated with
one's own.

We will be describing examples of these difficulties in greater
depth later in the book, but some brief examples may at present bring

---

[3] Typical scientific meetings in psychoanalytic societies involve a forty-minute presentation
and perhaps an hour and a half discussion. We started with three hours for each presentation. Later, we were to allocate ten or eleven hours to one presenter (described in Chapter
6). Hinz (Chapter 5) sees this time allowance as highly significant.

matters into focus. In Chapter 3, Tomas Böhm describes how some presenters in Prague 'looked rather anxious, as though they were about to dive from a 10-metre platform into a small pool'. He also comments that it seemed obvious that the declared intention to look at work in detail, to compare styles, to explore implicit models and to let the group analyse these models, could provoke anxiety because 'people believe they know what they are doing'.

In Prague, many reports indicated that there was 'a genuine uncertainty as to what a psychoanalytic model actually is. Did we understand roughly the same thing with transference, containment, countertransference and working through the surface? And what about *interpretation* and *analytic* models?' Also in Prague we were warned that

confusion and frustration about the task, about what and how to discuss, as well as about the roles of the different group members, influenced the work of the group, especially during the first group meeting. We all seemed tempted to fall back on the experience of clinical supervision groups with their more vertical hierarchical relationships between members.

Finally, the working assumption that the presenter *is an analyst* was not so easy to apply in practice as it was in theory, even though it was an important assumption for these groups to make.

When the analyst feels and thinks there is a psychoanalytic process going on, the group should assume that 'this is an analyst working'. This means that critical and/or upset feelings about good and bad practice must be set aside, which feels strange to us in clinical discussions.

The differences between ways of working that were to emerge from the workshop groups could at times appear extreme and incomprehensible to group members, for difference can threaten working assumptions. For example, many in one group were highly sceptical of a presenter who made twenty-three interpretations in one session and thirty in the next. In another group as many members found it difficult to understand how a session in which the analyst said almost nothing could possibly be considered effective. In yet another group some members could not understand (and were actually upset by) the presenting analyst's failure to draw the patient's attention to anxiety resulting from unconscious attacks on the analytic process, while others in the same group were quite astonished by the very suggestion of such 'attack' interpretations, which they imagined would be efforts to bully the patient.

Contrary to what might be expected, psychoanalytic theory and concepts did not provide a common language for communication. The meaning of key terms was not reliably shared, especially at the level of clinical examples. For instance, while many colleagues thought that the curative factor in psychoanalysis is transference analysis, they did not agree at all on how to describe the transference in a given session or what to do about this disagreement. Moreover, and perhaps most seriously, the groups inevitably dealt with such a wide range of concepts in order to describe and understand an analyst's way of working that each individual in the groups, as well as the groups themselves, raised quite different issues when discussing and comparing each presenter's work. So many were there, in fact, that we ended up with a two-page list (presented in abbreviated form in Chapter 3). This confirmed an observation I had made in Brussels: when it came to comparison (and despite our very best efforts), none of us had tools with which to do it. After Prague, one moderator put the issue succinctly: 'the wealth of ideas amounted to a logical multiplicity of models, viewpoints, assumptions and positions which were not always easy to juxtapose and compare because they were not at the same logical level nor in the same class.'

Between Prague and Sorrento, the main task was to develop a comparative instrument. I thought that without some framework to proceed we would continue to be lost in supervision and general discussion of the cases. Eventually, I suggested that the way forward might be to ask each of the workshop groups, after an initial discussion, to structure their proceedings by focusing on each of the presenting analyst's interventions in the session, one by one. I thought this would focus them on the analysts rather than on every last aspect of the cases. To do this rigorously, they were asked to consider several predefined categories, into one of which each intervention belonged. I thought about the categories as a predefined typology (with components influenced by a variety of theories of psychoanalysis), but the method soon came to be known as the 'grid'.

As Arne Jemstedt describes in Chapter 4, many colleagues in Sorrento made a real effort to do what was asked, treating the resulting exercise as a game or as a means to an end. They grasped that the process of discussing the exact category into which an intervention fitted would stimulate a more rigorous examination of the implicit models the presenter was using, and by and large this was the case. But some colleagues misconstrued the intention of this system of categorization – treating the 'grid' as a concrete rating exercise with an end in itself, which they felt would lead to some abominable results.

I knew in advance that to propose to colleagues to divide a session up into its component parts (rather like a jigsaw puzzle) so as to try to determine as rigorously as possible whether an analyst's interpretive behaviour fell into one or more categories, might seem a somewhat foreign and an emotionally dead activity compared to what psychoanalysts usually do in clinical work (that is, trying unconsciously to sense at depth what is happening emotionally and to construct a whole intuitively from a presently fragmented emotional picture – see Chianese, 2007). I thought the way to meet any potential prejudice and concern would be to try to warn participants in advance in a preparatory letter (Tuckett, 2002b). In that communication, I tried to demonstrate that what was being attempted was not as radical as it may at first sight have appeared. To support this, I stressed that reaching a rounded picture of anything complex usually requires careful attention to a number of small details, as well as imposing a sense of shape. Therefore, I pointed out that classification into segments was not per se an attempt to abandon unconscious or emotional sensitivities – which in any case, I thought, were facts of life, which could not be abandoned even if we wished. I also mentioned that I hoped that thinking about each intervention and how it could be divided into different categories was not to be an automated process but would require judgement, which in turn would require focus; but that the whole process was to be based on complexity – on intuition and feeling (and so on unconscious processes). For me, categorization was far from banalization. The value of the exercise would have to be judged not a priori but on its results; whether it helped us or not to look together at how the presenter was working, to identify different methods of working and to determine where they were and were not coincident.

I also knew in advance that there were significant problems with the classification scheme. First and foremost, it had too many categories that were not very well defined, something that was often experienced as frustrating, especially if it was taken too concretely.

For such reasons, I was prepared for some degree of the negative reaction that we got from some people in Sorrento, and which Arne Jemstedt describes in Chapter 4. However, the depth of suspicion that exploded from some serious and experienced colleagues as to the underlying aim of the project did disturb me and in some groups was nearly overwhelming. Moderators (who themselves were naturally open-minded rather than certain that this would work) were put through a stern test in trying to keep groups focused on the task at hand. Some colleagues in the workshops told their moderator that they were not going to stand by and put numbers on a psychoanalyst. It was to avoid that sort of activity that they had become psychoanalysts and not psychiatrists or psychologists. A significant minority became angry with the project and either tried to subvert the activity in their group or threatened to walk out.

In retrospect, the signs for this emotional difficulty were there earlier: I have mentioned that in Brussels none of us had really known how to make comparisons or along what axis to do so and, in that context, I had proposed that each group would be helped by having the same six questions with which to reflect with each presenter. The idea was not well received; I was told that the groups should not be subjected to prior restriction. It was clear, therefore, that restriction on discussion stirred up discomfort. Many thought it vital to preserve in the group the free and unstructured environment in which most analysts conduct their clinical meetings. To support this contention, free association was invoked as the only true psychoanalytic method, and any interference with free association was deemed likely to make discussion artificial and even non-psychoanalytic – a view which might have warned me that complex anxieties had been stirred up.

So, after one set of unstructured workshop meetings in Prague and a second set of structured workshop meetings in Sorrento, the project had a growing following and a considerable degree of enthusiastic support, but we had also generated a degree of anxiety and hostility. Following Prague, it had seemed clear that some structure was necessary for the discussions, but Sorrento had taught us that introducing it was no simple matter.

In Prague and Sorrento we had observed fear of presenting, anxieties about questioning what people were doing, fear of structure, fear of the loss of psychoanalysis, great uncertainty as to what a psychoanalytic model actually is, confusion over terms, group regression, an overwhelming tendency to become judgemental, fear of comparison, a difficulty comparing, a great deal of anxiety, considerable hostility and so on.

Whether because the problem of resolving differences has always existed in psychoanalysis or for other reasons, psychoanalysts have historically organized themselves into professional schools based on emotional allegiances and identifications, strongly influenced by transference identifications and counter-identifications during training, which themselves are the result of each analyst's own engagement with personal psychoanalysis (Bergmann, 2004), as well as the particularistic nature of psychoanalytic institutes. (The distinction made here is between particularistic and universalistic forms of social organization: Parsons, 1951; Tuckett, 2005.) The form of theoretical and clinical pluralism to which we have arrived in psychoanalysis is not 'disciplined' (Tuckett, 2004), which is to say that it has not in general been arrived at by an identifiable process of embracing or eliminating approaches and innovations because they do or don't 'work' according to some shared empirical criteria, such as agreed outcome.

However, while there is no doubt that developing such criteria for psychoanalysis is no simple matter, *not* to have developed any also has serious consequences. A creative response would have been to develop ingenious ways of addressing the problem, but efforts to construct criteria to resolve differences beyond using personal authority have instead been constantly suspect in psychoanalysis – with quantification and even empiricism regularly misrepresented, mocked and dismissed (for example, as simplistic 'straw men') – as happened in the Sorrento groups.[4] These responses are discussed further by Helmut Hinz in Chapter 5, with the general case for empiricism as a way forward for psychoanalysis made there and in Chapter 2 by Paul Denis.

The way differences in psychoanalysis have hitherto been managed

---

[4] Writing of her experience in Sorrento, Iréne Matthis (2003) stated:

> Relating to the Categorization System – using the Grid . . . – one or two were positively in favour to start with. One or two were vehemently against it or were very critical and could see no meaning in 'putting numbers' to an analyst's interventions and then compare the outcome.

Putting numbers was not, of course, the actual purpose of the so-called grid.

and the response that this project received in some quarters suggests to me that what Bion (1952) has called 'basic assumption' organization is significantly present in psychoanalytic groups, but that this has not been properly recognized or tackled. Freud's own social theories, as set out in *Civilization and its Discontents* (Freud, 1930; Tuckett, 2007), might have alerted us to the problem of managing difference within a group, bearing in mind what Britton (2003: 126) refers to as xenocidal tendencies arising from the management of the destructive instinct.

Whereas work groups (Bion, 1952) are constructed and function in relation to an external task, which provides feedback on performance, basic assumption groups 'evaluate' themselves to avoid external feedback, particularly by offering members a degree of security about the virtues of belonging to the group. In basic assumption mode, members of groups treat external pressure and outsiders as 'not us'; that is, as objects to help form the group's identity.

Insofar as psychoanalytic groups and institutions are basic assumption groups, it is unsurprising that they face such boundary problems, which the project was intended in part to make it easier to consider. There are obvious difficulties in codifying the boundary between psychoanalysis and related therapeutic disciplines just as there are in codifying the boundary between different psycho-analytic orientations. However, lack of clarity over boundaries means that variations in clinical work and technique gradually develop within a group orientation so that variation within groups starts to match variation between groups. Such processes have the potential to be creative but only if matched by discipline – that is to say if there are structures that negatively evaluate deviations that cross one boundary 'too far'.

A particular anxiety created by the 'grid-typology' in Sorrento was that it was derived from non-psychoanalytic social science methods. A further cause for anxiety was that it directly implied that existing group orientation labels are not necessarily indicative of common practice. For these reasons, the 'grid' was experienced as a violation of existing principles of social and emotional organization, and thus was inevitably anxiety-provoking. Questioning taken-for-granted procedures does create disturbance (Garfinkel, 1967).

In Chapter 4, Arne Jemstedt reports on some allegations made in Sorrento about the comparative methods project, including that it was anti-psychoanalytic. There were antagonistic statements made, arguing that putting 'numbers to people' as required by the grid was unethical. One way to interpret these allegations would be as basic assumption group phenomena emanating from professional groups under a perceived threat. When there is underlying anxiety or uncertainty, this threat can be managed by splitting, in which case the comparative methods project could be treated as a dangerous and concrete intrusion from 'outside' and which must be defeated if 'safety' is to be restored. Alternatively, the uncertainty could be treated as a signal of a need to address a problem, in which case the project can be one among several ways of trying to do so, and it can then be used instrumentally.[5]

In any case, with the benefit of hindsight, it is now apparent that the response in Sorrento and our reaction to it proved to be a major impetus in the project's overall evolution. As explained, I had underestimated the anxieties that colleagues had about difference, had not taken sufficient account of what I knew about the structural situation of the presenter and listener, and had not thought hard enough about many years of observing difficulties with psychoanalytic discussion and debate. Moreover, I had underestimated the anxieties that exist around empirical study and the deep misgivings in the psychoanalytic community concerning abstraction and the annihilation of the unconscious. Finally, I began to realize that the project involved a series of unfamiliar methodological assumptions which up until that point in time had been implicit. If we were to progress, these needed to be made explicit so as to be shared and debated. In short, progress was going to require a major re-examination of methods, epistemology and assumptions – the topic of Chapter 6.

Fortunately, I had adopted the strategy of workshop meetings followed by opportunities for reflection and had an extremely able and

---

[5] The work of two other EPF working parties was also relevant. Research within the Working Party on Education (WPE) had highlighted the quite fragile basis on which qualification into psychoanalytic societies rests. A complex duality seems to operate in which on the one hand we have many complex procedures in our training institutes and on the other apparently we find reasons – notably the absence of real criteria of competence – to qualify almost all those who complete the course so that in reality we let almost anything go. Meanwhile the Working Party on Interface (WPI) had accumulated evidence of all kinds of highly non-specific but powerful anxieties about contamination if there is work across interfaces. Some anxiety about the grid might be seen in this context: as anxiety based on a real fear of the fragility of the psychoanalytic 'plant' and its capacity to stand scrutiny – perhaps a deep lack of confidence in psychoanalysis itself. But this potentially initiates a vicious circle – lack of confidence, lack of rigour, anything goes, poor work, lack of confidence, and so on.

thoughtful group of moderators and consultants around me.[6] It was at this point, therefore, that I consciously discovered what I had previously known only intuitively, namely the function of working parties (discussed in the Appendix). This discovery was enabled by my role as chair for the Working Party on Comparative Clinical Methods, which provided a setting for a group of colleagues from several countries and psychoanalytic approaches to reflect on and share the actual experience they had been having.[7] There was also the useful pressure of having to organize a new set of workshops for the following year – and not wanting a repeat of the more difficult aspects of the Sorrento experience!

Additionally, thanks to the generosity of a small grant from the International Psychoanalytical Association Research Board, I was able to add some backroom preparatory research input and prior consideration. This meant that at the first two meetings of the new working party, we met much better prepared and my research colleague (Naama Ben Yehoyada) was able to spend time going over a number of published psychoanalytic presentations and other material. Together, we adopted the principles of grounded theory (Glaser and Strauss, 1967; Tuckett, 1994), and I was able to arrive at what became the framework of a two-step method for discussing, describing and comparing how analysts work.

The problem of discussing difference

Because the problems I have been describing took some time to apprehend, it may be that the reader of this book will also need time to grasp how fundamental the difficulties really are. One way to illustrate the problems that psychoanalysts have in discussing and compar-

---

[6] Haydée Faimberg played a very important role. As chair of the Working Party on Clinical Issues, she had selected the moderators of the groups in Prague and later Sorrento – many of whom are the authors of this book. She attended the crucial meetings we had in Paris and brought her clinical acumen to bear when we first tried out what was to become the two-step method. Jorge Canestri, chair of the EPF Working Party on Theoretical Issues, also offered helpful criticism and advice, as did Paul Denis, Iréne Matthis and Roger Perron, who acted as consultants in the moderators' meetings.

[7] After Sorrento, it was decided that Track 2 of the Working Party on Clinical Issues would become the Forum on Clinical Issues and Track 1 would become a new Working Party on Comparative Clinical Methods. I was now in the final year of my EPF Presidency but the new President-Elect, Evelyne Séchaud, invited me to chair the new group. Further details are in the Appendix.

ing how they work, and also to understand the importance of my argument, is to look at some of the presentations and discussions that have been appearing in the 'Psychoanalyst at Work' series published in the *International Journal of Psychoanalysis*. Most of the discussions exemplify the features that I think are relevant, but I will comment on two: the presentations by Rudi Vermote (Vermote, 2003; see also Goldberg, 2003; Rousillon, 2003) and Jean-Claude Rolland (Rolland, 2006; see also McGuinness, 2006; Stein, 2006). I was prompted to discuss the latter partly after a visit to an international conference in the United States, where I saw some colleagues shaking their heads in disbelief and commenting on how astonished they were that an analyst could respond to a patient in the way Rolland described himself doing.

In his presentation of an anorexic patient, F, who is described as improving markedly, two points, among many others, captured the attention of discussants. First, Rolland decided to take the patient into psychoanalysis although in the initial meeting the patient remained entirely silent. He comments:

> The end of the interview was approaching, and all we had shared was this silent presence. I said to her that I would like to meet her again, and asked if she wanted to make a new appointment then and there. She nodded. We agreed to meet the following week, same day, same time. I make that point because I wonder if, somewhere inside myself and without my being able to be fully aware of it, I had already in my counter transference, decided to embark on an analysis with her.
>
> (Rolland, 2006: 1433)

Second, Rolland briefly summarized a session (it was not one of the four he presented in more detail) in which the patient arrived after Rolland had received a telephone call from her psychiatrist to say that something terrible had happened: that the patient had thrown herself from a bridge and into the Rhone. During the session, however, the patient talked about the event with a note of jubilation in her voice, and said that she had done something 'heroic'. Taking account of the circumstances, Rolland states that:

> it was easy enough to link this piece of acting out to what had occurred in the previous session: it was both a kind of glorious and

liberating abreaction of her phallic position and a means of giving up what attracted her specifically, her sister's femininity.

(Rolland, 2006: 1437)

The comments I overheard at the conference suggested Rolland was irresponsible not to be making interpretations about an attempted suicide. This is a valid viewpoint, but the assumption behind it is that Rolland did not know what he was doing or was himself acting out in some way; in short, the implication was that Rolland needed supervision. The two published discussions of Rolland's work are by Trudy McGuinness (2006) and Ruth Stein (2006). They are thoughtful, ingenious, polite and respectful – perhaps models of what we have come to expect. But in both cases essentially what we get is a rereading of the clinical material from the discussant's point of view. This was McGuinness:

I do not quite understand the description of the patient throwing herself into the Rhone. Was it a dangerous act or not? I can appreciate it can be understood as a glorious and liberating abreaction of her phallic position, a kind of omnipotent folly; however, it also sounds as if it was a suicide attempt. Dr Rolland was in the best place to judge, so I'm curious about how he felt. I think my interest might have been in the playing out of the conflict between life and death incorporated in such an act and also in the interplay of the triangle, psychiatrist, analyst and patient enacted in the transference.

(McGuinness, 2006: 1445)

The patient's silences and the analyst's own silent response also receive comment:

I am intrigued not only by the shared silences at the end of the session, but also with the belief that it facilitates the transference forces to do their work. I don't think I have the same confidence that transference work of this kind will necessarily bring greater insight.

(McGuinness, 2006: 1446)

McGuinness' own views on how to manage silence follow.

The point for me, however, is that Rolland did not explicate his theory of how psychoanalysis works in his presentation, yet it is only his theory of psychoanalysis that can make sense of what he is telling us. It is partly as a consequence of my five-year involvement in the comparative project that I can guess something of it. It appears to me that, fundamentally, Rolland is relying on a theory of mind (the topographical model) and an associated theory of language and the development of unconscious representation and of the role and function of verbalization (and its negative consequences). From this point of view, he aims to make condensed polysemic comments that progress an unconscious, not a conscious, process. He has no interest in 'translating' (as I think he would see it) matters into words which the patient can hear and work over consciously. The capacity to be silent – to facilitate an unconscious process in which the analyst as a person is as unobtrusive as possible – and the introduction of minimal ego-level communication is the central part of the technique. Enactment is not part of the theory.

In the context of such an explanatory model, it makes very limited sense to me to discuss how Rolland might or even should have talked more to the patient about what she was thinking and feeling, as would happen using a different technique based, say, on the structural model.

Once we have really understood them, we might usefully discuss the relative strengths and weaknesses of different approaches, but this too is questionable in this context. We cannot try out the different technique. Rolland's patient has apparently improved quite markedly. To me the interesting question is not what else he might have done, but how we think his method actually achieved what it did.[8] And one

---

[8] I make this point although my colleague Trudy McGuinness demonstrates in her discussion how she is in fact a sophisticated and respectful thinker. She is aware of the need to understand that Rolland's method follows from his theory – explicitly recognizing that his

> emphasis on maintaining the setting and not interrupting the flow of the free association is rooted in his belief about what he is doing as an analyst. In his view, if he can foster the bringing into consciousness of repressed thoughts and wishes, this will fundamentally force internal reorganization of the psychic apparatus, very much following the thoughts of Freud pre-1923.
>
> (McGuinness 2006: 1443)

> Clearly Rolland's 'theoretical understanding of the patient underpins his interpretations,' she adds, before saying that 'because he says so little it sometimes seems, on reading the progression of the sessions, that there are some aspects of the material that might seem fundamental to me, that he chooses not to interpret' (McGuinness, 2006: 1443). It is in this sense that I am suggesting that what I am calling supervision, exploring an other's work in terms of one's own, is the only present method of discussion differentiated only by degree.

aspect of that method is that he does not in these sessions see it as useful to talk to his patient about psychiatric reality at all.

Stein (2006) proceeds along similar lines to McGuinness. She identifies a pattern in the material thus:

> We see that, as soon as the analyst relates to F's dread of helplessness, she can move to the transference and link the 'brick wall,' as she calls her analyst, with her father and note her greater freedom and safety with the analyst. Dr Rolland doesn't pick up this bid to clarify her transference fantasies and perceptions about her father and himself. He connects instead her fear of putting on weight, and her shutting the door when she has sex with B, with her father. These interpretations seem to point F toward . . . to which F assents and follows with expressing her fear of loss of bodily control, the sources for which we seem to see differently.
>
> (Stein, 2006: 1450)

As with McGuinness, Stein's point is apparently not made to elucidate how and why Rolland works as he does but rather to suggest what he might or ought to have done, and that he should see the material in the way that she does. We see here how the tradition of discussing a colleague's clinical material is, so to speak, to supervise it.

The point is clearer still in Arnold Goldberg's (2003) discussion of Rudi Vermote's presentation. This is quite an unabashed supervision. First, he sets out at some length his account of the way he listens to patients and what he does with what he hears. It is an interesting and lucid account of an aspect of what I term his explanatory model (see p. 27 et seq). Then he applies this approach to the presenter's work:

> After gathering together these sorts of data one must next turn to the activity that makes of analysis a process, that is, interpretation. Since I rely so heavily, if not exclusively, upon the interpretation of the transference I can almost automatically look to it to answer my question of how I know what is relevant for me or presumptive of an analytic call for self-scrutiny. Yet Vermote's interventions seem directed to essentially leaving himself out of the equation and more fully exploiting facts and information about the patient's childhood. More and more today we remain with the patient in the

'here and now' with the use of childhood material for confirmation and reconstruction.

(Goldberg, 2003: 1423)

To judge from these discussions it is perhaps unsurprising that the
experienced colleagues who met in Brussels or Prague at the beginning of the project soon became 'supervisors' – albeit articulate, very
polite and respectful, as per most of the discussants in the *International
Journal* series. This is the way psychoanalysts talk to each other. This is
the pattern we notice also in many scientific meetings in psychoanalytic societies, where the supervisor mode seems to take over very
quickly and particularly in discussions between analysts of different
schools. This is especially the case in many international meetings,
as will be elaborated further in the next chapter. We can recall
Winnicott's experience at the New York Psychoanalytic Society in
1967 (Ilahi, 2006), the debate between André Green (1993) and Ted
Jacobs (1993a, 1993b) at the IPA Congress in Amsterdam in 1993, the
debate between Evelyne Séchaud (2000) and Ekkehard Gattig (2000)
in the EPF Training Colloquium of 1999 in Budapest, or the discussion of Michael Feldman's paper in the 2005 Vilamoura conference.
Many readers will be familiar with the problem in the 'scientific
meetings' of their own psychoanalytic societies.

Perhaps the witnesses enjoy the spectacle of these discussions. Or
perhaps they enjoy taking sides, whether with the outraged discussant,
who feels entirely justified in correcting the errant presenter, or with
the victimized presenter, who is hurt by unfair misunderstanding. If
so, are these little more than ritual events in which by participating
in identificatory or disidentificatory processes colleagues receive an
endorsement of their faith? Like Shakespeare's Henry V, do we fight
foreign wars to bind together potential discontent at home?

One might counter this by asking whether the articulate alternative formulations are interesting and themselves also provide examples
of differences. At the risk of overstating my case, however, this now
seems questionable to me. It is not actually that difficult for an intelligent psychoanalyst to offer a rereading of someone else's clinical
material – especially if he or she is not hampered by having to work it
out with the patient in the next session and the next and the next.
More significantly, the deeper differences that are generating the
observable features of difference are not usually explicated heuristic-
ally. Was Vermote simply ignorant of how to listen and interpret the

transference? Is Rolland simply unaware of the value of making verbally explicit what is going on between him and his patient? I doubt it in Vermote's case and have already argued that it is not so in Rolland's. In fact (and with the benefit of what I have learned through the method to be described in this book), it is likely both were operating with what in the discussion were implicit theories of the way psychoanalysis works, based on fundamental ideas about the nature of language and of the unconscious, which, right or wrong, render irrelevant the feedback and comments that they received. There is as much point in telling Rolland that I would verbalize what is happening in my patient's mind as there is in a Frenchman telling an Englishman he speaks English with the wrong accent.

Unless the core ideas underlying differences are elucidated and explicated, it seems to me that, if the aim is to understand and learn, discussion is both rather pointless and misleading. If such differences are not understood in depth, what do we really learn? That Jacobs spends his time lost in his own childhood thoughts when with his patients? Or that Rolland takes horrendous risks with potential suicide? In effect we witness a dialogue of the deaf and the blind with many possibilities for error.

In fact, following this line of thought, if one reflects on what presenters or participants get from many clinical discussions, it is rather little – unless those in the discussion actually understand (whether explicitly or intuitively) enough of the presenter's approach to make comments relevant to it. (Very often it leads to suppressed hostility or masochistic submission.) In part this may explain why many psychoanalysts are not very willing to go to international conferences and also why psychoanalysts have broken up into ever more tribal orientations – perhaps attempting to reduce their experience of difference and pointless debate, a point made by Helmut Hinz in Chapter 5. But even isolation is not necessarily successful. I have noticed that what even close colleagues in fact share is not always so clear (see, for example, the so-called Contemporary Kleinians in London), although for the sake of living together, such differences are often coded and obscured.[9]

I hope I have said enough to set out the extent to which I think

---

[9] In the UK, independent and contemporary Freudian analysts do not form homogeneous groups; when they share the way they work with their colleagues there are substantial differences. I think this is also true of Kleinian group colleagues, but that disagreements are less openly explored.

the comparative project has somewhat unwittingly blundered into a deep problem that exists in psychoanalysis today, and perhaps the very problem that lies at the heart of the difficulties that the project was intended to address: that is, we simply do not know how to discuss another person's way of working psychoanalytically except by responding to the material with ideas of our own about it and how we would do it.

This tendency to 'supervise' seems to arise from several sources, including the desire to prove the superiority of one's own model and to compete successfully in a discussion group. This behaviour has many motives but, it seems to me, these are amplified by the situation of discussing clinical material in psychoanalysis, which is an inherently emotional process: deeply held emotional responses and beliefs are observably at stake, for both presenters and discussants. The discussant tends to talk as though the presenter should listen and adjust to the suggestion made for fear that otherwise the patient will be damaged or the treatment irretrievably stalled. This is as may be. But more centrally what is indicated is that something very vital is felt to be at stake: supervision in this context seems to mean not just the idea of knowing more than the presenter but also the idea of protecting the patient from harm. Thus to the potentially libidinal opportunities to display oneself in these discussions can be added the observation that we are clearly in moral territory (superego more than ego) and in very deep water indeed – not least because all this also takes place in human groups.

The problem of comparison and the problem of discussion

The difficulties that have been outlined so far can be conceived in two ways. The first set of difficulties concerns the whole framework for comparison: what does comparison of psychoanalytic clinical work actually involve and how can it be done? The second concerns the process of discussing clinical material and the experience that this creates for participants. To take the project forward, both sets of difficulties had to be tackled, particularly as it was also clear that both sets of difficulties could exacerbate each other – as happened in Sorrento.

We needed to find a way to address the various problems both of discussing psychoanalytic material and of comparing ways of working

– cognitively and emotionally, as well as at the individual and the group level. After our initial experiences in Prague and Sorrento, we had to reflect more deeply on the stark fact that discussants (including ourselves) had difficulty in trying to put themselves in the mind of presenters in order to try to imagine what they were trying to do. This was a task that required two capacities: the ability to accept the existence of what a social anthropologist might term an entirely strange explanatory model, and the emotional and intellectual willingness to be curious about it.

I have mentioned the idea of 'explanatory model' several times without defining it – in the hope that its meaning would be taken at face value. However, as the discussions led to the development of our method, I became aware that, to further the tasks of comparison and the discussion of difference, we would need to determine an appropriate methodology, and that this would indeed need to draw on work in the social sciences as well as in psychoanalysis. Three sets of ideas from social science seemed relevant to the problem of comparison and of discussion. I shall describe them in Chapter 6 and will show how the workshops were gradually transformed thanks to the participants' and the moderators' ever-improving understanding of how to use these ideas from social science. They moved from groups that tended mainly to function, after Bion (1952), as basic assumption groups, towards groups that could function mainly as work groups.

The concept of an 'explanatory model' (Kleinman, 1980; Tuckett, 1993; Tuckett et al., 1985) is a social anthropological device used to help explain underlying but often observable patterns of social interaction based on implicit beliefs. It starts from the proposition (perhaps not so foreign to psychoanalysis) that most things that do not make sense from the outside do make sense if understood from the inside. It was designed to deal with the situation where a doctor is telling a patient about a treatment option but just does not feel that the patient agrees. In this situation it might seem obvious to the doctor what needs to be done, but if this is so, why does the patient not see it? To the doctor, it just does not make sense. Yet, from a different perspective, perhaps it does. People, especially those from different cultural backgrounds, often have very different ways of understanding illness, its consequences, and how best to treat it; in other words, they have a different explanatory model. Thus, to understand a presenter such as Rolland, it is necessary to understand his explanatory model – the complex mix of emotionally charged and interconnected implicit and explicit beliefs that cause him to act as he does. Among these is, I have suggested, a theory of language and the unconscious which he left implicit.[10]

The concept of 'ideal type' (Schutz, 1953; Weber, 1920) is another sociological device designed to assist comparison. It is useful when facing the difficult question of how to derive generalizable comparisons from individual instances of observation. Weber was interested in understanding social organizations and the problems they had with change. He conceived three types of organization: traditional, charismatic and bureaucratic, each identified in terms of the way authority was 'typically' exercised within them. He defined a number of elements that exemplified each type. Although no individual organization would be exactly the same as others in the same type, they were usefully considered similar in terms of the identified characteristics. This might be one way to explore different ways of doing psychoanalysis: we would need to identify some common elements that we could identify for each type – for example, the way unconscious latent meanings are understood in different approaches.

The concept of role (Mead, 1934; see also McCall and Simmons, 1966) is a third sociological device that we can use to explore the underlying regularities in social interaction, for example in human groups. A role is a set of connected behaviours, rights and obligations as conceptualized by members of groups in a social situation. As a concept, it assists with reflecting on some aspects of the way presenters and discussants relate to one another and what might be the 'role' of the moderators.

One cause of the problems in discussing psychoanalytic clinical material can be seen as structural in a role-specific fashion: when discussants seem to have to 'supervise' presenters, it seems possible that the 'roles' of presenter and discussant might become confused. In fact, I have argued before (Tuckett, 1993) that we need to recognize that

[10] I used explanatory models in a study of physicians and patients (Tuckett et al., 1985). Concurrently, Joseph Sandler (1983) was applying similar ideas to psychoanalytic practice – notably in his idea of implicit models. I am very grateful to Jorge Canestri, whose EPF Working Party on Theoretical Issues had determined to pursue Sandler's ideas, for encouraging me to return to the elucidation of psychoanalysts' implicit models when we discussed the problems that had come up in Sorrento. Before Prague, the term 'model' had been dropped because it was thought too mechanistic for psychoanalysis. This argument may be part of the wider problems being discussed, but it also reflects cultural and linguistic difficulties; the result, in fact, of implicit, and so unrecognized, explanatory model conflict.

the presenter in any discussion has a specific and privileged role; he or she is the sole provider of access to knowledge about the psycho-analysis being discussed due to a long immersion in the many details of his or her experience with the patient, which is naturally both con-scious and unconscious. At the same time, the presenter also has all the potential blindness of that immediate position within the analytical relationship, with its necessary potential for *unconsciously* skewing or disturbing his or her thinking as a member of the analytic field.

When it comes to presenting clinical material within a workshop like ours, we could expect the analyst to have a view of what is happening and to have formulated interpretations and constructed an account of the session accordingly. But, precisely because the analyst's view is developed as a participant observer within the relationship, it cannot but be part of what is at stake in the relationship, and therefore open to scrutiny. The result is a rather curious situation. Presenting analysts, however skilled and distinguished they may be and with however many hours of dedication and thought behind them in their work with their patients, find that listening colleagues, who have none of this investment or experience, nor perhaps even the analyst's skill, are very likely to detect new and important meanings in the material that they have not seen. This is something a presenter needs to know. Small wonder, perhaps, that clinical presentations – particularly by senior colleagues to junior ones – are rare and often tense, and that there are such divergent reactions to clinical discussion.

Discussants, on the other hand, not only have the advantage of a different perspective, because of the different explanatory models they bring to the material from their own way of doing psychoanalysis, but also have *potential* access to information the presenter does not, and therefore to a different potential role competence. They have heard or read the presentation and have observed aspects of its construction; they can sense matters that are not brought up or which are repeated. These have an emotional effect, which possibly parallel unrecognized emotional situations in the sessions. Discussants, therefore, have both the *advantages and disadvantages* of their position outside the analytic relationship.

If this structural role asymmetry is not very carefully allowed for, discussion can become judgemental and insensitive (or even enactive), and presenters can become defensive. A more hidden form of the same difficulties might be to engage only in superficial or entirely uncritical discussion.

31

From the point of view just set out, the potential richness of group discussion in psychoanalysis is that it necessarily allows for the unconscious and implicit ideas of both presenter and discussant to emerge. Analysts' choice of material, their way of speaking about it and the words they use, all provide information about the analytic situation and about the patient's pathology and transference *of which the presenting analyst will not be fully aware*. This *aspect of the narrative*, rather than being a weakness, as it would be from the viewpoint of more objective approaches to observation and truth, is the quintes-sential aspect of a psychoanalytic clinical presentation:

> The central point of a psychoanalytic process is that it cannot rely on rational verbalisation alone, and in his attempt to communicate the analyst says more than he consciously knows. This is a strength, not a weakness – like free association in the analytic process itself, it is what makes things possible.
>
> (Tuckett, 1993: 1184)

The workshop groups that we organized were deliberately con-structed so that their membership included psychoanalysts from many of the available traditions. Inevitably, this meant that we all had difficulty understanding each other – as was so apparent in Prague – which, once recognized, could also be an advantage. We could say that within the group we had present most if not all of the universe of explanatory models that currently exist in psycho-analysis. Thus, the group as a whole could be relied on through their understanding or misunderstanding to inquire in interesting ways into the particular explanatory model the presenter was using – once, that is, they had engaged in sufficiently detailed discussion and assuming that they took care to explore what they were meaning. They can in fact go further than this, because members of the group respond to the presentation both consciously and unconsciously and also respond to each other and their ideas in the same way; in other words, the scene is set for them to become aware of implicit or unconscious models as well. But all of this is an advantage only insofar as participants, with the help of the moderator, are clear about roles and help the group to maintain a constant state of inquiry. Insofar as anxiety or other emotional factors cause indi-viduals to move out of role and to become supervisors, this inhibited the curiosity of the group and basic assumption processes might be expected to occur. In Prague and Sorrento, we simply did not realize enough of all this.

Managing and conceiving difference: the development of the two-step method

The working party reflection that took place after the Sorrento workshops led to a deeper understanding of the issues we faced and of the methodology that we would need to address it (see Chapter 6). At this point the emotional difficulties in comparing began to seem more predictable and more manageable. They were perhaps a function of the very difficulties the comparative clinical methods project had been designed to address: namely, the longstanding problem of discussing differences and of finding a way to define when work is truly psychoanalytic (and of what type) beyond its appeal to charisma and authority.

In Sorrento one group had in fact experienced serious conflict (as described in Chapter 4) and, to a large degree, successfully overcome it. They had done this by understanding the negative reaction to the 'grid' and, to a large extent, by learning from our failure to communicate properly to group members what we were trying to do. Specifically (and as formulated by Iréne Matthis (2003) on behalf of the group moderated by Dana Birksted-Breen) they had shown that where sufficient numbers of colleagues in a group were able to use the grid *instrumentally* (i.e. as a function, in a process of engaging with a task in a group), then it did seem mainly to facilitate discussion and to provide a focus that had not been present in the less structured environment that was Prague. Where, on the other hand, the grid was experienced as an *instrument* (i.e. as a fixed defining structure, like an externally imposed 'thing' in a context in which the overall task was received passively and not identified as an activity directed towards a meaningful end), then both the grid and the task were considered exploitative. The task threatened to become monstrous and then to stir the bitter reactions mentioned. In that emotional situation, dividing a session into the individual units of each intervention and then also trying to decide if an intervention was in one category or another was particularly dissonant. The activity ceased to have much meaning, caused anxiety and outrage, and became dreary and non-psychoanalytic.

The above group clearly managed to resist basic assumption regression and began to turn itself into a work group. In this group, as in the others, the leadership of the moderators, as well as the willingness of enough participants to stay on task and to keep trying to achieve it, was fundamental. This provided a clue for a way to help moderators support such regressive tendencies. Drawing on this experience and developing ideas based on the methodological issues discussed earlier, a new method was planned, drawing on four main principles.

First, still more time was allowed, removing the pressure of having to move on too quickly and allowing the workshop groups to engage more deeply in the cases presented; the groups would now meet for about eleven hours and discuss only one case. Each presenter's work would be explored using the same framework, and comparison of the cases would be done afterwards in the working party. This decision allowed more time for colleagues to warm to the task (Antonino Ferro called these earlier stages Step −1 (minus 1) and Step 0 (zero) – see Chapter 7). The decision also created opportunities for the group members to get to know each other over two days, and removed the difficult task of having to compare two people when they were both present within the group.

Second, a revised version of the grid-typology was developed; the new version was more precisely refined and with fewer categories, allowing us to keep them in mind more easily and understand their point. Step 1 in the workshop discussion would take about three hours and would be devoted to looking at the presenter's interventions one by one, but with the explicit purpose not of arriving at numbers and scores, but of generating an in-depth exploration of what the group thought the presenter was implicitly and explicitly trying to do. The aim of Step 1 was now to ensure that the group focuses primarily on the presenter rather than on the case, and to try to make the discussion as deep as possible. It is made explicit that it is a means to an end and not an end in itself.

Third, the focus was to be on the presenting analyst's explanatory model, which was assumed to be generating the observed events described in the session (the linked beliefs he or she appeared to have about what, psychoanalytically speaking, was the matter with the patient; how psychoanalysis works to transform those difficulties; what must be attended to and apprehended in the 'listening' for that to work; how the situation in a session between analyst and patient is conceived; and what exactly the analyst believes is the point of the things he or she says or does to bring about the process he or she wishes to achieve). The various psychoanalytic theories of language, transference, resistance, construction, memory, etc., would in this way be studied in situ. This was Step 2.

Fourth, the role of the moderator was understood as crucial and gradually became specified. Moderators needed to internalize the two steps and to hold the frame, thereby creating a relationship with both presenter and participants before the workshop meeting actually began, a relationship allowing the moderator firmly to hold to the task during the group meeting. The moderator's task included trying to ensure the presenter selected appropriate material (for example, avoiding sessions with very difficult patients where the presenter wanted supervision) and continuously trying to inject curiosity into the group – for example, by pushing the discussion at Step 1 by provoking the group to play with potential disagreements between them. It also involved being clear and creative about the different roles of presenters and discussants and, indeed, about the differences in the group.

The details of how the two-step method was developed and of how it works in practice will be discussed in Chapters 6 and 7. In Chapter 8, Johan Schubert discusses the way in which the discussion method evolved from the viewpoint of group dynamics, and also reports some of the data we gathered from presenters and participants about their experience. We undertook a small questionnaire study of the presenters and participants who had taken part over the years. Many comments were interesting and are reported in various places below. However, one colleague who attended in Prague, but who did not attend again until the Athens meeting four years later, is instructively quoted by Tomas Böhm. About Prague, this colleague wrote:

> Throughout my experience . . . I was feeling quite sceptical as to whether the main aim of the group, which was to try to draw inferences from the study of the material of the sessions in order to identify the presenter's implicit psycho-analytic theory, was at all possible; the aim seemed to me at that point a rather untenable goal . . . The main interference with achieving the aim was, in my experience at least, coming from the ubiquitous and almost automatic response that we have as psychoanalysts, and certainly it was true for us members of the working party in Prague, to assume the role of a supervisor/consultant when we listen to clinical material.

The strength of this response is related, I can hypothesize, to its being multiply determined by factors which all carry great intensity. I left Prague being quite pessimistic of the viability of this, to my mind, very important project.

The same participant found the usual tendencies alive and well in Athens, but

> not in a crippling manner however; it was now contained by the structure and this is, I believe, very promising.

In Chapter 9, Roberto Basile and Antonino Ferro reflect on the way in which what we have learned so far might provide feedback on other activities, such as ordinary clinical supervision for training or other purposes. What they suggest is a further surprise: the possibility that a method that was originally developed to avoid the difficulties created by the tendency to supervise in discussion groups might be of some more general application to supervision itself – in those situations where an important part of the work is not to suggest alternative meanings of the material, but to help supervisees to understand and to adjust their explanatory models. We can make the tentative suggestion that the methods developed in the project may have a wider application in most psychoanalytic discussion. This will be something for the reader to decide.

Chapter 2 of this book discusses why empirical study, broadly conceived, is a valid way forward. Thereafter, Chapter 3 discusses the Prague experience, which we might summarize as the attempt to achieve the comparative task without a predetermined structure, while Chapter 4 considers the difficulties we had when we first introduced structure in Sorrento. (A time chart intended to help the reader to place the different meetings and developments is on page xix.) Chapter 5 reflects further on the various difficulties and on why the very nature of the Freudian unconscious makes difference inevitable. Chapter 6 elaborates in detail on the work to evolve the new method, and Chapter 7 describes taking parts in groups using this new method with recent examples. Chapter 8 discusses the workshop experience in terms of some aspects of group processes and group dynamics, as well as using the feedback we have received from a questionnaire sent to participants. Chapter 9 looks to applications of the method in supervision and teaching and Chapter 10 summarizes the kinds of comparisons we are becoming to be able to make. We hope eventually to publish a comparison of the different methods that we have identified of doing psychoanalysis, but this will be for a further volume.

2

In praise of empiricism

Paul Denis (France)

Misunderstandings between psychoanalysts from different schools or different countries are not common – they are the norm. Any international psychoanalytic congress can provide numerous examples of this, although we shall deal presently with a misunderstanding that arose between Theodore Jacobs and André Green at the International Psychoanalytical Association Congress in 1993.

To illustrate the benefits of taking into account the analyst's psychic functioning during the sessions, Jacobs (1993a, 1993b) has given a detailed report of a session during which his own intercurrent thoughts had given him a better understanding of what was happening for his patient. Calmly reading this paper today, it is very obvious to see both a psychoanalyst at work, listening to his countertransference reactions, and a patient who is truly engaged in an analysis, experiencing a fairly characteristic form of father transference. Although, when presenting the case, Jacobs refrained from doing so, any analyst reading this material can perceive the homosexual aspects of the situation, including Jacobs' comments about his own past submission towards his elder brother. Any readers who are psychoanalysts will also think about their own clinical cases and sequences from their own work, a product that in some ways demonstrates the integrity of the clinical account. Although he did not, should Jacobs have explained this homosexual aspect and detailed the personal fantasies that are likely to have been activated in this session – despite being in front of the three thousand participants at a congress, including some of the analyst's former patients and supervisees? My own response is that Jacobs was under no obligation to mention the homosexual subtext of the analysis, and that, as it was, Jacobs' paper was more than adequate to launch the discussion and to benefit everyone. With this in mind, it seems that André Green's comments were extraordinarily acerbic. Far from reading between the lines and crediting Jacobs with current psychoanalytic knowledge, and far from taking into account the limitations imposed on his report by the very circumstances of its presentation, Green (1993) not only criticized Jacobs, but also pronounced an anathema: the homosexual aspect of the transference had neither been taken into account nor interpreted by Jacobs, no consideration had been given to the patient's relationship with his mother, and Jacobs had restricted himself to an analysis of the ego in the pure tradition of ego psychology, thereby demonstrating the limitations of this way of thinking; furthermore, Jacobs had, in Green's eyes, demonstrated the *non-psychoanalytic* nature of the account presented.

This dissension, arguably exacerbated by Green's personal style, is of interest because it exemplifies the difficulty that psychoanalysts have in appreciating the (equally) psychoanalytic work conducted by another practitioner (here, Jacobs) who has received a different training and who belongs to a different theoretical movement. Let us look at the misunderstanding in more detail: Green begins by suspecting Jacobs of some form of dishonesty, believing that the associations that Jacobs presents as having arisen during the session had in fact occurred to him afterwards in the process of writing it up:

> I find it difficult to believe that Jacobs was able *at one and the same time* to listen to what the patient had to say to him *and* to allow himself to listen so much to his own thoughts. Is it possible to listen to two communications at the same time, even if there is some resonance between them? If Jacobs was able to let himself dwell on his associations, he must, almost of necessity, have stopped listening to the patient during this time. But, you will object, what about evenly-suspended attention? This, it seems to me, is different from the implicit bipolarity of the work in the session presented by Jacobs.
>
> (Green, 1993: 1133, emphases in original)

Green argues that the way in which Jacobs says that he worked runs counter to 'true' analytic work. Ergo, in Green's eyes Jacobs is not a psychoanalyst and what he says is consequently worthless.

Green continues in his attempt to discredit Jacobs by contrasting his work with that of Dennis Duncan (1993):

In the first case, the patient's psychic material is considered from different viewpoints according to the line of interpretation being favoured, whereas in the second (Duncan's case) the analyst allows himself to be penetrated by the personal evocations aroused in him by the analysand's communications, which then provide some answers to the analyst's questions and effectively impose a 'ventriloquistic' interpretation.

(Green, 1993: 1134)

We might, moreover, question this praise of ventriloquism in the analyst. The ventriloquist cannot function without a puppet; who, therefore, is the puppet? The patient? Certainly not. Is Green then suggesting that it is the analyst who is the puppet of his own unconscious?

Regardless of these unresolved questions, Green continues by arguing that Jacobs was deeply 'penetrated' by what the patient said to him and by his attitude. Jacobs confesses to feeling poorly dressed and inferior in relation to his patient – an open admission of the 'penetration' of the analyst's psyche by the patient's words, but, for Green, this admission is of no consequence; it must only be demonstrated that Jacobs is not an analyst, while Duncan (and Green himself by extension) is the true analyst. Green therefore asserts that Jacobs cannot possibly work all the time in the way that he has described: 'It seems to me somewhat doubtful whether Jacobs is able to work on his own inner experiences in this way in every session and with all his patients' (Green, 1993: 1134).

So Jacobs is apparently an absolute impostor – even if he never said that he always works in this way and regardless of the fact that he is well aware that this is a specific patient and a specific session. Green does not relent:

Excessively close attention to the patient's ethnic, social, economic and 'psychological' (in the strict sense of the word) background has the same effect as the trees for which the wood cannot be seen. Such a view confines the analyst within a somewhat limited view of analytic psychopathology.

(Green, 1993: 1134)

It is entirely possible that, in general, excessively close attention to a patient's 'ethnic, social, economic and psychological' context may prove an obstacle to seeing all of his psychopathological wood but, in the particular case presented by Jacobs, where is this excessive attention? Is it not the patient's very personality that makes itself felt in an appeal to the analyst's psyche? No matter. For Green, this analyst from another school must be wrong, and probably because he is North American – since that is where this evil comes from: 'Had I been an analyst on New York's East Side and exposed to the influences of my local society, I would no doubt have felt comfortable with the standpoints adopted by Jacobs' (Green, 1993: 1131).

However, Green feels that the New Yorker's dishonesty is even more serious: he fails to quote his sources and has donned a mask:

> Jacobs's contribution, unlike others' . . . is completely devoid of references . . . This is tantamount to a statement of theoretical virginity, with attention focussing exclusively on the clinical aspects of the treatment. . . . Even when our opinions appear to have been shaped by the practice alone, they may in fact be inspired by an implicit theory concealed behind the facts. How, in fact, could it be otherwise?
>
> (Green, 1993: 1132)

Green is not to be deceived; to him, Jacobs' theory is visible and perceptible, and when theory takes priority over interaction, this is bad. In fact, it is anti-analytic:

> There is no place in the analytic session for acts, on the part of either the analysand or the analyst. Models based on a reference to action – 'interaction', 'trans-action' – represent not so much a step forward as a dangerous digression.
>
> (Green, 1993: 1135)

Such is Green's conviction that he confuses figurative with literal meaning, unless, for the sake of the cause, he is merely feigning ignorance that an interaction – here between two psyches – does not necessarily involve an act or an action. The scale of the misunderstanding and the accusatory nature of Green's account would have Jacobs carry out a moderate intervention in response to the key points of his prosecutor's indictment.

This incident, therefore, illustrates the difficulty that characterizes clinical discussions between psychoanalysts from different schools. If we consider Green's account as a whole – of which the quotations here give an indication – it is striking to observe that it brings together two disparate discourses: on the one hand, it puts forward a viewpoint concerning psychoanalytic treatment, a perfectly acceptable one that is palpably held by an experienced analyst well-versed in the practice of supervision and the labyrinths of theory, while, on the other, it sets forth an ideological discourse, according to which *ego psychology* is no longer at all psychoanalytic, and that, consequently, no analyst trained in this movement can truly be a psychoanalyst. Green in effect dismisses an entire psychoanalytic movement. It is a matter no longer of discussing a colleague's work, but of combating heresy.

During some highly productive meetings in small groups between the British Psychoanalytical Society and the Paris Psychoanalytical Society, participants have found themselves enmeshed in some confrontations and misunderstandings of a similar nature to that of Jacobs and Green. In terms of clinical work, the four or five weekly sessions presented by some 'Kleinian' analysts were compared to the three weekly sessions presented by the French analysts, and the gulf between the two at times seemed so wide that one wondered why the same term – psychoanalysis – had been used in both cases. Nevertheless, the discussion generally proved to be mutually beneficial for the participants. From a reading of *The Freud–Klein Controversies 1941–1945* (King and Steiner, 1991), it would appear that the internal discussions in the British Psychoanalytical Society were at the time no less problematic. It is probably no coincidence that David Tuckett, the instigator and principal architect of the working group from which this book has emerged, should be a member of this highly composite, if not divided, British Society.

A plausible explanation for one school damning another can be found in the constant tension that exists in psychoanalysis between its scientific ambitions and its fundamentally empirical nature. 'Empirical' here stands at perhaps one remove from the meaning associated with the so-called 'hard' sciences. For, based as it is on clinical experience, psychoanalysis lacks any possibility for experimentation and cannot adduce the same type of evidence as the 'harder,' natural sciences.

Psychoanalytic empiricism therefore operates on the margins between two types of clinical observation: treating symptoms, on the one hand, and treating the unconscious, on the other; that is, between treating what is manifest and treating latent psychic processes. This treatment of unconscious phenomena is deductive, hence the term 'metapsychology' (the psychology of psychology), which refers to its formulations. It has thus been possible to develop an entire body of reliable knowledge, verifiable by the practice of the treatment. However, clinical experience has also formed the basis for the construction of different, albeit occasionally interconnected, theoretical systems, which often either accord new meanings to what are considered classical terms, or use different words to describe analogous concepts that have arisen from similar, but not identical, experiences. Despite these similarities, however, every psychoanalytic treatment is in fact unique simply because there are no two identical patients nor any two psychoanalysts who have emerged from the same mould. Even two identical twins analysed by identical twin psychoanalysts with exactly the same analytic training experience with the same analyst would not provide an example of two identical analyses. Psychoanalytic method is intrinsically monographic and statistics are completely inapplicable here – meaning that 'empirical' research into psychoanalysis is, in the common sense of the term, rare. In fact, the scientific 'voluntarism' of analysts, instead of having a unifying effect, has produced such theoretical Babelism that accounts of clinical cases, if they are presented in theoretical language, basically become obscure to a psychoanalyst from a different culture. The diversity of the models that have developed is not the whole story; fundamental difficulties arise when analysts are too fiercely attached to their own model – as perhaps exemplified by the Green–Jacobs debate.

In order better to understand the attachment that analysts feel to their own model, it seems to me important to take into account the traumatic quality of the psychoanalyst's work. If they are not to limit themselves to indoctrinating their patients with ready-made formulas, psychoanalysts must allow themselves to be taken over by their patient's psychic functioning; moments of anxiety and guilt and various emotions will be aroused during the sessions, unsettling the analyst's own usual reference-points. In confronting this trauma, which is probably moderate but repeated indefinitely in the course of the day, the psychoanalyst's elaborative capacities are stretched to the utmost, and it must be admitted that they may at times be overwhelmed. In the desire to avoid being disorganized or made too anxious, analysts undergo the chronic temptation of a fetishistic solution: to cling to the method that they have been taught, to hypercathect it, and to remain faithful to ideas that, at any moment, have served them almost as an ideology of analysis, an ideology that is cathected with greater religious intensity the more harrowing their patients become. Psychoanalytic culture thus turns into a culture of *persuasion*. Every other technique is interpreted as a challenge to this counter-phobic belief system and consequently rejected on the basis of the (seemingly universal) formula of psychoanalytic anathema: 'this is not psychoanalysis'.

Discussions between authors from different groups, when they compare theoretical elaborations, are often characterized by these ideological viewpoints and by belief systems based on a tradition that idealizes the way in which revered masters proceed. Behind the arguments is concealed, often rather badly, a confrontation that is the equivalent of one child saying to the next, 'My dad's bigger than your dad', or to that exchange attributed to two patients: 'You see, to my analyst, your analyst's unconscious would be absolutely transparent.'

When debate (as opposed to anathema) does take place, one may often notice a divergence between practices, particularly when discussing clinical examples, but one might also notice that there are often common elements between theoretical approaches, which can also appear compatible on other levels. The opposite is also true at times: whereas the theoretical languages are different, the way of proceeding is ultimately similar and identifiable by a psychoanalyst from another culture as close or ultimately analogous to his own.

'Scientific' discussions are therefore generally problematic: the concepts, even those that might be considered fundamental, have sometimes assumed completely different meanings from one country to another. While every author may not have introduced their own vocabulary, they have often moved on from the classical notions: among authors such as Grunberger, Kohut or Rosenfeld for example, 'narcissism' no longer refers to Freud's definitions. This reinterpretation of terms can happen to such an extent that if at an international conference someone says that a patient experienced a 'narcissistic regression' at a particular moment in his treatment, it is more than likely that lengthy explanations will be required to prevent any misunderstandings.

Returning to the example of Green's attitude towards the clinical material presented by Jacobs, we might speculate about its historical foundations. During his training years, Green was confronted with clashes that led to schisms in the French psychoanalytic movement and ultimately to Lacan's resignation from the IPA after the revocation of his training analyst status following a site visit from the IPA.

The training candidates at the time were caught between a simplistic teaching of psychoanalysis that was strongly influenced by the prevailing ego psychology model and, on the other hand, the powerful attraction exercised by Lacan and his theories. Having lost his official status as a psychoanalyst, Lacan adopted a very specific position that consisted in presenting himself, on the contrary, as *the only* psychoanalyst, whereas all the others were worthless 'IPA-ists' who were only pseudo-analysts, for they had lost the spirit of Freud that he, Lacan, claimed to have preserved. The 'Americans' were especially targeted, and in particular the proponents of ego psychology, a movement to which Loewenstein – who had been Lacan's analyst (apparently with limited success) – belonged. Having been 'excommunicated', Lacan made some pronouncements that would likely have been anathema to outsiders. Green's attitude towards Jacobs becomes more understandable, therefore, when we remember that he was close to Lacan for a long period. Without ever having been in analysis with him, Green participated in one of Lacan's working groups on some clinical cases, faithfully attended Lacan's 'Seminar', and for a long time sought to draw benefit from Lacanianism. Even if, ultimately, Green recognized that Lacan's entire approach was leading him away from psychoanalysis, he has preserved something of the Lacanian trait of discrediting the opponent and claiming exclusivity as a psychoanalyst (which is not, admittedly, to mention Green's own propensity for polemicizing debate).

We can imagine other similar scenarios: for example, in Great Britain, the anathema pronounced on Melanie Klein by Glover probably continued for a long time in clashes between Kleinians, 'Contemporary Freudians' and the 'Middle Group' – until it became necessary to establish a formal agreement that candidates should not carry out their entire training under a single banner. Furthermore, discussions concerning Kohut's latest viewpoints and the debates concerning 'self-disclosure' by the analyst are no more amicable.

That said, while psychoanalysts may pronounce that practitioners and/or theorists from other schools are anathema, we must also distinguish between that which belongs to the realm of psychoanalysis and that which genuinely has ceased to do so. Jung, among others, clearly left psychoanalysis (see, for example, Bergmann, 2004: 14 et seq.), but the temptation gradually to abandon the excessively restrictive demands of the classical psychoanalytic treatment is something felt by each of us to a lesser or greater extent, and within all psychoanalytic societies.

To avoid conflicts, premature judgements and purely theoretical debates, one solution might be to take refuge in what I will call a form of pragmatism. Everything that happens when a treatment is set up in a particular framework could arbitrarily be defined, for example, as psychoanalytic. In this way, any treatment, say, in which a patient is seen *x* times a week for a duration of *y* minutes per session would be deemed psychoanalytic. Such a method, whereby the 'psychoanalytic' status or otherwise of a certain method was determined by the frequency and duration of the sessions, would settle every debate. However, it would place little value on the unique nature of psychoanalytic work and the *content* of what takes place in the otherwise 'psychoanalytic' framework. Any interpretation at all that emerged during these sessions would be reckoned psychoanalytic. The inadequacy of such a definition is clear, however; such an 'anything goes' approach only creates or reinforces psychic chaos – something that we could claim to know *empirically* (albeit not in the conventional sense of the word) from reflecting on experience, such as in supervised analyses. As such, we see that what I am calling a pragmatic definition of psychoanalysis would essentially be based on methods and results; it would be a means of limiting the space for reflection and, above all, a means of avoiding theory – the third term mentioned by Dana Birksted-Breen in her Introductory Foreword. In this way, what I want to call empiricism here constitutes an elaboration of the experience that what I call pragmatism merely records; or, in other words, empiricism recognizes that which is psychoanalytic, while pragmatism defines (and thus limits) it.

In this way, the reference-points indicated by Freud for recognizing what is psychoanalytic – the unconscious, infantile sexuality and the Oedipus complex – are ultimately empirical, facts of our experience or not. For we must bear in mind that these three elements are only theoretical at one remove; Freud does in fact implicitly refer to the discovery of the unconscious as a personal experience, to the experience of infantile sexuality as a presence within us, and to the experience of our oedipal feelings and their organizing power. The reference to reality, that is to experience, is for him essential:

Not even the most tempting probability is a protection against error; even if all the parts of a problem seem to fit together like the pieces of a jigsaw puzzle, one must reflect that what is probable is not necessarily the truth and that the truth is not always probable.

And lastly, it did not seem attractive to find oneself classed with the schoolmen and Talmudists who delight in exhibiting their ingenuity without regard to how remote from reality their thesis may be.

(Freud, 1939: 17)

From the outset, Freud's approach proves to have been fundamentally empirical, based on experience; this is why 'research' and 'therapeutics' are always connected in his works (see Chapter 5). It was by reflecting on his own experience of dreams and comparing it with his patients' dream experiences that he established the existence of the unconscious and a 'science of dreams'; that is, a body of knowledge about dreams that nevertheless remains limited by its empirical foundations. The theory of neuroses was conceived in the same way.

The analytic experience is hindered in its scientific ambitions by the undecidable and irreversible nature of its subject matter. Psychic causality is not pathognomic; a trauma that clearly seems to have produced a particular symptom in one person seems to have no effect on another. Moreover, there is no point at which it is ever possible to go back. While discontinuing a medicine generally involves a return to the *status quo ante*, discontinuing a psychoanalytic treatment stops nothing but the meetings with the psychoanalyst; what has been experienced during the sessions remains in our experience and something continues that cannot be measured. What analysts observe is connected with their own history and their own analysis.

In psychoanalysis, the object of knowledge must be constructed from two objects of study: what takes place in the patient's psyche and what takes place in the analyst's psyche. In no other discipline are the object of knowledge and the object of study so closely interconnected; a characteristic that psychoanalysis shares with the social sciences is the impossibility of any recourse to experimentation. If it cannot entirely be a science in some senses, metapsychology can at least claim to be a form of empiricism, in the highest sense of the term, an empiricism based on experience but one that is capable of formulating principles. A comparison of the various ways in which different analysts proceed, both within a single group and between different cultural groups, cannot therefore be based on comparing 'scientific' results or evaluating the theories that have emerged from these practices, even if this comparison may have much to recommend it (as would a comparison of the clinical profiles of patients treated by analysts in different countries).

The method that we are here proposing entails not only listening to a clinical account, such as that of Jacobs, but also completely reversing the antagonistic mode of listening that is so well illustrated by Green's indictment. The speaker's status as a psychoanalyst is regarded a priori as an established fact, and his interventions are considered in terms of their effect – both intended and actual – on the psychoanalytic process at that moment in the treatment. Beyond the elements of this method that have already been described, and which serve both for finding reference points and as a basis for comparisons, this involves a similar approach to Freud's comparison of his own neurotic pathology with that of his patients, or conducting the experiment of this comparison. In the method set out in this book, the experiment of comparison is conducted in small groups of ten to twelve psychoanalysts. The psychoanalysts who take part in this adventure – for adventure it is – reveal not only a clinical case, but also their way of proceeding; that is to say, their personality and, so to speak, their professional symptomatology. Those who listen to it and then discuss what has taken place during the sessions presented also take a risk in revealing their capacity to understand another person's patient and to identify with a colleague from a different background. Empirically, this experiment of comparison has two types of results. First, there is for each participant a private result that comes from a different perspective on his or her own conceptions, expanding in some sense the field of vision; and second, there is a 'collective' result that comes from the shared endeavour of applying the method.

As clearly emerges from the chapters specifically dedicated to it, this method has started from the description of experience and so has been empirical in its very formulation. From the initial attempts to the most recent working groups, the aim has been to elaborate shared experience and this has made it possible to develop an investigative method that can be applied by psychoanalysts who have not directly participated in its construction. Just as psychoanalysis, according to Freud, combines research and therapeutics, this comparative method combines research and reciprocal training.

However empirical in nature, this method also brings results. As there is no possible recourse to experimentation, we must indeed be satisfied with a 'principle-based empiricism' while accepting its limitations, which have been emphasized with faint contempt by Claude Bernard (1999: 204): 'Empiricism . . . is only unconscious and/or non-rational experience, acquired by every-day observation of facts'.

We must recognize that this formula applies almost too well to the psychoanalytic approach. However, lacking any possibility of an 'experimental' psychoanalysis, empiricism is our sole option: comparatively reflecting, in a *test of comparison*, on the form of unconscious experience that is constituted by psychoanalysis in its very custom and practice(s). This approach provides a way of moving forward from sterile confrontations, drawing benefit from other people's perspectives and testing the general rules that are commonly accepted. It is on this condition that psychoanalysis will be able to continue its development and, in clear distinction to other methods, assert its field of operation and its unique nature.

Acknowledgements

This chapter has been translated by Sophie Leighton with support from the European Psychoanalysis Federation scientific initiative.

3

Before the method, underestimating the
problem and the meeting in Prague

Tomas Böhm (Sweden)

Prologue

Prague is a beautiful city with unforgettable sights, like the Karlbridge
or Charles Bridge, the old Town Hall and the Jewish cemetery. When
we arrived for the EPF Conference in 2002, it seemed as though the
good soldier Švejk and his relaxed friends were waiting for us in the
restaurants with Knödl and Staropramen beer. The conference took
place in the local Hilton, which was situated in a peripheral part of
the city's kernel, and which resembled a modern, displaced American
monument in the midst of a central European historical capital.

We, the moderators in the conference's clinical groups, were
recruited by the organizers of this first Working Party on Clinical
Issues because they knew us personally and because we all spoke
English (as well as several other languages). I had myself been in
supervision groups with Haydée Faimberg, who set up the groups
(see the Appendix). I was interested in the problem of different psychoanalytic schools, in the differences in views about technique, and,
above all, in the absolute conviction of many analysts who thought
that they were right in what they were doing. But I knew very little
about what we were supposed to do in these new working groups
when I arrived in Prague, although we had received some correspondence about the aims of organizing them. We had been told that
there should be no supervision in the groups and we should assume
that all presenting analysts *were* analysts, which meant that we should

50

not evaluate different methods into better or worse, or into more or less analytic categories. We had also received a suggestion from the organizers to raise six basic questions with the groups about the presenting analyst's way of working – but these questions were to be more like a fallback in case the work didn't develop spontaneously. Sure enough, it seems that in most groups the questions were not used.

And so, we knew in advance only a little about the explicit aims of the project, but, as the conference went on, we learnt more about these aims in the real life of a group that was struggling for a new kind of comparative structure. At the first meeting, the moderator had no real instruction or instruments and, although we had received some hints about what we should *not* do, the task of discussing analytic material in a meta-technical and neutral way was new to us. That said, the role of moderator could be understood as a parallel to the analyst's role; that is, providing the presence of another person for doing analysis of associative material.

The aim of the groups

This is a shortened version of how the aims of the group were explained in a letter to the moderators from David Tuckett:

> The task of these small groups is to help to develop a mode/language of discussion for psychoanalytic work and particularly to find some relatively unsaturated conceptual tools to permit description and comparison of different ways of working.
>
> Each presenter has been chosen through a consultation process in the wider working party with the aim of selecting colleagues whose reputation in their own society is for sensitive and competent psychoanalytic work. A starting assumption, therefore, is that each presenter is doing psychoanalysis. The challenge is to define what doing psychoanalysis actually means in each particular case: for that presenter in that case based on what is actually described and demonstrated in those sessions.
>
> We can refer to each presenter's way of working as demonstrating in practice his or her method or model.
>
> There are a number of underlying reasons for wanting to try to conceptualize better and in the most detailed way the different METHODS (models) that each of the colleagues presenting uses.

Formal structure

This new style conference in Prague was the first attempt in the EPF to use working parties (see the Appendix). Our Working Party on Clinical Issues had ten groups of twelve colleagues each. These 120 analysts were selected in the following way. Half that number was proposed by the representatives of each society as being experienced analysts; the representatives indicated those more suited to be presenters and those more suited to be discussants. From this list of sixty, we also chose the moderators and reporters.

The other half of the vacancies were left open as a pre-registration option for colleagues wanting to attend the conference and to take part in this kind of clinical discussion. One person was asked to be presenter, both being prepared to register very early and being known for his competence.

Three hundred analysts applied to participate in the small groups; this led inevitably to exclusions – a situation which was quite unexpected. (In the event, three ad-hoc groups were added, with presenters found only a few days beforehand; these groups ran on later days in the conference.)

First impressions: chaos is our beginning

I remember a crowded lobby at the Hilton, with lots of lists on noticeboards about groups and group members – and a note that the moderators should get together in a room before the groups started. People everywhere were trying to understand where and when to go and what their role was and why. I escaped from the chaos of the lobby to the moderators' preparation room, where we were curious and a bit tense. What was this about? Why did I volunteer to do this chaotic and seemingly unstructured work? As I remember it, Haydée Faimberg was there assisted by Paul Williams, and perhaps also David Tuckett. They looked friendly and a bit rosy-cheeked and excited, and they talked again about the goal of comparing different psycho-analytic languages, different ways of conceptualizing analytic work and how to create a better clinical understanding between analysts. It all sounded wonderful in theory, but soon we would be out there in different groups trying to do it in practice.

In each group there were two different presenting analysts whose clinical work we were supposed to compare. They looked rather anxious, as though they were about to dive from a 10-metre platform into a small pool: no one could be certain that there was water down there. In a way it is very odd that, after years of conferences and so-called scientific discussion, such a basic thing as trying to find out what you really mean could be so difficult. But obviously this way of looking at details, comparing styles, exploring implicit models and letting a group analyse these models could provoke anxiety because 'people believe they know what they are doing', as someone in the noisy lobby said.

In addition to a moderator and two presenters, each group had a reporter, who would take notes on the discussion, as well as discussants who had prepared thoughts about the clinical material. This being our first attempt to structure the groups, not everyone had an active role, but in later conferences every group member became responsible for different issues. As for the reporters, their role was at first somewhat controversial, since we had to resolve confidentiality issues: we started by having reporters disguise all identities of presenters and patients.

The reports from each group were then made available for further reflection. Upon rereading them four years later they give a vivid first impression of the difficulties that we had in most of the different groups. The first word that comes to mind is 'over-ambitious'. Maybe this is a necessary phenomenon when you introduce some kind of pioneer work. One finds oneself wanting to do too much, which seems somewhat naive in retrospect, but which seemed realistic at the time. For instance, what does one make of the idea of comparing two analysts in the same group when we didn't even know what to look for in *one* analyst. Beforehand, this task seemed reasonable, as though we expected the comparison itself to bring out the factors that were different and make them more clear. Actually performing this task, however, made us realize (and gave us the opportunity to work out) how much we would need to develop in future conferences.

Warming up with clinical discussions

I always find it a fascinating experience to recognize that colleagues all over the world seem to do the same kind of work, seeing patients that are not that different and struggling with similar problems sitting in practices that look quite a bit like my own. On the other hand, our task was to find out what the hidden *different* agendas were and where we took similarities too much for granted. By hidden agendas I mean not only theoretical and technical differences, including private theories, but also power struggles about having the 'right' opinion and wanting to convince others or make an impression with one's own convictions.

Most groups seem to have started intuitively, with a clinical discussion of the cases in a way that the members were used to. Group members came from different European countries and in my English-speaking group no one seemed to know anyone else more than superficially. From the beginning it struck us, that whatever else came out of this, it would be a great way to get to know European colleagues professionally and maybe also personally. In this way we would also come closer to understanding – and tolerating! – the differences between us. The task was to get a grip on *what* these differences were and how to describe them.

Even if we tried not to spend too much time on background facts, it seemed necessary to get acquainted with the material and the way the group members heard it and understood the dynamics. To prepare ourselves for the unknown task of defining and comparing, we needed this warm-up and process of feeling safe with each other. Here are some comments from some of the reports:

> trying out our clinical hunches about the cases is actually a necessary step towards forming a picture of how this analyst works – he or she knows the patient and what it is like to be with her, but we do not.

> Once there was a sufficient grasp of what might be going on psychoanalytically, there seemed to be enough confidence to begin exploring and trying to systematize what the analyst might be doing. However, here I think the group came up against a problem. There was a genuine uncertainty as to what a psychoanalytic model actually is. Did we understand roughly the same thing with transference, containment, countertransference and working from the surface? And what about *interpretation* and *analytic* models?

> We were lucky in a way to have two presenters who worked very differently. One presentation was of work very different from what most people recognized as analysis, so one had to work very hard to

really see what the presenter was wanting to do and not just think of it from one's own frame of thinking. People said they thought this presenter was Kohutian to which he/she responded that he/she was Kleinian! We never got to discuss concepts because we only got to the stage of beginning to identify differences.

Such experiences were typical of what was happening in most groups, and, as one of the reports I will discuss more in a moment makes clear, it seemed that, if this project was to develop, it would need some work on a conceptual framework that permitted working analysts to grasp what precisely a model is, so that we might orientate ourselves more towards the group task.

Confusion about the task

Confusion and frustration about the aims and purpose of the group task, about what and how to discuss, as well as about the roles of the different group members, influenced the work of the group, especially during the first group meeting. We all seemed tempted to fall back on the experience of clinical supervision groups with their more vertical or hierarchical relationships between members: supervisors, experienced analysts, young members and candidates. The difficulty here was to find a *horizontal* relationship between group members where no one was supervising and the moderator had only the task of focusing the group on its aim. As one reporter described it:

> Most of us apart from the moderator tended to different degrees to fall into formulating the patient's problems and/or supervising the analyst, and into discussing the presenter's model with an (implicitly critical) comparison with our own. However, our moderator was a cheerful but determined taskmaster. The six questions were not referred to for guidance, even though some were spontaneously raised.

Below are some extended excerpts from a group report showing how a group is struggling to find clarity about the aims of finding models of work in the presenting analysts. Many clever viewpoints are found here, but the confusion about the task still seems to dominate. It may also be an illustration of how hard it is for readers from outside really to understand a report made from someone on the inside of a group.

Warming up

There seemed to be much goodwill and effort in the group to establish a sense of mutual understanding and to respect the presenting analysts' positions. The objective of the gathering – to try to grasp the analysts' models – seemed to be a rather ambitious one, requiring first a number of steps before the group was in a position to address models. For example, in this group there was a clear need for a process of mental negotiation with the presented material in order to establish a sense that this was psychoanalysis being practised. The group brought their own models to bear on the material and flexibly tried to establish connections so that enough common ground was laid for a discussion. To this reporter, the ensuing discussions in the meeting were a kind of 'retroactive' comparative analysis of ways of thinking: inter-subjective and intra-subjective responses to the material were subsequently unpacked and elaborated in an attempt to reveal similarities and differences. This process of defining where one stands in relation to the material and then reflecting on various positions seems to be the core of this kind of group work.

What is a psychoanalytic model?

Once there was a sufficient grasp of what might be going on psychoanalytically, there seemed to be enough confidence to begin exploring and trying to systematize what the analyst might be doing. However, here I think the group came up against a problem. There was a genuine uncertainty as to what a psychoanalytic model actually is. It seems that if this project is to develop we need to do some work on a conceptual framework that permits working analysts to grasp what a model is in order to orientate ourselves more towards the group task.

A reference to Bowlby (from one of the analysts) indicates that the presenter believes that, as long as the patient can come back and 'find' the analyst, this will help her. Is this one of the presenter's models? The notion of 're-finding' the object in order to deal with her confusion is the way in which the analyst feels it is best to approach this patient.

From a theory viewpoint, how does the analyst formulate this attitude or model into forms of intervention that will help the patient? The presenter mentions Green, Winnicott, etc., who inform his ideas and interpretations.

The presenter seems to look for supervision

The presenter reflected on how the fourth (somewhat overwhelming) session made it hard for him to use his countertransference to good effect. Contact was too difficult to maintain. The patient seemed not to respond to most interpretations; the process faltered. This pressed the analyst into being even more explanatory in approach . . .

It was suggested that it might be important to focus on her destructiveness given the extent to which she destroys the good object . . .

The presenter says he felt overwhelmed by anxiety in this session – there was too much happening – hence his rejecting interpretation. He feels that he was forced into a position of not being able to understand; he felt like a puppet in her hands. He couldn't use his countertransference feelings because the patient was paralysing his thinking.

The group oscillates between supervision and looking for the 'model'

A participant refers to the patient's attacking behaviour and to the analyst's reaction. The session is a fight, but it is not oedipal. It is more linked to the comment about the loss of the object (weekend) leading to attack. She has lost her good object and her idealized object so she attacks the bad object and the analyst reacts losing his normal capacity for containment.

One discussant thinks that the presenter's model contains a number of aspects including oedipal and pre-oedipal 'sub-models'.

The analyst has a Winnicottian 'ideal–typical' model which is his preference and this then appears to become disrupted by the patient's pre-oedipal functioning.

The presenter replies that his model is very much linked to countertransference fantasies. These fantasies are unconscious and not immediately understandable and there is no model available at that point – it is invoked in order to give shape to what is happening. The idea of 'enactment' is unavoidable and must be taken into account.

The discussant says that countertransference is a psychic reality, whether or not one has a model. Interpreting at different levels, even if one makes mistakes, generates new ideas.

Somebody offers an analogy: the analyst falls into the water and has many ways of getting to the surface for oxygen. He has lost oxygen, rather like the patient. The patient tried to get to father's bed as a defensive way of dealing with this but the primary issue is the loss of oxygen and how to recover it is the fundamental issue.

There was general agreement that a model is not an abstract notion but a complex combination of personal, internal, historical, bodily experiences that are in communication with intellectual and theoretical perspectives.

This lengthy vignette seems to be an example of our first lack of structure in Prague, where we tried to structure roles in groups, but were not experienced enough to know how to. It seems obvious from this group report that group members in Prague were talking much more about their own models than trying to focus on the model of the presenter, something that we learnt gradually to do in later conferences.

To supervise or not to supervise

From the beginning of the clinical discussions in Prague, I noted a strong temptation and tendency for group members to supervise the presenting analyst. This might also be part of the common clinical discussion experience: someone presents to get viewpoints on a problematic clinical situation, and supervision seems like the natural thing to do. It is also probably a way to define your position in a group – that you are someone who can contribute with fruitful thoughts. But this time it was supposed to be different.

One reporter formulated it like this:

I would say that the group found sticking to it [the task of studying the style of clinical work being used] very difficult. Most of us except the moderator tended to different degrees to fall into formulating the patient's problems and/or supervising the analyst, and into discussing the presenter's model with an (implicitly critical) comparison with our own.

The same reporter also added that the clinical discussion – apart from supervision – in itself seemed to be necessary.

As a moderator, I found this task new and challenging. There were both more and less experienced analysts present in the group, but I had to stop all of them – sometimes with considerable verbal force – from supervising in an implicitly critical way. What we were supposed to find out was the way the analysts themselves seemed to think about their work and how they worked – not what *we* thought or liked or disliked about it! This also meant that the presenting analyst might have an implicit theory of the way he or she worked and a different, explicit theory that came out in practice. The moderator also had to protect the presenting analyst from the invading viewpoints. Another moderator comments on this:

a lot of my energy over the meetings and afterwards was to protect the presenters or make them feel better afterwards. Maybe this is because the task was nebulous and so people tended to 'supervise' instead of what the task was meant to be (more so in Prague than in subsequent years, where there was a 'grid').

To understand the other's perspective

The following quotation from one of the reports sums up the problems involved in understanding the perspective(s) of the other participants:

Prague was particularly interesting because my group had a presentation of a very different point of view and it was remarkable how difficult it was for people not simply to look at this presentation from their own perspective, or even to realize that the analyst had something in mind with her way of working. I even had virtually to rewrite the reporter's report, which wiped out the understanding that I think had been achieved. It is also clear that many people believe they are working in the transference, even though from someone else's point of view they often are not. One has to get beyond common assumptions about words to begin to understand another perspective.

I also got the impression that the reasons some groups 'loved each other' was because they felt they thought the same, which I think says something very important about how much people hate difference and how gratified they feel by sameness. (Also I think they had felt quite threatened by the task and were happy to 'stick together'.) I also discovered how some people don't want to be bothered with a different point of view (some of my best friends . . .!) and thus happy when it's the same.

Other observations about the group work

Considerable effort was made in the groups to try to find a framework of comparison. For instance, it was suggested that perhaps many of the contrasts between the presenting analysts hinge on the *being versus doing* dichotomy – to accompany the patients through their journey versus having to offer new understanding actively. This dichotomy was sometimes also compared to mother versus father and nurse versus doctor. Here is one report:

> Many of these contrasts seem to hinge on the being versus doing dichotomy – do we trust psychoanalysis to do its healing work (of nurturing mental development) and see our role as to accompany the patient through this journey, or do we see ourselves as having, actively, to offer new understanding which will promote new ways of relating . . .?

None of this is intended to imply that those in the groups were not valuing their experience. They were: many individuals in groups expressed the wish to meet again with the same members, because of the good working atmosphere that was being created in the relatively long and intense time spent together.

That said, time was also found to be too short properly to accomplish some kind of relevant comparison. It was considered a difficult task to reach a third hermeneutic level, investigating the concepts used in psychoanalysis, even if this was preceded by second-level work like inter- or supervision.

Some groups underlined the importance of transference and countertransference feelings for understanding the patient. Also it was underlined that transference interpretations were given in the here and now so that the patient can grasp them. My own attitude towards transference interpretation is that these assumptions often bear the characteristics of confessions of faith in a religion. By underlining views about different transference interventions, it seemed as if members wanted to make certain that they belonged to the right tribe.

One group emphasized that they wanted to focus exclusively on the clinical material without relating to the presenter's own statements. This is also how some moderators later developed group work in subsequent conferences, where presenters were asked to sit passively and to listen to the group discussing their work, and maybe comment afterwards on their reaction to this discussion. This is also a way of discovering the difference between implicit and explicit theories. Another group wanted to ignore the presenter even more.

So, the following issues were in need of elaboration and discussion: where/what the data is, imposing theories, implicit theories and examples. In short, the group sessions posed a lot of complications for the task.

Summarizing the main difficulties

As indicated, the non-supervisory goal at first proved almost impossible, and demanded a great deal of insistent intervention from the moderators. Maybe this had to do with confusion about the new structure, the unfamiliarity with more horizontally working clinical groups in our hierarchical/vertical system of candidates, non-experienced and experienced supervisors, and renowned analysts. In the clinical groups of the later conferences, some experienced analysts have testified to feeling that this kind of learning experience has many advantages compared to conventional supervision. The analyst will ideally feel helped to see his or her own way of working more clearly, which is a good starting point for development, rather than trying out someone else's model without realizing one's own. On the other hand, there have been experienced analysts who found it very difficult, both in Prague and later, to let go both of their supervisory role and of their tendency to decide what is good/right or bad/wrong analysis.

The assumption 'everyone is an analyst' is not so easy to make in practice, even if it is an important assumption for these groups. When the analyst feels and thinks there is a psychoanalytic process going on, the group should assume that 'this is an analyst working'. This means that critical and/or upset feelings about good and bad practice must be set aside, which feels strange to us in clinical discussions. This, of course, also connects to the non-supervision difficulty. One way to reflect about this is to wonder whether all analysts have moments during their sessions with patients when 'a psychoanalytic process is going on' and other moments when it is not. The art of analysis may be to an important extent connected to the ways an analyst can increase the frequency of such moments in the process. When in later conference workshops the presenters were asked to select sessions where they thought a process was going on, it was a way of helping to define that it was an analyst who was working.

The 10-metre drop into a too-shallow pool, I mentioned before, is an image of the unknown and uncertain quality of these groups. In a way, this was not unexpected. The working group presented a structure that made many participants anxious. Some prominent and experienced analysts could not change from their usual supervisory or judging habits; other experienced analysts would hide behind their laptops and rationalized their behaviour as making notes on interesting viewpoints. In general, the less experienced members seemed to be more flexible and open to this new structure.

It became apparent that we lacked the tools to describe other people's work or even to listen to it and really hear it on their terms. This meant there was no comparative instrument either. This also contributed to the uncertainty and to the tendency to fall back on to well-known vertical, hierarchical structures, or even the basic assumptions described by Bion (1952).

This leads to thinking about the *Babelization* issue. Since the group members mainly used the same technical language, it was assumed that the same terms also meant the same things for different people. It soon turned out that this was not the case. Terminology regarding transference, countertransference, interpretation, frames, setting, perversion, narcissism and so forth turned out to be differently interpreted by different individuals and nationalities. When the moderators tried to get group members to leave technical jargon aside, the members tended to feel threatened by not being able to hide behind terminology. A central aim of these groups was to find better ways of understanding each other, and one way was to talk without terminology, so that we could be more certain about what the other person meant. In this way the confusion about implicit assumptions also diminished.

In some groups analysts presented problematic cases where they more or less explicitly needed supervision. When the analyst presented a case in which he or she was so much under siege that analysis was difficult, the group felt invited to wade in. Instead of focusing on the analyst's model, the group felt it would have to work on saving the analysis from a breakdown.

Most groups experienced the paradox of having too much to do and too little time to do it. Almost two days' intense work, with one or two sessions per day from two analysts, meant that groups had more time than in most comparable clinical seminars. This structure was designed to provide enough time for reflection, to change one's mind, to go back to earlier parts of the session, to try different ways of comparison and to discuss the aim of the group, but in the end there was too little time for all of the change and uncertainty that came with the new structure. The combined time limitations and uncertainty made some groups unstable; some members came too late, or could not participate the whole time or had not 'understood' that joining this kind of group meant 100 per cent presence.

The character of groups with members from different countries meant that people for the most part did not know each other or their ideas before the working groups took place. In traditional supervision groups, this arguably has fewer consequences, since the group members try to learn from a leader or teacher of some kind. In these more horizontal groups, however, the members tried to find sameness, not least because everyone shared the same profession, but instead they found difference, which no doubt felt threatening. People did start to get acquainted, and even made friends, but often they felt more threatened than curious about their differences of ideas. That said, sometimes the differences were so unclear or hidden that there was an illusion of sameness.

The confidentiality issue was similar to that in other clinical groups but there was also a special aspect to it here. The presenting analyst was exposed here in such a way that his implicit and explicit ways of working were analysed by the group. Confidentiality therefore involved protecting both the patient *and the presenting analyst* from being discussed outside of the group. This issue would be better resolved over the course of future congresses, but it was already a major issue in Prague.

One group's attempt to compare

One possible difference that was considered particularly important in assessing differences between working methods concerned the way in which the patient appeared to be *seen* by the analyst, which may be a basis for what is *done* by the analyst. It also seemed possible that the basic understanding of the *aims of psychoanalysis* was different between the two analysts. Certainly in Prague we underestimated the full extent of the complications in comparing aims. Both Snow White and Cinderella are fairy tales about young women who eventually meet a prince; but they are also very different stories and difficult to compare. Although impressionistic rather than systematic, Table 3.1 illustrates one group's attempt at comparing and shows in some small way what we were able to accomplish in that respect in Prague.

In spite of the differences outlined between them in Table 3.1, the similarities between the two analytic styles were more striking. Moreover, the group's discussion also suggested that the differences in the work described might be accounted for more by differences between the stages of analysis and the patient's ways of presenting, rather than by differences between the basic styles of the two analysts.

Nonetheless, the themes identified in this group's discussions have in fact recurred in later work, and in retrospect can be seen as good predictions of that against which we later came to try to discriminate. We were frequently to consider how to compare:

- the analyst's 'style' as a trait versus his or her way of working with a particular patient
- (interpretive) 'activity' versus (supportive) 'passivity' in the analyst
- focus on trauma or deprivation versus drives, e.g. aggression and destructiveness
- putting things into words versus leaving some things unspoken and giving patients space to find their own understanding over time

Table 3.1 A comparison between two analysts presenting in Prague

Presenter 1	Presenter 2
Development of the relationship to the object (analyst) is in the centre.	Withdrawal of the patient from the mutuality of relationship is not a spontaneous concern.
Considers the main task of the analyst as accepting affect precursors, detoxifying them, and giving them back to the patient.	Considers the main task of the analyst as creating links, integration, between mental areas, in the effort to create a picture of the patient's mind.
Tends to view the analysis mainly in terms of a 'two-mind psychology'.	Tends to view the analysis mainly in terms of a 'one-mind psychology'.
In some instances responds 'as an object', possibly with the idea of being a 'developmental object' for the patient.	Has more the stance of a 'participant observer'.
Interprets the transference. In some cases interprets 'in' the transference.	Avoids transference interpretations unless direct reference to the analyst is made by patient.
Holds a firm belief in the patient's capacity for development when given a good enough environment.	Holds a firm belief in the patient's capacity for development when given a good enough environment.
Draws the patient's attention to her behaviour in and outside sessions, and to her active responsibility for the situations she comes to be in.	Omits reference to the patient's behaviour in and outside sessions unless he makes direct reference to it.

- reassuring versus confronting
- working at the conscious or preconscious level versus interpreting unconscious meanings
- looking at what the patient is experiencing or suffering versus what he or she is doing (unconsciously repeating)
- speaking to the patient in 'ordinary language' which can be confidently understood versus using special terminology
- being drawn into countertransference (e.g. by showing when worried about the patient) versus using it to understand what patient is actualizing (but we seemed to agree that all of us would do the first en route to trying to do the second)

- seeing the patient as containing the seeds of healthy functioning, and naturally tending towards health in the right conditions versus suspecting the patient of maintaining pathology and resisting change unless we get her to see what she is doing (seeing the glass as half-full or half-empty)
- being a self-object (formulating and reflecting patient's feelings) versus being a whole object with an analytic function – the first might be a step towards the second
- needing to be a good object versus being willing to wait and seem impotent
- feeling that the patient brings out the best versus the worst in one as an analyst
- selecting one clinical fact versus another
- using one's own metaphors versus adopting those of the patient
- working consistently with one's conscious theory versus doing something different
- having a conscious theory of the patient's mind versus working with a primarily clinical theory.

I have mentioned how the patient's pathology, the length of the psychoanalysis and the stage in the analysis from which the sessions were chosen might possibly have important effects on the different presentations and how they are interpreted by the group. Even when these issues were specifically scrutinized and valued, it remained difficult to compare technical issues and the handling of the cases, since the differences regarding the aforementioned basic variables were too great, and so tended to invalidate the comparisons.

Proposal for the future

Sticking to the task, members of many groups had thoughts about how to progress with future work. Several groups proposed that it would be important in future groups to focus exclusively on the detailed clinical material in order to reveal the presenter's way of thinking and working, without relying too much on the presenter's own explicit statements on how they worked. One point of departure could be the scrutiny of the different technical concepts in relation to the clinical material (transference, countertransference, reconstruction, resistance, internal/external reality etc). The presenter could then listen to the discussion, without participating. After the discussion one could then let the presenter introduce his or her working model and compare it with the conclusions of the group. This presupposes detailed reports of the sessions, perhaps with a description of the presenter's own thoughts and feelings during the session, but one would in this way really approach the task psychoanalytically, trust one's method and one's tools, and hopefully arrive at a common understanding of concepts etc.

Thought was also given to the number of sessions presented. Four or even five sessions from a whole week had been presented in some groups. This was a lot to prepare for the presenter and an overwhelming amount of material to deal with. It put too much pressure on the group to get through and it reduced the time and space for reflection and discussion. It also put increased pressure on the moderator to watch the clock. There was doubt as to how far the last two sessions added to the process, and it was clearly necessary to reflect in future on exactly what presenters should be asked to do.

Three challenges

Looking at the reports from Prague, three challenges were immediately apparent:

- First, because discussion in the groups inevitably focused on so many different aspects of what it might be useful to conceptualize in order to describe and understand an analyst's way of working, some clarification as to how and what to compare was necessary. One moderator suggested that the wealth of ideas amounted to a logical multiplicity of models, viewpoints, assumptions and positions, which were not always easy to juxtapose and compare because they were not at the same logical level or in the same class.
- Second, in some sessions there was doubt as to whether psychoanalysis was going on at all. In future, in any session being discussed, the presenting analyst must believe that he or she is at that moment doing psychoanalysis successfully – that is to say, he or she must feel that something is happening which in his or her view is creating psychic change, and so has been 'caught'. Only then does it make sense to start trying to work out how this is

being done. In some of the presenting sessions, it was not always clear that there was any recognizable sign of an established process that would create psychic change, and thus be 'caught'. Perhaps this was because the analyst had used the setting (consciously or unconsciously) to seek help with a difficult case, meaning that the treatment being described was overwhelmed with difficulties that the analyst had not yet been able to grasp. In some cases, it certainly seems that analytic skill was being used to hang on to or to create the conditions for later work. Such sessions may need to be understood, but they greatly complicate the picture. Haydée Faimberg had anticipated this problem, but in the future she thought it could be clearer still that only sessions illustrating what the presenter believes to be an ongoing and developing process should be the focus for this work. A similar problem may exist with very early sessions where the work has not yet taken off.

- Third, the six questions that the group moderators were given in order to help them make comparisons were not much help. It is possible that their utility was reduced because their underlying intent and purpose was not explicated in relation to more familiar ways of describing our work. It may have been insufficiently clear that traditional concepts such as 'transference interpretation' (together with its oft-stated role in creating psychic change) had in fact influenced the questions. It also seems likely that their utility was undermined by a lack of clarity in the task itself – something that only became clear after attempting it. In future we would need some facilitating structure – and it was precisely such a facilitating structure that we developed over the next few years.

From Prague to Athens: four years later

Marina Perris had attended meetings in Prague as a reporter, but for practical reasons did not attend again until Athens four years later. Her post-Athens report helps us to recognize what progress was made in the interim:

The difference between the two working parties was very impressive. The change in the way the task was approached was quite an achievement. I consider this difference to be a testimony of the quality of work that colleagues have been able to do over the years. Throughout my experience in Prague I felt quite sceptical as to whether the main aim of the group, which was to try to draw inferences from the study of the material of the sessions in order to identify the presenter's implicit psycho-analytic theory, was at all possible; the aim seemed to me at that point a rather untenable goal. The main interference with achieving that aim was, in my experience at least, coming from the almost ubiquitous and almost automatic response that we have as psychoanalysts: to assume the role of a supervisor/consultant when we listen to clinical material. The strength of this response is related, I can hypothesize, to its being multiply determined by factors that all carry great intensity. I left Prague feeling quite pessimistic about the viability of this project, even if, in my mind, it was very important.

In retrospect, the beginnings of the project in Prague seem to constitute the necessary first steps that have led us to where we are now. The project has taken many further steps since then, but already in Prague, there are clues leading towards these later steps, even if these clues have only become visible with time: already in Prague we were discussing how a degree of structure needed to be created; how there might be only one presenter in each group; how many different ways to conceptualize psychoanalysis there are; and modifying the role of the presenter, who is often asked now to step back from the group's discussion in order to prevent discussion from being blocked by more consciously located or rationalized theories. This has created a move away from explicit theories and towards thinking about more preconscious or implicit views. But there will be more about these things in the next few chapters, so let us for the time being join Švejk for one last dinner of Knödl and Czech beer before we move on.

4

The Sorrento experience
Chaos replaced by too much structure

Arne Jemstedt (Sweden)

After Prague

In Chapter 3, Tomas Böhm described the 2002 EPF Conference in Prague. He concluded that several difficulties had interfered with the basic aim of the workshops, which was to find ways of describing and comparing different ways of working psychoanalytically. These difficulties included confusion about the task, including a lack of tools for listening to and describing an analyst's work, the tendency to focus on the patient and to adopt a supervisory position rather than to try to understand the presenter's way of doing psychoanalysis – and thus also to try to leave aside one's own favoured theories and models. Böhm did, however, note the participants' interest in and enthusiasm for the project, and suggested that to move forward future groups would require a clearer sense of the purpose and the method they were using.

The Prague experience gave the members of what was then the Working Party on Clinical Issues much food for thought,[1] especially on how best to proceed with the project: would it be possible to find a way of organizing discussion in the groups so as to focus on the task of describing and comparing analysts' modes of working, thereby lessen-

---

[1] Prague was organized by the Working Party on Clinical Issues. After Prague this developed into two tracks and one eventually developed into the Working Party on Comparative Clinical Methods (see Appendix).

ing the difficulties of Prague? The discussions that followed split the working party into two 'tracks', both of which had the same starting point and the same end point or aim: to study experienced and competent psychoanalysts' actual ways of working while understanding their differences and respecting them as such. However, the proposed methods to reach this end point differed. As described in Chapter 1 and the Appendix, Track 1 (chaired by David Tuckett) was based on a decision to address the problems in Prague by being more structured. To achieve this, we would first have to construct a typology of the technical differences in the actual work of analysts, and use this as the basis for understanding and describing different ways of working psychoanalytically. For Track 2 (chaired by Haydée Faimberg), the idea was to explore the basic assumptions (explicit and implicit) that underlie a particular analyst's particular way of working through a fairly traditional free discussion method, where the emphasis is on listening to and explicating the assumptions made by presenter and listeners. Doing this would allow us to 'compare how the presenter believes he works and how his mode of working has finally been understood' (Faimberg, 2002). (Track 2 has continued very successfully at subsequent conferences, but as yet has not produced further reports.)

It is Track 1, later dubbed the Working Party on Comparative Clinical Methods (WPCCM), and its development and transformation, that is the theme of this book.

Issues in constructing a typology

As Böhm indicated (see Chapter 3), the six questions given to the group moderators in Prague were not much help. Something else was needed to provide groups with a framework for exploring dimensions of the way an analyst worked, and to help them focus their attention on this, rather than on the case itself.

As outlined briefly in Chapter 1, David Tuckett embarked on this task by turning to some clinical examples; that is, by looking at several sessions from five cases presented in groups that he had attended or which were well reported. They all involved presentations by well-known analysts from intuitively very different psychoanalytic traditions. He wondered what was really different about them and decided to try to study the specific interventions that the analysts made in the sessions (including the decision to be silent), and to think about what might be their underlying function. What might the analysts be trying to do by participating in the sessions in that particular way?

Focusing on each intervention in turn, Tuckett asked himself what the analyst might be seeking to do, and gradually developed a scheme to typify interventions into functional categories, creating different categories in which to place each intervention so that they had approximately the same functional meaning. It was of course apparent that many interventions had multiple functions, but the idea from the beginning was that it might be more useful for discussion in the groups if an effort was made *to try* to determine the 'main' point of an intervention. That approach appeared to lead to deeper considerations about what the analyst was doing.

This meticulous study of interventions in a number of clinical cases – and the clinical theories that seemed to underlie them – resulted in a preliminary typology of interventions consisting of three main categories and thirteen subcategories. On the face of it, the interventions of the five analysts, when differentiated in this way, seemed to demonstrate different patterns of working. It perhaps seemed that the device of asking a group to think about the function of what analysts actually did with patients *before* discussing together the possible nature of the theory behind it, had the potential to harness the group's ability to think about the analyst's work. It could introduce a different perspective, which might facilitate deeper thinking about the specifics of different analysts' actual techniques.

It was and is, of course, patently obvious that to propose to colleagues to divide a session up into its component parts in order to determine as rigorously as possible into which category an analyst's intervention falls, would seem a foreign and emotionally dead activity compared to what psychoanalysts do in their clinical work and what psychoanalysis is about. From the start, however, David Tuckett noted that categorization was not an aim in itself. The idea behind it was to see if it could facilitate a deeper understanding of analysts' ways of thinking and working and enable comparisons between these different ways.

The typology was presented and discussed at a moderators' meeting in Paris at the end of January 2003. This was the first meeting of the EPF Working Party on Comparative Clinical Methods, and was attended by almost all of the Prague moderators and a number of experienced consultants.[2] At the meeting, several further analytic sessions were discussed in terms of the typology and some misgivings were aired, all of which led both to some changes in the categorizations and to some attempts to find anchoring examples. The discussions led to a decision to try out the new method at the forthcoming EPF Conference in Sorrento. The thirteen categories, as defined after the meeting in Paris, are set out in a summary form in Table 4.1. (To save space, only some of the examples of each subcategory are given in the table.)

The typology – which was soon referred to as the 'grid', in spite of its somewhat misleading association with Bion's Grid – together with a letter explaining the method and the ideas behind it, was sent in advance to all those who had registered for the WPCCM workshops in Sorrento. I will be quoting from reports where in relation to Sorrento the terms 'grid' and 'typology' are to be understood interchangeably.

Sorrento and the application of the method

The second, new style EPF Conference took place on 24–27 April 2003, at the Hilton Palace in Sorrento, a beautiful town on the dramatic, rocky coastline of the Bay of Naples, which enjoys a tremendous view over the Mediterranean and the island of Capri, with Vesuvius hovering in a slightly threatening manner behind.

In spite of the confusion and difficulties in Prague, our European colleagues were very keen to participate in Sorrento. There were several reasons for this interest: the unique opportunity to spend almost two days in a group with colleagues from other countries discussing in detail clinical material presented by two experienced analysts; the opportunity to find out – in a much more elaborate way than usual – how psychoanalysts from other schools and traditions think and work; and a much more vague interest and curiosity (as well as doubts) about the project and what it might lead to.

Approximately 120 people took part in the nine WPCCM work-

---

[2] The meeting was chaired by David Tuckett and was attended by Eva Berberich, Dana Birksted-Breen, Julia Fabricius, Antonino Ferro, Helmut Hinz, Arne Jemstedt, Paola Mariotti and Johan Schubert (as moderators) as well as Paul Denis, Haydée Faimberg, Iréne Matthis, Roger Perron and Evelyne Séchaud as consultants.

Table 4.1 The Sorrento typology

1 'Managing the setting' interventions

To a greater or lesser extent every analyst says some things to the patient whose purpose can be described as 'managing the setting'. Of course, there is a way in which every intervention signifies or not the specificity of the psychoanalytic setting. Here, however, we are referring to a specific limited class of interventions that some analysts may sometimes use to create minimal conditions for the work and to encourage a patient to participate and to associate – what some analysts may call the therapeutic alliance. These kinds of interventions are mostly aimed at consciousness and appear to fall into three subtypes.

1.1 Acknowledging or describing affect or predicament	1.2 Seeking associations	1.3 Basic information housekeeping
These will be comments or exclamations apparently expressing some kind of empathy with what the patient is feeling or experiencing, whether consciously or unconsciously.	*These will be comments apparently aimed at eliciting more from the patient but apparently aimed more or less at the patient's conscious capacity. It would include 'asking for associations'.*	*Simple statements of fact necessary to keep the treatment going.*
For example:	For example:	For example:
• Mmm!	• What are you thinking?	• It's time.
• You don't sound too sure.	• Can you tell me more about why you decided that?	• You forgot your coat.
• You feel sad.	• And the little black cat?	• We are going to have to discuss your fee (insurance claim, etc.).
	[Note – There could be situations where comments that look like those above are used by the analyst with care and subtlety to elaborate linking and so facilitate an unconscious representational process. On those occasions the comments would not (as it were) be questions requiring answers at the conscious level. There would need to be some supporting comments from the analysts for this intention to be considered.]	

2 Making observations seeking to understand the patient but not specifically directed at or linked to the unconscious process in the room with the psychoanalysts at that moment

The aim is to separate comments an analyst makes that specifically refer to feelings and ideas considered present in the room at that moment (hic et nunc) from those which involve more general observations. The comments in the next three categories are for situations where it seems the analysts in some way or another tried to prompt the patients to reflect more or less consciously or unconsciously on the content of the things that he has been saying but does NOT link this to the experience of being in the session right now.

2.1 Past and present life

Comments on the conscious or unconscious meaning (or other aspect) of relationships with employers, spouse, parents, colleagues, siblings, use of time, work plans, etc.

For example:

- You were terrified of your mother.
- You do seem to look down on X.
- You are very worried if the treatment can continue if you can't pay.

2.2 Current (or anticipated) fantasies and fears

Comments on ideas and possible fantasies (including unconscious fantasies) the patient has in relationships, current activities etc.

For example:

- You fear the termination . . . your advances may prove ephemeral.
- You seem to need to be on top or you will collapse.
- That sounds like wishing to keep a father who would solve all problems.

2.3 Meaning of dream content

Comments made about the possible (unconscious) meanings of a dream or attempts to develop interest in such meanings, which go beyond asking for associations.

For example:

- It was a nightmare in the first part . . . threatening in the second . . . but then you became a winner.
- Your dream seems to be about whether you can face change or not.

[These comments need to be more interpretative than seeking associations.]

3 Making connections directed at or linked to the unconscious process in the room at that moment

All of the comments in the categories below involve direct attention to the ongoing situation in the patient's unconscious mind in the session whether involving direct linking to the situation between analyst and patient and patient or not.

3.1 Facilitating unconscious representational process (draw attention to unconscious connection or word to facilitate elaboration and linking)

This category is designed for comments (which will often be quite ambiguous) apparently specifically designed to widen the patient's unconscious capacity to represent emotional situations in his or her mind. They are, therefore, comments believed to address unconscious rather than conscious percepts and will often take the form of linguistic linkages bringing together ideas previously apart.

For example:

- Foutre?
- Time is flying.
- An exhibition of you as a man?

[These judgements will often require understanding the analyst's intent and being convinced by it – requiring explicit support from an understanding of the analyst's way of working.]

3.2 Describing behaviour in the session

This category covers comments made to draw a patient's attention to specific behaviour in the current session – with implicit or explicit unconscious meaning. (The fact this takes place in the relationship to the analyst is not made explicit.)

For example:

- I observe you say 'I don't know', quite often.
- (Mentioning slips of the tongue.)
- You talked about x then y.

3.3 Linking affect or behaviour to analytic situation

Here the comment is explicitly linking affects and behaviours in session to the experienced presence of the analyst in the room with the patient.

For example:

- You're sad because of my holidays and my lack of understanding how you feel.
- You feel my silence not as listening but as disinterest and feel I am letting you down and leaving you alone.
- If you could look at me you feel you could separate from me.

3.4 Designating current emotional situation with the analyst

This category is for the variety of comments that designate meaning, defensive or exciting mental processes, wishes or unconscious phantasy in the session. [It is the meaning of the words not the explicit formulation that matters – see examples.]

For example:

- You are frightened to be alone with me. [Alone with me?]
- You are asking me not to be like your father, to be there for you.
- It immediately feels dangerous and frightening to be here.
- You are right, I had not understood quickly enough how quickly things change in you.
- Something good happened here between us yesterday which made you feel better but now it's in shreds and you feel like shit.
- You don't know if I have come back or if I am still away. It is not so much that you don't know what to tell me but if you can tell me.
- The bubble is the device that you find to separate from me in order that the contact with me would not crush me.

3.5 Specifying a core organising unconscious phantasy

Here an analyst seems to try to draw together a number of observations about what has been learned about the emotional and unconscious phantasy experience with the analyst and sets out a deeper structure.

For example:

- When you are being friendly to me I think you feel like a 'good girl' who is performing me a service, but at the same time false – I think you are only real when hating me.
- You believe I think that and that it is my way to extract myself from you and not take the weight of your feeling.

3.6 Specifying unconscious links between session experience and the patient's present life or difficulties

Here comments are made linking the current emotional and unconscious phantasy experience (including any core phantasies) with the analyst to the patient's present life or difficulties (symptoms).

For example:

- You are trying now with me as with your friends not to care. . . . To not worry what I am thinking.

3.7 Specifying unconscious links between session experience and the patient's past

Here comments are made linking the current emotional and unconscious phantasy experience (including any core phantasies) with the analyst to the patient's past history and experience.

For example:

- [Lengthy interpretation describing how, as with her mother, the patient feels horribly involved with analyst and made horribly worried by what her analyst is thinking.]
- You like me but you are afraid, you're afraid that it might give you the strength that your father had [which was disastrous].

shops that were arranged. As in Prague, there were two presenters in each group. The presenters were experienced analysts and – to avoid one of the problems from Prague – they were asked to present what in their view was good enough but also progressing psycho-analytic work, from which their 'process' could be discerned. The aim was to minimize the risk of a situation where discussion in the group would be obscured by difficulties or impasses in the work being explored.

The moderators were well acquainted with what we were trying to do in the groups, most of them having been moderators in Prague as well as taking part in the moderators' meeting in Paris. Still, it was a new experience for them to apply the grid-method of discussion in practice and to moderate complex group discussions based on it.

Obviously, the participants in the groups were not so well acquainted with the new discussion method or at any depth with the ideas behind the project. Although some had participated in Prague and all had received a description of the proposed discussion method before going to Sorrento, they did not have the experience of reviewing and discussing the work done in Prague. To distribute the responsibility for recording work in the group, some members were given the task of taking notes during the discussions, which were also to be tape-recorded in order to allow detailed exploration at a later date.

The moderators underlined that the task of the group was not to provide supervision of any kind (which, as mentioned earlier, had also been one of the major problems in the Prague groups), but to try to get as clear a picture as possible of each analyst's way of think-ing and working without evaluating it. We knew that this was easier said than done, for we are all prone to arranging what we perceive according to our own mind, following the theories, models and ways of thinking that have become our professional personalities, and thus subtly – or not so subtly – to dismissing what seems alien to these personal inner patterns, and to suggesting other ('better') ways of understanding the patient discussed and to offer other ('better') inter-ventions and interpretations. One major purpose of the Sorrento model (and the models that were constructed after Sorrento) was to diminish this tendency towards what might be called isomorphic projections.

The task of the group, then, in relation to the clinical work presented, is not altogether different from the task of the analyst in relation to his or her patient: to sense and to understand the speaker's inner state and the working of his or her mind without falling back on our own pre-formed ideas and theories. Freud's (1912: 115) notion of 'evenly suspended attention' and Bion's (1970) thoughts on 'without memory and desire' are relevant here.

The structure of the group sessions

The structure for the two days' work in the groups had also been given some thought. It was as follows.

Free-form discussion

First, the two cases (two or three sessions as verbatim as possible with or without a short background) were to be discussed in a free-form way for about two hours each, to get the group acquainted with each case and each analyst's way of working and the interplay between the analyst and his/her patient. This also, of course, enabled the group members to get to know each other and to lay the foundation for an open-minded discussion.

The moderators had different ways of moderating these and the ensuing discussions. Several used a method where the presenter took a back seat and allowed the group members to associate to the material presented, discussing it among themselves without turning to the presenter for questions or clarifications. The idea was that this would generate a more spontaneous and playful discussion, with greater opportunity for unconscious communication and for unexpected ideas to emerge. At suitable moments, the presenting analyst would then be asked to join in, giving room for an interchange of thoughts between the analyst and the rest of the group.

Examining interventions

Second, each session in each case was to be examined in terms of the interventions made, according to the typology described in Table 4.1. To reiterate, there were three main categories of interventions:

- 'Managing the setting' interventions.
- Making observations in an attempt to understand the patient but not directed at or linked to the unconscious process in the room at that moment.
- Making connections directed at or linked to the unconscious process in the room at that moment.

There were thirteen subcategories in all. Thus the analyst's interventions were to be categorized as 1.2, 2.3, 3.6, for example, with the aim being to find the category that would best fit each intervention.

As explained, the idea behind this was that the categorization, and especially the discussions leading to it, would provide a way of establishing a picture of the analyst's way of thinking and working. As it was, the categorization process took up a large part of the discussions. Despite the moderators' warning that categorization according to the 'grid' was not an aim in itself, but should be seen as a method of facilitating a process of understanding the analyst's way of working, the use of a typology for interventions provoked doubts, objections and misunderstandings – which we shall discuss shortly.

Comparison

Third, time was to be devoted to comparing the two analysts' ways of working, using the categorizations made and the discussions around them. In other words, by defining interventions, we might explore differences in the two analysts' clinical theories and how these were employed in the relationship between the analyst and the patient. This concerned both the conscious, explicit theory to which the analyst seemed to adhere, and (more importantly) his or her implicit, not-consciously-formulated theory, whatever that seemed to be. The task of comparison naturally involved uncertainties, doubts and objections.

How did it all work out?

On the morning before the workshops started, David Tuckett gave a short introduction to the project. After this, we formed our respective groups, with some colleagues enthusiastic, while others were sceptical but interested in taking part, and other colleagues were already expressing opposition to the idea of categorizing an analyst's interventions – in their eyes, this seemed very alien to the nature of psychoanalysis. However, being well-mannered and mature psychoanalysts with a capacity to contain tension and contradictory feelings, the participants set to work.

I will now recapitulate the experiences from the workshops in Sorrento using and giving examples from the moderators' often extensive reports (including my own), written comments from presenters and participants, and a summary report prepared for the EPF Council – hereafter known as the Sorrento Report – written by David Tuckett and placed on the EPF website (Tuckett, 2003).

General discussions of the two cases

Leaving aside the common inconveniences at conferences (difficulties in finding the right room, some participants being late, others leaving the group before the work is completed, etc.), this was the easiest part of the workshop, being very much like ordinary group discussions of clinical material: trying to understand and get a feeling of the analysand's problems and inner state of mind and of the analyst's way of understanding and working with the analysand.

Nevertheless, there were some difficulties: in a few instances there were questions about the suitability of the patient for analysis and about the analyst's way of handling the analysis, which of course influenced the rest of the work in the group.

The use of the 'grid'

After the general discussion of the cases, the group began the categorization of the analysts' interventions, devoting about two hours to the two-to-three sessions of each case. Even though it had been emphasized that the grid had no value in itself, and that it was only a tool to help the group understand the presenters' ways of working and to facilitate a comparison between them, the application of the grid to the clinical material evoked many (and sometimes strong) reactions, ranging from appreciation to doubts to annoyed opposition.

These different reactions were reflected in the climate of the discussions: in many groups there were lively and productive discussions, despite questions and objections related to the structure of the grid, while in others the opposition to the grid per se coloured the discussions and made them thorny.

Reactions to the 'grid' as a method

At the beginning of the Sorrento Report, David Tuckett wrote:

> Among those taking part in the groups, some raised anxieties and doubts about the project. Among these were worries that something as subtle and subjective as psychoanalytic practice could not be rigidly clarified, let alone assigned to categories. Some of these doubts were linked to perceived difficulties with the grid itself – for instance, doubt about focusing only on the analyst's interventions to the exclusion of the interaction between patient and analyst; or concern about the usefulness of a procedure that can appear to classify very different approaches as the same.
>
> (Tuckett, 2003)

These doubts and worries came through in the reports from the workshops. There were, however, also several positive and appreciative reactions. Below are some quotations from the moderators' reports and also comments from participants and presenters:

> When we started using the grid on the clinical material, we had to look closely and systematically at the analyst's interventions. In several cases this was interesting. I felt – but not everybody agreed – that the grid helped us to concentrate, and to be anchored, so to speak, on what was happening in the session, rather than floating off on all kind of interesting but vague topics. However, the grid generated strong reactions. The group, probably in its entirety, felt doubtful about the categories' usefulness, and more importantly, about what I would describe as the status of the grid in relation to psychoanalytic work. It was felt that such typology does not address and convey what is specific to psychoanalysis.
>
> (Moderator's report)

[One presenter] expressed a strong feeling of being somewhat limited by the grid. In my understanding of her argument, the point of an analytic intervention is that it is at the nodal point of different levels and different currents of meaning – its *polysémie*. Forcing an interpretation into one category strips it of its essential meaning and undermines – violently – the analyst's function and identity. [The other presenter] felt less strongly, reporting that she had found the clinical discussion interesting and that the grid helped by focusing the discussion.

(Moderator's report)

This last presenter was not alone:

The experience did not fit with any familiar data; it was completely a new experience . . . in Sorrento I was [in a group] with another presenter, it was my impression that also for him the experience was new, unexpected and different from the kind of presentations we are all used to.

1. The freedom, aliveness and directness of the discussion. People seemed to say what they thought, there was no other agenda but the clinical work, there was no reputation to be careful about, no sidestepping the truth, no concerns about protecting the presenters' sensitivities either.
2. The complete change of focus from the usual one on the patient. Now being on the analyst's mind, how the analyst arrives at what she says, where the responses come from, where the interpretations have their origin. I think the 'transformational experience' factor (this has been mentioned by several presenters) comes from this shift of focus. In fact the presenter gets a piece of good analysis for free . . .
3. The move away from supervision, especially if a good moderator keeps the group on the task, otherwise supervision does creep in.

(Presenter's comment)

But there was still trenchant criticism:

Some of the participants agreed with [X] who felt that the group was engaged in a work of research of a traditional kind . . . quantifying the analyst's intervention, and eventually representing the analyst in a pie-chart. He felt he did not want to take part in this kind . . . of research.

(Moderator's report)

Finally, this is a comment from a colleague who participated in Prague as a group member and in Sorrento as a presenter:

In Prague 2002, I was just curious. And indeed the groups were very interesting. But I expected that the participants would try to discuss the material without valuing; without knowing better. And in this regard I was disappointed. The discussion was done in supervisory style. Many group members did not even understand the aim and method of the group. The moderator was quite helpless and uninformed himself. In Sorrento 2003 [it was different]: I presented a case together with a colleague from another society. This time the group extensively used the categories. But the way we used them ended up to be not very fruitful. But in this respect I had been very sceptical before. My expectations were met from another point of view. This time we better succeeded in discussing the presented case material in a new way: not supervising, not knowing better, trying to understand the models of the presenter. Although we did not reach the latter aim it was a new experience.

This sample from reports and comments shows the great diversity of reactions to the application of the grid. As mentioned, some participants felt that the grid was alien to the nature and spirit of psychoanalysis; they thought it was positivistic, that it did not at all do justice to the subtleties and complexities of the interaction between analysand and analyst, that the sequence of interventions and how they influence each other as well as the analysand's response to them were not taken into consideration, etc. Some of these reactions were very strong; one participant even felt that it was 'unethical for him to stay in the group'.

Other comments, as exemplified by some of the quotations above, were much more positive, even enthusiastic. Despite uncertainties about the application of the grid as a whole, and not least about the distinction between different categories and subcategories (to which I shall return shortly) the discussions in many groups were constructive and creative.

I wish to consider three aspects of the more positive statements. The grid helped the groups to have more structured discussions, to shift the focus from the patient to the analyst, and to steer away from the usual supervisory position and instead to try to put oneself in the presenter's shoes. Thus the Sorrento model helped to alleviate some of the major problems that had been encountered in Prague the year before.

Thoughts and comments on the specific categories of the grid

Ideally the working process would consist of a creative balance between the association of the group to the intervention in question – without involving the presenter – and, at suitable moments, the presenter's thoughts about the thoughts and feelings behind his or her intervention. This oscillation between the group members and the presenter would, parallel to the process of categorization itself, lead to a deeper understanding of the presenter's way of thinking.

When the discussions were not thwarted too much by confusion and objections to the grid, such creative moments took place in many of the groups. However, benefiting from the experience of later conferences (in Helsinki 2004, Vilamoura 2005 and Athens 2006), it is obvious that the quality of discussions improved considerably after the Sorrento workshops. This is due to the fact that the grid was developed into the two-step model and that the moderators (and the participants) became more and more experienced in this kind of work, which lent more depth and complexity to the discussions.

Let us now take a look at the details of the categories and subcategories of the grid, the extent to which they were useful or deficient, the extent to which they helped the group to get a picture of the presenter's way of working or confused this picture, whether the categories were too few or too many, and so on.

The categorization of each separate intervention led to intensive, extensive, and sometimes to chaotic discussions, all mixed up with discussions of the relevance of the different categories in the typology. To give a picture of these discussions, I shall quote some passages from the moderators' reports. I start with two simple examples:

There was a 10-minute *silence* at the beginning of the session. This was meant to be ignored when using the grid, but it is of course very much part of the exchange between analyst and patient.

[The analyst says:] 'Yes.' Here it seems very important to hear the tone of the word yes. It is . . . important to distinguish between the three main categories [in the typology]. Category 1 has to do with the therapeutic alliance, category 3 with the unconscious process with the psychoanalyst.

There are some proposals for category 1: 1.1, because the psychoanalyst says 'I've heard you'; 1.2, because the psychoanalyst asks for associations.

There are also some proposals for category 3: 3.1, because of the information the psychoanalyst gives. The psychoanalyst seeks a deeper sense of what the patient brings in and he doesn't want simply to encourage the patient. When there is a question mark [following 'yes'] it should be more category 3.

The following two examples capture more complicated discussions:

The interventions made by the analyst of the first case were quite extensive. It became obvious that each separate intervention harboured different intervention types according to the grid. For instance, an intervention was started with some sort of acknowledgement of what the patient was feeling (category 1) and was then followed by connections being made to unconscious meanings (category 3). It was suggested that statements having ambiguous contents actually quite often are used by analysts to promote the process. This makes the classification task difficult and some participants found it counterproductive in the efforts of really getting to grips with what was clinically relevant.

However, working through the interventions did allow the group to see some areas where the typology needs further precision. For example, at the start of the second session the patient comments that so few people understand one's needs. Maybe, he says, this (having needs understood) is more important than having them fulfilled. But he does not think he really wants to be known and says that in the end there is only dirt to be found. He then goes on to speak of being reminded of a legal case, about an expert who finds in a simple shop a very valuable goblet that he buys for next to nothing from the ignorant shopkeeper. According to the Supreme Court he acted legally but not decently. The analyst replies: 'So there is some treasure hidden in the dirt. But to whom does it belong? To analyst or patient, to mother or baby?'

This intervention was classified as 3.4, although it was noted that in referring to 'analyst or patient' and 'mother or baby' there are two levels, the analytic situation and a level more concerned with core phantasy. In discussion the group thought that more than one level in the same intervention was, in this example, designed to facilitate links and associations (it was not intended to refer to actual history), but that in some interventions several levels might indicate either a difficulty in understanding or a countertransference difficulty or a fragile situation in which the analyst wants to touch all sides of the meaning delicately.

In answering questions, the analyst clarified that her intended meaning was that the hidden treasure in the dirt belonged to the patient/baby and he feared the analyst/mother might claim it. But, in discussing this piece of material it was pointed out that another analyst might have seen it as the patient feeling he might acquire something valuable from the analyst without her knowing. But then we realized that even if the analyst had understood and interpreted the material the other way round, we would still have categorized the intervention as 3.4. And yet which way round it is taken is a quite significant difference. In other words, we thought the typology did not differentiate between subject and object, who is active and who passive, in the way material is interpreted.

After this further discussion it still seemed that what is not captured [in the typology] is whether the subject and object are defined or whether this is left open or whether it is stated as a question. The group thought it might be important to try and capture this as it would relate, for example, to whether material was taken up in projection (or in an 'analyst-centred' way) or whether the analyst tries to return the projection to the patient (a 'patient-centred' interpretation).

This last quotation, apart from showing some of the deficiencies of the grid, also, I think, conveys the level of complexity and sophistication in the discussions that the categorization often led to.

Several, if not all, of the groups, found that some of the categories, especially the subcategories in category 3, overlapped, making it difficult to distinguish between them, e.g. 3.3 and 3.4 seemed too close to differentiate. In some instances there were vivid, if not to say wild, discussions where the categorizing of an intervention oscillated between all three main categories, moving for example between 1.2, 2.1 and 3.3 until the group settled finally, but with some reservations, for one of them.

Several other problems of the grid were pointed out. For example, 'the difference between an early/premature (pseudo)transference interpretation and a well-thought-out [transference] interpretation' was not captured by the grid. Also, the limitation introduced by a focus on only the thirteen grid (sub)categories was underlined; there were suggestions for adding more categories, e.g. a category for empathic communication, for interventions where analysts give a deep interpretation without referring to themselves as a transferential object, etc.

One major issue concerned difficulties in judging the interventions according to explicit or implicit criteria, i.e. how much weight should be given to what the analyst actually says and how much to the silent thoughts behind the intervention. This issue is clearly related to the above consideration of how much the presenting analyst should be drawn into the discussion, i.e. the balance between associations in the group and the presenter's information and thoughts. But this issue also relates to the implicit meaning that the group could sense in an intervention. One member of a group wrote to his moderator after Sorrento:

> Especially in the 3 category, it has been of some confusion for me whether we had to judge the intervention from the explicit, literal meaning or from the implicit meaning of the intervention. As far as I remember, in both cases . . . there had been interventions, where there [was] no direct reference to the situation in the room, although it was obvious that both [analyst and patient] knew that the interpretation meant their relationship.

Certainly the whole exercise of applying the grid would be meaningless if the *intention* of the analyst's intervention was ignored. At the same time, it would be just as meaningless to rate an intervention according to what the analyst told the group about his or her intentions. The constructive and creative feature of the grid – in the instances where it was allowed to develop – was the interplay between the thoughts of the group and those of the presenter.

As a by-product of sorts, many presenters found it 'very enlightening and broadening' to listen to the group's associations to the details of their work, giving new and sometimes unexpected perspectives on it. The comment from the presenter mentioned earlier ('in fact the presenter gets a piece of good analysis for free') works in the same vein. In other instances there was more of a clash between the assessments of the group and the presenter's view:

> for instance, the group did not think that the presenter was addressing unconscious material, but was engaged in some sort of acting out with the patient, whereas the presenter thought differently and meant that his interpretation was a type 3 intervention.

Before going into the last part of the workshops, which involved an attempt to compare the two presenters' ways of thinking and working, there are some conclusions to be drawn here: the grid provoked objections and criticism; nevertheless, it generated vivid, rich and sometimes sophisticated discussions about psychoanalytic work, and it certainly helped to shift the focus from the analysand to the analyst.

Nonetheless, from the examples given above it was clear that the grid suffered from considerable deficiencies. In *Learning from Experience* (1962), Wilfred Bion discusses the optimal relation between a 'realization' (in this case the session presented) and a 'model' of this realization. The model should be close enough to the realization to capture the essential elements in it, and at the same time remote enough and flexible enough to be applied in a meaningful way to other, similar realizations. The grid model fell short in this respect: it was both too close and too remote from the realization. Too close in the sense that it contained many detailed categories, and too remote in the sense that many relevant elements in the realization were not considered. There were enough voices in the groups to justify the addition of (probably many) more categories and subcategories, even though such additions would render the grid overwhelmingly complicated and impossible to use.

It should also be noted that the grid seemed to have a 'British slant' to it: category 3 was the most elaborated of the three main categories, having seven subcategories, most of them specifying direct interventions aimed at the 'here and now' relation between analysand and

analyst. That is, these interventions were aimed at transference interpretations, while other interventions, such as short, unsaturated comments that pick up on details in the patient's flow of associations, had
a less prominent position. This was pointed out by several people. For
example, one participant commented that he 'was happy with the
workshop. Perhaps one objection is that the method was designed
according to object relations theory as it has been worked out in
England.' This of course was a weakness in the Sorrento model since
its purpose was to catch and describe the different ways in which
psychoanalysts think and work. This issue is related to the final part
of the workshops, the comparison of sessions, to which I shall now
turn.

Comparing two analysts' way of working

Each group's final task was to compare the two presenters' way of
doing psychoanalysis. This was handled very differently in different
groups. Some groups felt they could not attempt it. Iréne Matthis
wrote in her commentary at the panel discussion on the last day of the
conference:

> Maybe the reason was that the judging attitude, which was sus-
> pended during the discussion of the case material, reappeared at the
> moment of comparison. We defended ourselves against identifying
> with the 'harsh judge' that we thought or feared we would become,
> by deciding not to compare. We need a lot more experience before
> this second task can be achieved.
>
> (Matthis, 2003)

There were similar reactions in other groups. Furthermore, factors
relating to the different pathologies of the two patients, such as different lengths of treatment, etc., made comparison difficult and
meaningless. Wrote one moderator:

> The approach to this task was hesitant and cautious . . . and it was
> obvious that the situation created anxiety. The handling of this
> difficulty was met by focusing on the pathology of the two patients
> in question instead of on the analysts . . . thus, from this perspect-
> ive, it was the patient's pathology that had major importance to

the choice of interventions rather than the working style of the analyst.

Apart from these complications I think one major reason for the difficulties in comparing sessions was the fact that the group had not been given any tools for doing this. While the grid provided an elaborated (probably too elaborated) model for the task of categorizing interventions, only a few general remarks were given to the groups beforehand about comparing methods, and there was no structure or model to contain this second task apart from looking once again at the interventions – with the same eyes as before. The group was still anchored in the typology, therefore, without a tool to lift the discussion to a 'meta-level'. This was expressed in one moderator's report:

> The most difficult task was to compare the two presenters, and therefore the group did not undertake this task. The group was too uncertain about what they were looking at to make comparisons and thought it impossible to make meaningful comparisons without judging who was better (e.g. who made more transference interpretations because most members felt that transference interpretations were more valuable than other interventions).

To return to Bion's ideas about realizations and models, what was lacking here was a meaningful and elaborated model that could be applied to the realization – in this case the categorizations of interventions and the discussions that accompanied them.

Nevertheless, in some groups attempts were made to make a comparison between the two presenters, although not necessarily using the grid, and in one group this was done quite extensively. This comparison was based on a theme that surfaced in several of the groups (and which is not new in psychoanalytic discussions): namely a comparison between 'British' and 'French' models of psychoanalysis. This is of course a simplified division, since most analysts consider themselves to have multiple functions and thus to move between different vertices when listening to patients. However, on a generalized level this division and comparison make some sense, e.g. concerning the use of 'saturated' versus 'unsaturated' interpretations. In this group it happened that one presenter (A) belonged to the French school and

Table 4.2 A comparison between two analysts presenting in Sorrento

Presenter A	Presenter B
The analyst declares to belong to the French school, with many openings on Italian psychoanalysis.	The analyst declares to belong to the British school and to refer, among others, to Rosenfeld, Tustin and Bion.
The group sees a coherence between the declared formation and the way of working as it appears from the material.	The group sees a coherence between the declared formation and the way of working as it appears from the material.
The external reality is seen on the one hand as a representation of the world of precocious infantile sexuality but on the other as a constant picturing of the *hic et nunc* of the session.	The external reality is seen as a 'theatre' of the representations of the patient's object relations.
It is not considered necessary to supply classical transference interpretations at every single session.	'If there is not at least one transference interpretation during a session, I feel something is missing', says the analyst.
Interpretations are here defined as 'unsaturated', metaphorical, open. The interventions are less numerous. Among the theoretical reasons given for this one is a greater faith in the patient's ability to work by himself.	Interpretations seem to be more uni-vocal, aiming at a well focused point. The interventions are more numerous. The theoretical reason brought forth is that the patient can feel more contained.
In the formulation of the interpretation, the patient's words are employed.	In the formulation of the interpretation the analyst employs her own words.
There is frequent use of 'we together'.	There is frequent use of 'you–I'.
The analyst declares she never asks questions to the patient.	The analyst declares that occasionally she feels free to ask the patient a question.
The analyst attracts the attention more on the game of identifications and on the activity of metaphoric co-building.	The analyst attracts the attention more on the areas of aggressiveness, sadomasochism, envy and separation.
In some cases the analyst seems to show the patient what happens in the 'kitchen' of his thought ('C'est ça que j'ai pensée . . .', 'This is what I have thought . . .')	The analyst gives fewer disclosures on the train of thoughts that has led her to interpretation.

the other presenter (B) to the British school. The main differences between the two analysts enucleated by the free group discussion, are illustrated schematically in Table 4.2.[3]

In some other groups, efforts, often half-hearted, were also made to compare the two presenters, but all in all this part of the work did not turn out to be very fruitful, and in one group it was suggested that it would probably be more productive to explore one analyst's work with two different patients to get a deeper understanding of his or her way of thinking and working, instead of superficially and with some anxiety trying to compare the modes of working of two analysts who were present.

Concluding remarks

The work in the groups in Sorrento was very intensive. The participants spent almost two full days discussing in detail and with great concentration two or three sessions presented by two colleagues, and everybody (not least the moderators) was quite exhausted afterwards. In most groups there was a sense of having had a rewarding experience through this unusual opportunity for profound clinical discussions. As has been shown above, there were also doubts and objections, sometimes strong objections, against the grid as a method for formulating characteristics of different kinds of psychoanalytic work.

The following quotation from a moderator's report might be an apt way of summing up feelings about the workshops:

> We agreed that we had had a creative working group, a rich clinical discussion, that we were able to cope with very different opinions over the two days, and that the method gave us a structure for our discussions. However, the majority of us saw a potential danger of oversimplification of the discussions, in the form it has today.

The method in Sorrento certainly accomplished a shift in the focus from the patient to the analyst; it led to more vivid and rich discus-

---

[3] This was just an attempt at comparing French and British styles made at this moment by this group with these two analysts, and should, of course, not be seen as a sophisticated way of describing or differentiating these two styles.

sions; and it helped the participants to avoid a supervising approach in the discussions. But, apart from the objections raised against a model based on any kind of typology, there were several significant defects and deficiencies in the method. First, the grid was both too detailed and too narrow, i.e. it contained over-elaborated subcategories concerning different kinds of transference interpretations, while other aspects of the analyst's work was not taken into consideration. Second, there was no tool in the method for facilitating more sophisticated and complex formulations about a presenter's explicit and implicit way of working and thinking. Third, the idea of comparing the two presenters' work on the whole turned out to be unproductive both for psychological and factual reasons.

'Models are ephemeral', writes Bion (1962: 80), '. . . I have no compunction in discarding a model as soon as it has served or failed to serve my purpose'. After Sorrento, the question was: should the model be discarded on the basis of the objections against it and the deficiencies in it? Quite early on the answer seemed: probably not. In spite of its defects, many participants felt that the model could still be useful if changed and improved. This was the challenge, then: to try to construct a model that would make it possible not only to have rewarding clinical discussions, but also more truthfully to capture and describe different ways of thinking and working psychoanalytically. The efforts to develop a new model, and the evolution of it, will be the subject of the chapters to follow.

5

Some reflections on the problems of comparison and difference in the light of doubts and enthusiasm

Helmut Hinz (Germany)
With contributions by Manuel Fernández Criado (Spain)

Nothing is to be compared,
nothing is without comparison.[1]

The comparative project that is the subject of this book is concerned with trying to describe and specify psychoanalytical traditions as different as British, French, Kleinian, independent, contemporary Freudian and Lacanian, together with techniques and theories as diverse as drive psychology, ego psychology, object relations psychology and newer developments, such as relational psychoanalysis and intersubjectivism. The aim is to be able to get to know these traditions thoroughly, in sufficient detail, and from within. The comparative process brings to light similarities as well as differences, and, in the course of this process, we hope it may be possible to understand more precisely what psychoanalysis is. Or perhaps we will be left repeating Wolfgang Loch: 'One cannot *say* what psychoanalysis is; it becomes apparent' (personal communication).

My participation in the comparative methods project began when I was invited as a discussant to the first Brussels workshop (see the

---

[1] A paraphrase of Theodor W. Adorno's 'Nothing is to be affirmed, nothing is without affirmation.'

Appendix). I was a last minute moderator in Prague, where demand outstripped supply and we had to arrange three extra groups. I have been a moderator at every meeting since. In this chapter, I shall discuss some of the theoretical issues involved in comparing differences in psychoanalytic practice, as well as report on a small survey I undertook with Manuel Fernández Criado into both the doubts and the enthusiasm that the project has aroused.

I will begin with an account of my own ambivalently enthusiastic and doubting response to the invitation to participate, before discussing similar feelings expressed by my colleagues. I will then seek to explore at some length what I consider to be the main psychoanalytic reasons both as to why, in my opinion, comparison is a necessarily difficult process, and as to why there must inevitably be a significant range of really different approaches in quality psychoanalytic practice – all the while avoiding the pitfalls of 'anything goes'.

About my doubts and enthusiasm

From the beginning I clearly felt both the enthusiasm and the doubt that colleagues, moderators and participants later expressed. When I was first asked to join in the discussions in the EPF Working Party on Comparative Clinical Methods (WPCCM) in 2001, I looked forward to the prospect of enjoying stimulating and enriching discussions with a group of experienced colleagues from various European countries and with a variety of different psychoanalytical approaches.

My interest in different ways of working must in part stem from being deeply influenced by Wolfgang Loch, who was head of the Psychoanalysis Department at the University of Tübingen between 1969 and 1982. I believe he saw himself as a liberal in the field of analytic theory and practice, perhaps to the 'left' of the British independents in this respect. (Loch was inclined towards the work of Melanie Klein.) Thriving on the academic style, Loch immersed himself in nearly every psychoanalytical school of thought. Respecting their specificity, he took the best from each of the thinkers that he came across and, as a result, his teaching and writing were characterized by many quotations. My ambivalence towards this project perhaps stems from the fact that eventually I developed the wish to specify and deepen my own personal analytical stance. To do this, however, one need not find out about every psychoanalytical school (as Loch did); one can also achieve autonomy by studying one great psychoanalyst's work in great depth. Even Loch himself once told me not to fear being one-sided, for example when writing a paper.

So, when invited to take part in the comparative workshop at the EPF Congress, I recall a conflict emerging, in that my professional development no longer led me to be primarily interested in the variety of psychoanalytical concepts. I wanted, rather, to intensify and deepen my own personal analytical development through learning from daily psychoanalytical practice and the problems that this entails. The detailed analysis of clinical situations would help me to develop and perhaps formulate my own psychoanalytic models, practices and theories, as would reading clinical accounts and occasional supervision concerning the finer points of the analyst-patient relationship. It was these I wished to study and to make my own in order to remain flexible and yet firm, and to bring together my experience and my theoretical models in an authentic form.[2] It was at around the time of my invitation to the EPF Working Party that I began to take it as a compliment when colleagues classified me according to a particular school of thought (Kleinian). Previously, I had wondered whether being classified as someone's disciple was the equivalent of being seen as the victim of a strong ideological/'scientific' sect, i.e. deprived of one's own capacity to perceive, think, and to experience autonomously.

I make this point because I think that in scientific or academic disciplines it is important to make clear distinctions, although, as we shall see, too closely to observe distinctions can lead to closed-mindedness. Following the thoughts of George Spencer Brown and Niklas Luhmann, I think it makes sense that each scientific discipline starts off by making a fundamental distinction: for example, immanence/transcendence, justice/injustice, system/surrounding and unconscious/conscious are the starting points of theology, jurisprudence, systems theory and psychoanalysis respectively. In

[2] I am concerned here with several polarities: the polarity inherent in double contingency, that means the freedom of reciprocally constructing each other in a relationship on the one hand, and the unavoidable development of (new/old) stable structures (cf. Baraldi et al., 1998: 39). We meet this phenomenon in analysis: a multiplicity of options to interpret the same situation on the one hand and the often reduced number of repeated relational patterns. This polarity manifests itself to the analyst in other forms, e.g. as a combination of the following analytical functions: lawgiver/teacher and midwife for free associations; father and mother function and theoretical awareness that other 'parents' act differently; great responsibility and playful creativity; techniques of treatment and art of interpretation.

psychoanalysis, the crucial distinction at the beginning is that between the conscious and the unconscious. From this point on, our science was developed and differentiated, by further observations, questions and answers: for example, when do unconscious processes start? Different psychoanalytical schools answer these questions in different ways. For example, a difference between Winnicott and Klein, in my view, is the belief that rudimentary mental structures, which then play an *active* part in the process of early interaction and psychic development, exist at the beginning of psychic life. This has many consequences; for example, in how the concept of trauma is unfolded or in the way an interaction between perpetrator and victim is considered. In any case, psychoanalysis certainly begins with the difference between conscious and unconscious, and every psycho-analyst must in the consulting room take a position on what exactly this distinction means. From these beginnings, a young discipline, or, for example, a psychoanalytic school, will not constantly look to neighbouring disciplines, but will usually carry on research based on its own precepts in its own field of practice, with its own methods, concepts, models and theories, and be unworried by comparison. For example: I cannot study the analytical power to create insight and association by explicit interpretations of the *hic et nunc et mecum* (here and now and with me) as a possibly central means for psychic change if, at the same time, I follow the idea that transference interpretations are generally a seduction or damaging to the spontaneous inner process of representational functions and associations. At some point, however, I might want to address this latter issue. It is by pursuing thought in both directions separately that I believe I can open my eyes to consider the disadvantages of my theories and techniques when going into the depths of our approaches.

In my contact with colleagues from other schools within my own society and local group, I have frequently been struck by the regular reappearance of general patterns of communication and understanding, or rather ritualistic misunderstanding. Such repetitions have produced a certain weariness and unwillingness in me to find interest in any criticism other than that which had developed from within my own discipline. Criticism that arrived from outside – such as is frequently experienced in psychoanalytic institutes – often seemed redundant to me. Viewed from the opposite perspective, one could say that, in taking this attitude, I simply did not understand this criticism within my belief system, was unable to use it for my development, and could not adequately put it into clinical practice. Moreover, my own reflection within my technique had made me aware of personal weak points or areas of my analytical functions that I wanted to develop myself by going deeper into one school of thought and my own experience with it and my patients. This is what I had done since about 1990. Sometimes I had felt it was hard work, as difficult as some psychic change. I also felt content by this development of my analytical functions and enjoyed it. I did not think I had become narrow minded or simply stuck in 'tribal' thinking (see Chapter 1).

Nonetheless, when the opportunity to join the workshop came, I gladly accepted the offer of working on the WPCCM project. The prospect of meeting an interesting group of European colleagues and of moderating comparative workshop groups at the new annual meetings of the EPF was tempting in itself, although it was clear this was going to cost me a lot of time and money. Furthermore, the chance to see up close examples of clinical practice that were not available locally was too good to refuse. In other words, the conference provided me with an important opportunity to check whether, through concentration on my own psychoanalytical development, I had, perhaps, become too concerned with improving my own approach, and had not sufficiently questioned my own basic tenets, even though some of the reasons for this were, as explained above, good ones. It was immediately apparent that the lengthy clinical discussions would provide a new opportunity, and the groups demonstrated a real desire to examine the inner processes of the analyst. Moreover, the Congress showed sufficient and due respect for the presenters and for the difficulty of trying to understand from within another analyst's way of working and thinking – not just for one or two meetings, but perhaps over the course of several conferences.

Others' doubts

Talking to our European colleagues, Manuel Fernández Criado and I encountered dissatisfaction and doubts with the comparative project – both against the project as a whole and more specifically against the workshops in the EPF meetings. These doubts ranged from frankly uttered prejudices to clearly formulated judgements, from merely weak anxieties to elaborated critical thoughts.

The objections raised against the project were pretty heterogeneous. We will summarize them based on the feedback that the moderators picked up in meetings, on the specific statements and descriptions of the workshops in Prague, Sorrento and Helsinki, and on telephone and email interviews. Included are the moderators' own doubts and critical thoughts.

One of the first objections that came to our ears was based on a suspicion that the project was an unwanted attempt to make 'research' broadly established in psychoanalysis and specifically in the EPF conferences. Such critics obviously meant 'research' in the sense of formalized 'empirical' investigations. I will not enter here into the question of whether empirical, statistical or quantifying approaches are politically or scientifically important for the development of psychoanalysis as a science or for its survival in social healthcare systems. I would like simply to state that this objection seemingly involved a misunderstanding: those involved in this project understood it to be *clinical* and only in this sense to be 'empirical'.

I think of empiricism as being linked to experience; that is, sensing, feeling and thinking with one's own psyche and body in the presence of another soul and body. This is a definition of empiricism very near to the philosophical and epistemological term pragmatism. I think of clinical pragmatism as linked with suffering and the wish to suffer less. Sometimes this is a matter of survival, although there are always questions, such as how to live a more human life, a better life, or how better to tolerate unavoidable suffering? Pragmatism in this sense has to do with life, human life, and the protection of life/human life. From this point of view, the comparative workshops tried to address how different analysts assess the human condition by investigating the clinical psychoanalytical situation and experience in all its varieties. Extensive investigation of clinical material was the starting point of the whole comparative enterprise.

For Freud, psychoanalysis consisted of two inseparable partners – research and treatment – and the term research, although the cause of some doubt, has played a similar role in this comparative project. Research here involves investigation into the interactions of the analytical couple by means of detailed group case discussions and with the help of a changing and evolving set of terms to observe and describe more clearly how a specific analyst (with a specific patient in a distinct clinical situation) works.

A second objection was that the project was too formalized to be truly psychoanalytical. Thus, when the moderators first tried to introduce the new formal method of discussion, objections were raised that this could damage psychoanalysis, its freedom, its creativity, its individuality, its liveliness. One colleague said after his experience in Sorrento that

> the formal investigation was strongly imposed from outside (by the moderator) on to the free and creative approach to the clinical situation, and therefore experienced as disturbance. The aim of the Working Party to promote discussion and interchange between different methods is good. But the formalization as applied that time [in Sorrento] slays the rich and interesting contents.

I think that this impression applies to various participants in the early workshops – especially in Sorrento (see Chapter 4). But, as explained, the project used the experiences of Prague and Sorrento to learn and develop. Formalizing the comparative method served a purpose when group discussions were not working (as happened in Prague). Where formalizing the comparative method created difficulty, we tried to understand it and revise the method. As mentioned by Dana Birksted-Breen in her introductory foreword, anxieties on this score gradually lessened when it became clear that the workshops were working in an analytical spirit. The idea was to support, to catalyse and to deepen in a *first step* the discussion by looking at each intervention that was explicitly made (deliberate silence included), in order to assess and classify the possible functions, targets or aims of that intervention. In the *second step*, the discussion was continued by applying a prepared and pre-formed network of several terms, psychoanalytical foci, a chart and a grid. These terms or foci were formulations to represent the inner templates that psychoanalysts might use to answer the following questions: What is wrong? What is listened to? What is thought to be the psychoanalytical situation? What is thought to facilitate psychic change? What brings psychoanalytical transformation about?

Third, 'categorization' was often objected to as a term (just as 'formalization' had been before it) and was deemed anti-psychoanalytic or worse. Such a formal approach (formal for being in written form) is judged as hindering free association, suspended attention and the spontaneous emergence of a selected fact. Categorization and classification were seen as mechanistic and lacking subtlety; they interrupt something that otherwise could evolve freely. This objection raises an old controversy: is psychoanalysis a process or a technique? As one sceptic has put it: 'Each analyst works with implicit and explicit theories. Each theory is a network or tissue of a multiplicity of motives. It is a big question if categorizing and comparing make sense at all.' Another colleague added: 'What will be the outcome at last of this big comparing project? Does the comparing finally help the clinician?' In Chapter 1, David Tuckett clearly points out to what extent we underestimated the depth of the anxieties that arose among some psychoanalyst colleagues while categorizing analytical interventions. He himself (and I think all the moderators) were far from using categorization in what would be thought of as a banal way. On the contrary, it is my experience that seeking a category for an intervention or interpretation often shows how complex thoughts and analytical talk really are.

Fourth, some colleagues found one of the underlying assumptions of the comparing project, namely that each presenter is to be seen as an experienced and competent analyst, unacceptable and even unethical, because such an approach might lead to non-differentiation. To project members, however, this precondition was necessary and congruent with the aim not to criticize or seek to improve others' work according to one's own views, but really to get acquainted with it, and to investigate the analyst's mental background, their inner template, and their experience, including their explicit and implicit theories. Such an assumption is necessary in order seriously to investigate the forms, contents and intentions of analysts' interventions and their ideas about the analytic process, be they implicit or explicit. This assumption also makes analytic sense because one can say that each analyst does his best; under the pressure of repetitive forces, he/she strives as much as possible to keep the analytic space open by reflecting on the forces that urge patterns to be repeated, and which evolve anew in the present relationship. This is independent of the version of relational theory to which the analyst is inclined (be it conceived as transference–countertransference interaction, bi-personal field, enactment or involvement of unconscious phantasies).

It is my experience that making the assumption of competence leads one to get to know better and from inside how other analysts work. But making the assumption is at times disturbing. Sometimes it means that you get to know better what you yourself are normally doing, which may involve the realization, for instance, that you are not particularly flexible and do not master the whole range of possibilities in the field of the art of interpretation. For example, from time to time I felt weakened in my analytical stance when listening to very different approaches, but, thanks to this awareness, I could describe more explicitly what I was thinking and doing when analysing my way. I do not think that this working assumption of competence is unethical or detrimental to the project. According to my experience, the working groups do not promote non–differentiation or non–differentiators. On the contrary, there is a big difference between *anything goes* and the awareness that several different analytical ways are obviously fruitful. Perhaps through comparing, one can develop a broader scope of options for work, although one might feel that one's analytical stance is at times weakened.

One further remark before proceeding to some rather different criticisms: we do not easily set aside the inclination to judge. In fact, we very easily become judgemental when confronted with ways of doing analysis with which we are not well acquainted. This is an experience I had in at least one group. I suppose there is a balance to be found between being judgemental and being a non–differentiator.

Money

Somewhat surprisingly, another significant element of suspicion and perhaps mistrust about the project concerned money; some people felt that the EPF's or the IPA's money was being used by a small group associated with the project for their own ends. Perhaps such misgivings conceal a deeper mistrust of the politics of the IPA and the EPF, and the belief that research is not valid as a scientific method, which leads people to disparage it on the basis of a wider concern regarding the use of EPF funds. There was even a suggestion of financing an underlying 'plot' inside the EPF to eliminate free ways of thinking and non–mainstream ways of practising analysis.

Reflecting upon this point reminds me that the working parties, of which this project is part, have in fact stimulated much interest among European colleagues, who have attended conferences in large numbers and so have self-financed the work. Certainly some people spoke cogently about the use of funds and clearly felt that work that did not benefit them was financed through them; from this viewpoint, it is natural to raise objections that, while rational, reflect many different kinds of feelings. Some of the opinions voiced expressed very raw concerns. However, I should mention that both I and many of my colleagues spent not inconsiderable sums of our own money in order to take part in the project.

Language

A final objection may on the surface seem mundane, but I think it hides a deeper meaning. It concerns the problems raised by the language barrier(s) at the workshops, where different group members had varying degrees of fluency in the two main languages, English and French.

The issue behind the language objection may relate to a problem that we have already discussed: difficulties in expression might well seem to reduce the credibility of a research method that relies on people's judgement and their ability to communicate, particularly when this ability is under scrutiny. People's concern with the language problem created feelings of mistrust towards the validity of the method and reduced the credibility of the whole process. Some of the opinions I heard about the project's defects were significant in this regard: people who could not attend these workshops for language reasons sometimes denigrated the procedure or idealized it and felt very left out. Thus, the language barrier kept some from participating and increased the sense of being excluded. People naturally resented their exclusion from the 'privileged' people in the groups.

A variation of this difficulty applies to those in the groups who spoke English or French as a second language only, and who grew tired during the day. As the day wore on, the doubts and scepticism of group members began to show more openly. Again this created doubt about the process, which depends on people's capacity to ascertain verbal input when this skill is under question because of the language.

Criticism even took the form of broad statements, such as: 'This will kill analysis', 'This is against analysis', and 'This leads to nothing helpful for analysis.' But I would like to stress my own experience as a moderator and say that a great deal depends on how the task is communicated. The more vividly a moderator can explain to the group how and why the categories and frames (which became known as the two-step method) did not have a sense or aim in themselves but were only means to support the detailed process of investigating, experiencing, thinking and feeling the way other experienced analysts do their work, the fewer objections there were. Once the group got down to work, they found it really a remarkable experience to encounter different levels and different ways of understanding the complex work that each analyst does, and that this was facilitated by the new template for discussion. It usually allowed one to hold on to this examination process or process of understanding the other analyst in a longer and more detailed way than we had experienced with other methods.

It has been important both to state and to explore the various objections that have been valuable to our thinking. But clearly these comparative clinical workshops would not have been the success they were had the criticisms I have mentioned been shared by the majority of participants. They were not, and the number of participants over six years was remarkable, with many repeatedly (and even yearly) joining the workshops. This positive reaction and enthusiasm is linked in my view to the following formative assumption: each presenter is to be seen as an experienced analyst; everybody else's task is to find out what that means. This process can, briefly, be differentiated from the more traditional practice of supervision. I confess to being astonished that many analysts obviously have had negative experiences with supervision. But the wish to find a respectful way of discussing and to have clinical material discussed seems to run deep, even if supervisors do not always realize that it is the analyst, and not themselves, who is in the front row with the analysand. Great interest, however, is evoked by the prospect of learning a different approach to discussing clinical material.

Naturally there are also other, non-specific factors that helped to draw people to our working groups: they form an interesting sort of working holiday, they take place in wonderful European cities, they involve getting to know a group of colleagues, and they provide an opportunity to further this experience and to learn a lot about psychoanalytic thinking throughout many parts of the world.

What is comparison analytically?

I now turn to the question of comparison. What is comparison analytically speaking and why might it be difficult? My idea (or hypothesis) is that there is apparently a conflict between the need to compare in order to differentiate and to test reality, and the problematic nature of comparison as an instrument for ironing out specific and subtle differences. Comparison seems to produce both levelling and differentiation.[3]

Hermann Beland, a German analyst, published a study about comparison. For him, comparison is

> a powerful ruler serving all processes in life and present in all, though working from hiding . . . In a ceaseless activity from the moment of conception the body compares every item of information requiring comparison and there are billions of these in every moment.

> (Beland, 1998: 197)

Beland (1998) says that it is through comparison of quality that the all-powerful pleasure principle reigns. It has to differentiate between 'pleasant' and 'unpleasant', while the reality principle differentiates between 'true' and 'untrue'. At times Freud explicitly gave *comparing* the central role to which it is entitled in the development of knowledge. When, for example, Little Hans regretted that his thirst for (sexual) knowledge and his desire to see his father's and mother's 'widdler' had not yet been satisfied, Freud writes: 'it is probably the need to compare which compelled him. The ego is the standard with which one measures the external world, one learns to understand it by means of a constant comparison with oneself' (Freud, 1909: 107, quoted in Beland 1998: 199). It is through comparison of 'good' and 'bearable' with 'unbearable' experiences that neurosis and psychosis are also set in motion, because, in Freud's words, the neurotic turns away from reality when he 'finds it unbearable – either the whole or parts of it' (Freud, 1911: 218; see also Beland, 1998: 199).

Beland observes that in normality and in neurosis, 'comparison' does not at first sight seem to be impaired. This impression is deceptive, for one soon notices that there are 'wise avoidances and other manipulations of comparison' (Beland, 1998: 200). He goes on to describe how children protect themselves from 'impossible'

---

[3] With immanent self-criticism and criticism, fundamental methodological guidelines and a number of basic concepts (in theory and technique) can serve as reference points, as values to compare with. For self-critical work, for example, the reference points could be the following questions: if and how free association is taking place, can free-floating attention be given, is the observation of manifestations of countertransference and the examination of current transference oriented to countertransference being used as an instrument in treatment, and does this serve resistance to the analytical process or an opening towards it?

comparisons but instead compare themselves sensibly with their own age-group in order to avoid total depression. A function of comparison with others, therefore, is that it fosters growth, with envy emerging as a normal side effect.

Roger Money-Kyrle (1971: 103–104) was able to show that misconceptions frequently form when an infant is confronted with the good breast and with the creative parental couple; these misconceptions help to reduce the shock and pain of recognizing the fact that, while the good breast and the creative parental couple are so rich, they are not at the infant's command. The processes in the analytical situation are for their part highly complex, too, and they create excluded third parties, within the analytic couple and outside it. Extending Money-Kyrle's thoughts, I would like to suggest that these processes are not only complex but also supremely beneficial and highly creative, and that they imply an experience of separateness and time. For, in the analytical setting there is resistance not only to analysis but also to what might be perceived as a natural tendency to get better, and one can assume that both analyst and analysand are trying as best as they can to overcome this resistance. If more were possible, it would occur, however, and so, given the intimate cooperation of the analytical couple (which, if all goes well, bears fruit in its own specific way and finds its own potential for development), misconceptions may well develop in the minds of observing third parties (be they colleagues, supervisors, case study working groups, etc.). The 'comparisons' from outside (thoughts, conjectures, interpretation) can create more or less subtle (even unconscious) manipulations of the material: ignoring alternative perspectives, omissions, the taking apart of things immanently connected (e.g. choice of words and atmosphere), or equating things that are really different.

Misconceptions can be of various types: the observer will perceive the connection between practice and theory in a different way to the analytical couple (and the perceptions of analytical couples will vary themselves); the observer's viewpoint can either be judged negatively, or recognized as different, or equated with the observer's personal experience. To judge negatively splits the theory–practice compound apart,[4] while following the second path denies the

---

[4] It consists of oppositional pairs: Interpretation and the current reality in the relationship, word and thing, word-image (in Strachey's translation: word-presentation) and thing-image, concept and observation, manifestly spoken texts and the emotional quality of the analytical situation.

perceived difference between *your* and *my* position, since it 'usurps' 'yours'. In both cases, 'the expression and content of our philosophizing begins to acquire an unwelcome resemblance to the mode of operation of schizophrenics' (Freud, 1915: 204). When 'we think in abstractions there is a danger that we may neglect the relation of words to the unconscious thing-image' (in the Strachey translation, 'thing-presentation') or that we 'treat . . . concrete objects as though they were abstract' (Freud, 1915: 204). 'Word and thing' (Freud, 1915: 299) do not match in either case. We are, then, dealing in word-presentations and giving up the thing-presentations, or vice versa, or we are taking a quality and equating it with the substance (Loch, 1991: 31). Through these thoughts and quotations about misconceiving and misrepresentation, I want to point out problems that can occur by comparing, especially when done in haste.

Comparing can either lead to the discovery of difference and self-knowledge, and to a testing of reality that subsequently can benefit development; or it can enlarge difference, delete it and undermine development. Are we not, at times, rather quick in our academic cleverness to think we already know the conceptual systems and mind-sets of others, including their strengths, which we are happy to share, and their weaknesses, which we are not.

Such reductions and enlargements of difference, such non-equations and equations of our own practice with that of another, fail to take into account the specific many-layered interactions in the analytical relationship and help to spare us 'the oedipal work of realistic comparison' (Beland, 1998: 202) and thus help reduce the painful responsibility for our own real but limited abilities. The comparative project attempts to address this problem. We base work on the assumption that realistic, differentiating comparisons will indeed be possible through insight into the inner workings of the analytical couple if sufficient time is given.[5] I would like to repeat in this context that, after Prague and Sorrento, the setting of the comparing

---

[5] In order to gain an impression of the 'case', it is advisable to proceed as in a classical group supervision; i.e. 'I see that quite differently' or 'a central unconscious phantasy may have been overlooked here.' We clearly draw inspiration and energy from these controversies and the exchange of differing ideas. In a second step, the clinical material will be examined in detail in the WPCCM and at this stage will be thought through as rigorously as possible from the perspective of the presenter in order to get to know his or her inner model of psychoanalysis, to hear what good reasons and theoretical background have led this colleague to feel, do, say or not say what is recorded in the minutes of the session.

workshops shifted dramatically. Before Helsinki the moderators' group had learnt that we needed twice the time for discussion than had at first been planned. It is my impression that after this big change, discussion deepened and became calmer, more reflexive and more precise. This is not only due to better-adjusted terminological instruments in Step 1 and Step 2, but also in part due to the adjusted timetable, which better fitted this enormously complex task.

I shall now return to the interaction between differentiating and comparing in psychic life, where both difference and comparison have a double function: since comparing is a main instrument for gaining access to reality, and since comparing leads to the recognition of differences, comparing can lead to more or less subtle misconceptions and misrepresentations, particularly when we are overburdened by the perception of differences that are too great. To recognize difference is the beginning of recognizing the richness of the universe of reality. I have mentioned Money-Kyrle and the importance and difficulty of recognizing the facts of life (the supreme good breast, the supreme creative parental couple, time and death), but I would like to add explicitly what is implicit: the ability to recognize the difference of sex, which provides from time to time high quantities of pleasure and is the basis for procreation, but all too often this (same!) difference can seem too big and causes trouble, neurosis or worse. Similarly, intense discussions in which we get to know our colleagues can be both the source of analytic pleasure, creativity and development and the source of (both good and bad) disturbance and hostility. Difference is sometimes very difficult to bear because we get anxious when we are in the middle of a strange world. I think we share a deep and strong need for identicalness. Trying to adjust the object, or to have the analyst behave according to unconscious expectations and archaic phantasy, is not only a strong force in our patients, but sometimes, in our contact with colleagues, it exerts itself in order to make us feel safe again. It is not always easy to question one's own work and style, especially for those with much experience of professional practice. No analyst can say that another analyst with a different approach to the same patient might have worked better, a situation that creates problems of responsibility and guilt-pain, because we work with our hearts.

The basis for difference in psychoanalysis

In the comparing workshops we have a great opportunity to meet different analytical worlds. We should try to have the same emotional experience as Freud when he had to realize that his understanding of hysteria and of sexual seduction was one-sided. In his famous retraction (Freud, 1887–1904: Letter 139), Freud had to acknowledge the influence of phantasy on memory, and thus correct his previously held opinion of the development of neurosis ('I no longer believe in my neurotica [theory of neurosis]'). He confessed that he no longer knew what he was confronted with. But, to his astonishment he was neither 'depressed' nor 'confused' nor 'exhausted', but rather 'proud that after going so deep I am still capable of such criticism' and of assessing the new situation 'as the result of honest and vigorous intellectual work'. There was no feeling of 'shame' or 'defeat,' but of 'victory' (Freud, 1887–1904).

I want now to elaborate my argument a bit further in order to show why it is quite inevitable that we will have very different ways of conceptualizing the analytical process, of fostering it and of completing it well. It is not, as I shall show, a question of 'anything goes', but it is a fact of scientific necessity: the existence of different analytic worlds is a product of the psychic reality discovered by Freud. This fact can be a problem (in that it can be puzzling), but it is also a pleasure because we can see the different ways in which the psychoanalytical project and psychoanalytical experience have vividly and freely developed since Freud started it — by drawing his crucial distinction between conscious and unconscious. The variety of different theoretical and practical forms of psychoanalysis follows as an expression of the liveliness and richness of the unconscious. The richness and multiplicity of forms and the different ways to do analysis have rational bases in each psychic apparatus and in the way they react to or communicate with their objects. It is this argument that I now wish to elaborate and to place alongside the other emotional and conceptual issues already raised in this book.

To start with, we know that there is no observation independent of theory. It is the same with psychoanalytic facts and experience. In terms of the theory brought to them, therefore, psychoanalytic experiences must be seen differently, and carried out and potentially completed in different ways. But there is a second reason, not as well known as the first, but which has to do with the fact that in every individual multiple layers of inner reality are repeatedly transcribed, retranscribed or constructed in a changed form and are brought to life in the moment. I am stating here my reason for arguing, as Freud did, that psychoanalysis has always implicitly been a constructivist discipline (see also Chianese, 2007). Later I will give a more adequate definition of constructivism. But, seen from the constructivist point of view, perception, attention, memory, experience and general insight all contain elements of construction. Various Freudian terms support this view: inherited schemata, primal phantasies, infantile sexual theories, unconscious phantasy, transcription, *Nachträglichkeit* and multiple determination. Three of them, Freud's concepts of transcription, of memory, and of multiple determination/multiple function/multiple meaning, will presently be examined in more detail.

The main facets of psychoanalytical theory (drive psychology, ego psychology, superego psychology, psychology of the self, theory of narcissism, object relations psychology and so-called intersubjectivity), together with the metapsychological approaches (dynamic, economic, structural, genetic, adaptive) and the well-known psychoanalytical schools of thought can be seen as focusing or reliving aspects of this multilayered and manifold internal function/structure/meaning/construction. From this perspective, for instance, the directions of the different schools of thought represent different choices of interpretation. The co-presence of different aspects, be they mutually contradictory or complementary, makes sense, for it is a question of a complex total reality which cannot as yet be represented in any simpler form and is therefore to be preferred to an over-neat theory. The sense and justification for the various forms of psychoanalysis (theoretically and in practice) is the starting point for the comparison of clinical methods in the project that forms the subject of this book. In this chapter, I have to put aside the question as to which psychoanalytical approach, methodology and technique is, in my view, the most appropriate to enable psychical change or to promote 'the best possible conditions for the functions of the ego' (Freud, 1937b: 250), although I shall conclude with some remarks about my personal choice in the range of possibilities.

Construction and psychical reality

In Freud's collected works (including his letters), he used the word 'construction' roughly five times more frequently than he used the word 'reconstruction' (about 250 instances compared to 50). I should like to take this as an indication that the constructivist perspective had already been an essential part of his theory, having been developed long before the appearance of *Konstruktionen in der Analyse*, which he did not write until 1937. It was through Wolfgang Loch that I first encountered this constructivist perspective in psychoanalysis (Loch 1976, 1988; see also Eickhoff, 1996), which has since become more widely known, with interpretation and construction in psychoanalysis being the themes of the 2005 EPF Congress. Freud anticipated the repercussions of this constructivist content and spoke to Hilda Doolittle of a major philosophy contained in his discoveries (Doolittle, 1976). However, he acknowledged its importance only with hesitancy and, as Feldman (2005: 52) has shown, Freud continued to adhere in part to the ideal of reconstruction of memory and of bringing historical truth to light in his techniques of treatment.

Constructivism is to be understood here as a heterogeneous quantity of theoretical approaches stemming from diverse disciplines (biology, neurophysiology, cybernetics, psychology), whose common ground can be found in the tenet: 'the world-as-it-is-perceived – in its variety and multiplicity – is the result of inner processes' (Baraldi et al., 1998: 100), i.e. of nerve cells, of the organism, the psychic apparatus, a system of phantasies.

As an initial example of construction, I shall mention Freud's term 'inherited schema'. At the beginning of psychical development, there is the neuro-physiological pattern, inherited schema (Freud) or pre-concept (Bion), which is an inherited expectation of the breast. This expectation is the precondition for the organism or rudimentary self to be able to make any connection at all with its environment in order to start the process of exchange. These inherited schemata are the starting point of psychical development, quasi-first interpretations of a situation or, alternatively, constructions, whose correctness will have to be proved in their compatibility with the environment.

Inherited schemata are, like the Kantian categories (quantity, quality, relation, modality), 'concerned with the business of "placing" the impressions derived from actual experience' (Freud, 1918: 119). In words attributed to Bion: when the inherited expectation of the breast meets the breast then the previously empty concept (I don't know what a breast is but when it is there I will recognize it instantly) becomes vivid and sensually filled; it gains meaning.

The inherited preconception is transformed into a conception through experience and also serves as a preconception for further encounters with outside events. In the process, it proves or does not prove its worth pragmatically in contact with life. Here, very clearly, elements of construction can already be seen. They are undertaken by an inherited schema, as a mental element of the drive to make contact with an object. What Freud referred to as primal phantasies (castration/primal scene/seduction) can be seen in this sense as mental working instructions designed to sort the infant's impressions. (These primal phantasies can, for example, be read as misconceptions and defence against recognition of 'the facts of life': Hinz, 2001.) Through these processes the objects make their appearance and 'making an appearance' is the literal translation of the Greek word 'phantasizing' (von Uexküll and Wesiack, 1988).

One can argue that 'being psychical' is synonymous with 'having meaning' (Loch 1988: 39), and the 'psychical' emerges when meaning is ascribed to the meeting of an unconscious phantasy with an outside event.

There is already in Freud's work an understanding of 'interpretation' and 'construction' as synonymous, although he simultaneously tried to hold on to certain differences between them (Freud, 1937a: 260). This constructivist view meets with dissent and provokes misunderstandings the origins of which lie, on the one hand, in colloquial usage and, on the other, in the justified wish of many to keep their distance from forms of 'postmodern' one-sidedness, as, for example, radical constructivism and radical intersubjectivism. Radical constructivism loses sight of the fact that there is a reality outside the construction, even if it is only through constructions or interpretations that anything can be said or thought about it. Radical intersubjectivism, meanwhile, loses sight of metapsychology.[6] In its extreme form it sees much so-called co-creation but no repetition compulsion and its manifestation in enactments specific to each couple and at first

[6] In so-called intersubjectivism the difference between psychology and metapsychology disappears: 'Intersubjectivity [is] no concept at all, it is simply a formula to fill a gap, showing one can no longer either endure the subject or determine it' (Luhmann, 1995: 169).

unconsciously repeated. The fashionable concept of the co-creation of the psychoanalytical situation is likely to be the expression of an underestimation of the power of the unconscious. In re-analyses, it can sometimes be observed that particular relationship patterns can assert themselves with successive analysts (independent of gender) (cf. Hanly, 2007).

In everyday parlance, statements such as 'that is a construction', or, in German usage, *das ist konstruiert* virtually mean 'put on', 'fabricated', 'artificial', not connected to any real observation, and/or forced into an inappropriate theory. In a similar way, 'that is an interpretation' usually means just one opinion among others, purely subjective, simply imagined, without connection to anything objective. These colloquial usages point to real dangers in overdoing interpretationism and constructivism. It can lead to such phenomena as thinking in a way that is quite disconnected from reality and which is escapist daydreaming instead.

The term construction is to be understood in a very different way in this chapter; namely, as synonymous with reconstruction, with interpretation to be understood as the absolute precondition for individuals to be able to find their way in their ('real') environment. In the same sense, unconscious phantasies are understood as constructions of reality. 'Compatibility relations' (Baraldi et al., 1998: 101) determine whether a construction or unconscious phantasy is acceptable or viable, or merely discarded like a key that does not fit. But – unfortunately – in psychoanalysis things are more difficult: if the patient were the key, then the analyst is the lock, and he tries to make the lock fit him. I shall expand on these problems, which can make for uncomfortable reading and which probably seem more philosophical than psychoanalytical, in order properly to clarify that construction does *not* mean that 'anything goes'. Not every construction is possible. It cannot be doubted that outside (and inside) of ourselves 'something' really exists, be that a reality or a psychic reality. But we cannot claim to have any direct access to it or knowledge of it. There is no simple correspondence between our knowledge and the 'something' we believe to know. Our knowledge corresponds to our inner structures, and not simply to the reality or psychic reality of the object. One possible way of checking if our knowledge is true or false is to talk to other scientists, a procedure that can lead to consensus. This consensus theory of truth, however, has its weaknesses. We know that large groups of scientists can be stuck in error and have delusional consensus – as can non-scientific groups and masses (and potentially more so). We also know that great scientific revolutions and discoveries are often created in relative isolation and face resistance from the scientific community.

If there is consensus, it has to prove its compatibility with reality and life. How we construct our surroundings and objects is constantly tested by the question: is it compatible with the needs of ourselves and of our objects? Is it bodily, psychically, socially in the service of survival? Is it useful enough, fruitful enough, human enough? What we describe as 'something,' as a reality/psychic reality, exists, or at the very least is an approximation in the sense that we are able successfully enough to interact with reality, as well as with our psychic reality and with other people. I know that we have needed to define 'successful' again, but I hope that this short epistemological sketch has given some orientation in this complex field. I shall now try to show how Freud and analysts after him dealt with the problem that the multiplicity of options and constructions does not end in omnipotent and destructive arbitrariness, but remains a source of freedom and manifoldness.

In 1937 Freud formulated explicitly what had been implicit in his previous thinking:

> Quite often we do not succeed in bringing the patient to recollect what has been repressed. Instead of that, if the analysis is carried out correctly, we produce in him an assured conviction of the truth of the construction which achieves the same therapeutic result as a recaptured memory. The problem of what the circumstances are in which this occurs and of how it is possible that what appears to be an incomplete substitute should nevertheless produce a complete result – all of this is matter for a later inquiry.
>
> (Freud, 1937a: 266)

The elaboration of the constructivist perspective inherent in psychoanalysis is, I suppose, part of this later inquiry and development, as happened, for example, in our comparing workshops.

In 'Konstruktionen in der Analyse' (Freud, 1937b), a clear move towards a consensus theory of truth can be seen. It is a question of a consensual giving of meaning, a construction between discovery and invention which is 'indispensable for the present and future of the subject' (Dantlgraber, 2002: 422; see also Loch, 1976: 885) in that it is 'life-sustaining'. This succeeds only when there is a relation to truth 'which has its origins in the past' (Dantlgraber, 2002: 422). This 'grain of truth' (Freud, 1907: 80), with its link to the past, is during analysis revived in changed form and made accessible to the sensual experience of both parties by factors that have their origin in the analytical present. Can we assess whether a construction/interpretation is compatible with an actual analytic reality and in 'contact with truth' (in the sense of 'viable')?[7]

Wolfgang Loch often mentioned Michael Balint's recommendation that analysts should not offer an interpretation until they have developed and had available a number of other possible ones. This recommendation was important to Loch in that it accentuated the constructivist character of the analytical process and the necessity to practice adopting changes in perspective. In emphasizing the optional character of interpretation, there is, however, a danger of intellectualization, of randomness and of arbitrariness. Wolfgang Loch was well aware of this danger and knew the critical objections to optionality: if one has more than one interpretation in one's mind, they may well all be wrong. A kind of supermarket of interpretations and interpretation fetishism can develop, which simultaneously recognizes and denies reality, and, in a perverse transference situation, can encourage the patient to remain in a pre-oedipal world. Or the work can freeze up if one or the other of the analytical couple regards themselves in a reifying manner as being in possession of reality (without inverted commas). Reality is, however, as 'un-ownable' as the unconscious is unconscious. Certainly more psychoanalytical research is needed here on what possibilities there are for deciding which interpretative alternative is to be rejected in favour of which. Any such decision would,

---

[7] In this footnote, I summarize some of the hints Freud gave in 'Constructions in Analysis' of how an apt interpretation can be identified. If in the course of this work in the *hic et nunc et mecum* of the analytical situation memories do rise to the surface, then that can be exactly what is most desired. One question now is: how is one to imagine this arising of memory or emerging of a piece of lost life history? Freud writes that after an 'obviously apt construction' 'surprising' and 'lively recollections' (Freud, 1937a: 266) can come up, recollections not of the historical event, which was the content of the construction, but of 'details relating to that subject,' for example recollecting 'with abnormal sharpness faces of the people involved in the construction, or rooms in which something of the sort might have happened' (Freud, 1937a: 266).

An apt construction thus triggers processes of remembering: not – as might have been expected – coherent additions of whole tracts of lost biographical narrative, but rather fragments, which are surprising, at first incomprehensible, detailed and vivid. Earlier inklings gain greater conviction and create connections to form altered webs of infantile impressions, memory, phantasy, insight, experience and lived recognition.

however, also have to be allied to the knowledge that even the interpretation now chosen cannot claim to be the only possible one. It can, at best, only be that which at the present moment seems most compatible with the experienced reality of the relationship and the assumed unconscious total situation.

Trace and transcription: memory as construction

As Ilka Quindeau (2004) clearly explains in her book, *Spur und Umschrift: Die konstitutive Bedeutung von Erinnerung in der Psychoanalyse (Trace and Transcription: The Constitutive Meaning of Memory in Psychoanalysis)*, 'historical' and 'constructivist' concepts of memory exist side by side in Freud's work (Quindeau, 2004: 9; see also Haas, 2006). 'Historical' concepts refer to the assumption that 'a past event or experience is stored in the memory and can be called up unchanged as a recollection' (Quindeau, 2004: 9–10). 'Constructivist' concepts of the memory, 'as they prevail today in the cultural and neuro-sciences, have turned away from this storehouse model'. They assume the 'alteration of earlier experiences through memory processes; (the act of) remembering is not the recalling of an earlier state but rather the present reading of it' (Quindeau, 2004: 10). In an extreme case, this would mean that memories depend entirely and exclusively on the present and not on the past. The past could then be arbitrarily 'constructed' according to the interests and needs of the present and come to be totally in the power of the subject (cf. Assmann, 1998: 132; Quindeau, 2004: 10). In this chapter, which takes Quindeau as its lead, a concept of memory is presented to counter this tendency to randomness, arbitrariness and omnipotence: one that 'does justice to the constructed character of memory but also grants the past a weight of its own' (Quindeau, 2004: 10), by reflecting on the limits of constructability. In a comparable way, the constructed character of psychoanalytical knowledge in general has to be considered, while the existence of psychical 'reality', with the limits of its constructability, must also be recognized.

Freud succeeded in observing remembering as a complex process of the memory without smoothing over the contradictions in his theory of memory. In this way his contribution to a theory of remembering is the precursor to more modern concepts, where transcription plays a great role.

In his letter to Wilhelm Fliess (6 December 1896), Freud writes:

As you know, I am working on the assumption that our psychic mechanism has come into being by a process of stratification: the material present in the form of memory-traces being subjected from time to time to a *rearrangement* in accordance with fresh circumstances – to a *retranscription*. Thus what is essentially new about my theory is the thesis that the memory is present not once but several times over, that it is laid down in various kinds of indications. I postulated a similar kind of rearrangement some time ago, (*Aphasia*), for the paths leading from the periphery [of the body to the cortex]. I do not know how many of these registrations there are: at least three, probably more. . . .

W [*Wahrnehmungen* – perceptions] are neurones in which perceptions originate, to which consciousness attaches, but which in themselves retain no trace of what has happened . . . For *consciousness and memory are mutually exclusive*.

Wz [*Wahrnehmungzeichen* – indication of perception] is the first registration of the perceptions; it is quite incapable of consciousness and is arranged according to associations by simultaneity.

Ub (*Unbewußtsein* – unconsciousness] is the second registration, arranged according to other, perhaps causal relations. Ub traces would perhaps correspond to conceptual memories; equally inaccessible to consciousness.

Vb [*Vorbewußtsein* – preconsciousness] is the third transcription, attached to word presentation and corresponding to our official ego. The cathexes proceeding from this Vb become conscious according to certain rules; and this secondary *thought-consciousness* is subsequent in time and is probably connected with the hallucinatory activation of word presentations, so that the neurones of consciousness would once again be perceptual neurones and in themselves without memory.

If I could give a complete account of the psychological characteristics of perception and of the three transcriptions, I should have described a new psychology. Some material for this is at hand, but that is not my present intention.

I should like to emphasize the fact that the successive registrations represent the psychic achievement of successive epochs of life. At the boundary between any such two epochs a translation of psychic material must take place. I explain the peculiarities of the psychoneuroses by supposing that this translation has not taken place in the case of some of the material, which has certain consequences. For we hold firmly to a belief in a tendency toward quantitative adjustment. Every later transcript inhibits its predecessor and drains the excitatory process from it. If a later transcript is lacking, the excitation is dealt with in accordance with the psychological laws on force in the earlier psychic epoch and along the paths open at that time. Thus an anachronism persists: in a particular province *fueros* are still in force.[8] We are in the presence of 'survivals'.

(Freud, 1887–1904, Letter 112 of 6 December 1896, trans. J. M. Masson)

This extended quotation may be justified because it provides evidence of the early existence of the idea of several rearrangements, registrations, transcriptions and translations, together with the accompanying conception of the coexistence of several layers of memory and of the psychical process as a process of stratification. Moreover, the concept of *Nachträglichkeit* is beginning to appear, in that there is mention of transcriptions in connection with successive epochs in life.

We will return to this letter a number of times. For the moment, what we shall emphasize is Freud's view that *no layer can be lost in the psyche* and, after a few comments on the first and second transcriptions, that the first registrations of perceptions or memories of concepts must suffice. In my view, the source of the richness of psychoanalysis lies in this description:[9]

---

[8] See footnote in the Letters, Letter 112 (Spanish) '*fuero*: older local or special privilege from before the establishment of a central legislation'.

[9] It seems plausible to me that both transcriptions can be imagined as phantasy systems existing alongside one another and that they can become active in oscillation, as happens, for example, in the interactions between paranoid-schizoid and the depressive position described by Bion, or in the way that Matte-Blanco has described the psychical modalities of symmetry and asymmetry. Simultaneous association and ordering according to similarity corresponds to total identification and projective identification, as well as to the equating of self and object and the equating of the word with the thing it describes. In the symmetrical mode, as Matte-Blanco describes it, there is, first, no distinction between space and time; second, the equating of opposites. If before and after are equated, there is no time, if inside and outside are equated, then there is no division in space and no separation of inner and outer reality. Third, if out of two wishes only what is common to both is perceived, there can be no contradiction and no negation. Fourth, if the part can be taken for the whole, then condensation and displacement are the rule. This corresponds to Freud's descriptions of the way in which the unconscious works and how they relate to the functioning of memory.

The first of these *Mnem (mnemonic)* systems will naturally contain the record of association in respect to *simultaneity in time;* while the same perceptual material will be arranged in the later systems in respect to other kinds of coincidence, so that one of these later systems, for instance, will record relations of similarity.

(Freud, 1900: 539)

We also find other workings of the unconscious in Freud, which could perhaps be remote pre-stages of the phantasy system of the depressive position; the second transcription, the 'causal relations' and 'conceptual memories', which are also inaccessible to consciousness, become easier to understand if one imagines them as psychical paths laid by sequences of events and patterns of actions. In this way, unconscious *if-then-* and *because-* relations can occur. For this reason, unconscious concepts (patterns, images) are formed as a second transcription via elementary interactional processes connected with the satisfaction of the most important needs of the body. At this unconscious level of functioning and phantasy, there is separation of space and time, of subject and object, of whole objects and representations of them in their absence. However, as already explained, this second transcription has no access to consciousness. It has to experience rearrangements in order to reach the official ego, or the secondary thought consciousness. Just like Bion's beta and alpha elements, these two transcriptions are not recognizable directly. And it is interesting to remember how Freud described unconscious phantasies:

On the one hand they are highly organized, free from self-contradiction, have made use of every acquisition of the system of Cs [consciousness] and would hardly be distinguished in our judgement from the formations of that system. On the other hand they are unconscious and are incapable of becoming conscious. Thus qualitatively they belong to the system Pcs, but factually to the Ucs. Their origin is what decides their fate. We may compare them with individuals of mixed race who, when taken all round, resemble white men, but who betray their coloured descent by some striking feature or other, and are on that account excluded from society and enjoy none of the privileges of white people. Of such a nature are those phantasies of normal people as well as of neurotics which we have recognized as preliminary stages in the formation both of dreams and of symptoms and which, in spite of their high degree of organization, remain repressed and therefore cannot become conscious.

(Freud 1915: 190–191)

In his later works Freud abandoned the notion quoted earlier on, that the successive registrations represent 'the psychic achievement of successive epochs of life' (Freud, 1887–1904: Letter 112). It seems reasonable, however, to suppose that the expression 'epochs of life' refers either to the stages of psychosexual development (oral, anal, phallic, genital), to oedipal/pre-oedipal stages, or, once again, to the crises of the entire life cycle (Erikson, 1956). It also seems reasonable to suggest that 'at the boundary between two such epochs a translation [or transcription] of the psychical material must take place' (Freud, 1887–1904: Letter 112). The connection between drive modality, satisfaction modality, the unconscious pattern of thinking, unconscious phantasy and transformation or transcription will only be briefly illustrated here. Devouring or eating up and being devoured or eaten up, as well as the desire to sleep, all belong to the modalities of the oral phase. These oral modalities organize inter-actional experiences and patterns of both experience and thought, which lead to the transcription of experience up to that point. The same is true for the anal modalities – holding, possessing, controlling and their counter wishes. In a way that is comparable to the phallic modalities, radical competition, such as castrated versus not-castrated and omnipotent versus impotent, can be seen as transcription models contributing to the organization of perception, experience and memory. The same is true of the genital modality with its closeness to reality, its richness and its pain. It creates great opportunities if it is lived, but actually living it involves inherent problems. If this modality is unbearable, pre-oedipal transcriptions will emerge. If bearable, the transcriptions can be stabilized. Here, too, there can be oscillations between the two, as for instance between the paranoid-schizoid and depressive position.

There are many unanswered questions that cannot be addressed in more detail here. For example questions about the form that these unconscious 'texts' and 'transcriptions' take. It is over these questions that psychoanalytical controversies, both theoretical and technical, start: are there, for instance, psychically unstructured areas where there are no texts that could be transcribed, but where texts would have to be freshly created or written? What is the relationship between actualizing and recalling representations, or presentative and representative symbolism? Does repetition in transference, involvement or entanglement provide direct access to the past? When no transcription was possible, and *fueros* or remnants remain in force, are these to be regarded as direct memories *stemming from the past* or only *memories of the past?* What is the relationship between 'repetition' in transference and 'recalling' of memory? What are these: reissue or revised issue or new edition?

Multiple determination

If the psychical mechanism consists of stratification of transcriptions, then one can also assume the coexistence of multiple transcriptions or translations. This results in the principle of the multiple determination and multiple meaning of every psychical phenomenon. Robert Waelder, who emigrated from Vienna to the United States in 1938, was the first systematically to think of this principle. In 1930, he was inspired and stimulated by the second theory of anxiety, as Freud (1926) had developed it in *Inhibitions, Symptoms and Anxiety*, and wrote that this second theory of anxiety was not intended by Freud to 'do away with the older conception or replace it', but that it was meant to mean that 'in a real case, both theories – the breaking in of anxiety over the ego and the formation of the anxiety signal by the ego with a biological function – in fact represented two facets in one real event' (Waelder, 1980: 57). On the one occasion the 'phenomenon is described from the point of view of the id and the other from that of the ego' (Waelder, 1980: 57–58). Waelder concludes from this use of the double perspective that in general 'it might not only be permissible but positively required of psychoanalysis to apply a multiple perspective in looking at every psychical act' (Waelder, 1980: 58). In his conception of the ego as a mediating instance, Freud had allocated three tasks to it; in its dependency on outer reality, on the superego and on the id, the ego must mediate the claims of these three, and in doing so has only relative autonomy.

Waelder adds a *fourth* task to these three: the *compulsion to repeat*. He sees the attitude of the ego towards the repetition compulsion as similar to its stance towards the life of the drives. The tasks that are 'imposed on the ego from its deepest psychical tendency' (Waelder, 1980: 60) are used by the ego to overcome threatening experiences, while the ego is simultaneously at the mercy of these tasks as representing the 'real event/act of repetition'. The observation of the simultaneously *using and being at the mercy of* lead Waelder to the conclusion that the ego has no less than *eight* tasks, or rather 'eight groups of tasks the ego tries to master, four of them are given and the remaining four the ego poses itself' (Waelder, 1980: 60, 61). Alongside *multiple determination* (in Freud, this is sometimes called *over-determination*), Waelder places the *principle of multiple functions* and the *principle of multiple meanings*. Multiple functions mean that every attempt to master or to solve one task simultaneously represents an attempted solution of the other tasks, no matter how unsuccessful such an attempt may be. Since the tasks are contradictory in nature, a 'completely successful simultaneous solution of all eight tasks is impossible. This is the root of the compromise character of every psychical action' – and is true not only of dreams and symptoms but also 'for every psychical action/happening/event' (Waelder, 1980: 62). Multiple causes, multiple motives, multiple functions and multiple meanings are a matter of course for psychoanalysis, although difficulties can arise when trying to bear more than one motive, reason or cause in mind.

The different varieties of psychoanalytical practice

Fundamental to the complex theory of psychoanalysis, the above aspects represent a rational basis for the different ways of conceptualizing, fostering and completing the analytical process in the 'real many-layered mental activity' of every analysand. The principle of layering, the concept of transcriptions, the complex concept of memory and *Nachträglichkeit* and the principle of multiple determination/function/meaning form a framework within which the differing psychoanalytical directions can be located and can form a specific possible meaning.

It has already been mentioned that the reason that metapsychological viewpoints (dynamic, economic, structural, genetic, adaptive), theoretical directions (drive psychology, ego psychology, superego psychology and psychology of the self, object relations psychology, intersubjectivism) and psychoanalytical schools have developed and persisted is that they are compatible with 'psychical reality' and, therefore, may continue to represent options for interpretation in a present-day psychoanalytical situation as long as they prove their worth.

The term 'options for interpretation' means that psychoanalytical interpretations have an optional character; every perspective, every interpretation represents a possibility of understanding. Both during the process of the development of an interpretation in the analytical situation and in the moment of its formulation, acts of faith, choice and decision are involved. Alongside inductive and deductive conclusions, the logic of abduction plays a role in psychoanalysis (Hinz, 1991); that is, educated guesses or abductive conclusions in Peirce's (1958, vol. 5: 171) sense. When Freud spoke of 'guessing', what he meant was an elaborate interplay of mental operations: exact examination starting out from the surface, the combination of multiple factors, the use of experience and knowledge and the intuitive deduction of general laws from single cases.

Found in this way, the 'selected fact' (Bion, 1962), which creates something ordered and comprehensible out of what had previously been disordered and incomprehensible, has, if certain conditions are fulfilled, relations to inner reality with its multiply-stratified transcriptions, which can now be translated after the event and can be rewritten in the analytical process.

The evaluation, which in the case of these selected facts is either an *idée fixe* or a telling construction, will also follow after the event through the observation of the reactions of the analysand to his or her own understanding or to the options offered. Following the principle of a multiple determination/function/meaning, every interpretation option will take up a determination/function/meaning, will intervene at a single point in what is happening in the unconscious, and will have repercussions on the entire inner structure and on the analytical couple.

Every metapsychological viewpoint, together with every perspective that is crystallized in one of the great theories, represents a part of the spectrum of what happens to the psychoanalytical situation as a whole. One can therefore make an analogy with the working mode of psychoanalytical case study groups, and speak of a psychical 'prism effect', as Loch described it with regard to the Balint groups. 'Just as the prism fans the light out into colors, the commentaries of the members of the group reveal the motive-structure of the doctor–patient relationship in its separate elements' (Loch, 1972: 281). This prism effect is a result of the spontaneous unconscious reactions of the member of the group to the description of a clinical situation. Particularly in the case of severely disturbed patients, it can also happen that the group produces a resonance-effect when it falls as a whole into a *unisono* countertransference to the case description 'by either identifying with the suffering patient or by producing a reaction-formation to the patient's hidden agenda' (Loch, 1972: 281).

This 'psychical resonance effect' (Loch, 1972) not only occurs in case study groups, but also characterizes the community of psychoanalysts and the history of their discipline. 'Resonance effects' or complementary countertransference reactions arise towards certain groups of patients until these patients can better be understood.

The great question still remains as to which psychoanalytical perspective and which interpretation is best for the analytical process. Waelder wrote (1980: 62) that it is 'fundamentally impossible that any one action [or that any one interpretation] should be the solution in the same manner and with the same success for every one of the tasks' to be solved in the web of multiple determinations, functions and meanings. Every attempt at solving represents a partial solution and may fulfil one task better and another worse than would a different approach.

According to Waelder, psychical actions are in a category of their own if they are near-successful in providing a solution for the multiple sides/functions/meanings of a conflict. He chooses as an example the sexual act in the context of orgasmic satisfaction and a happy relationship.

> While fulfilling the demands of the drives, of the darkest compulsion to repeat, satisfying the demands of the superego and the claims of reality, the act of love is equally the moment the human ego can discover and sense its self in the face of all these realities.
>
> (Waelder, 1980: 63)

Can this be taken as a model for analytical intercourse? Since the course of treatment must be carried out in abstinence, part of the first point will be missing: there can be no question of *orgasmic satisfaction* or fulfilment of drive demands. The drive demands themselves, the urge to repeat (enact, involve), the demands of the superego (ideals, idealizations, shame and guilt), the demands of reality (analytical setting, time, money, person of the analyst, interpretative activity) and self-discovery (ego function, regulation of self-esteem, insight and reactions to these) will, however, be very present and – if all goes well – brought into balance. Analysis as an inner process is interminable. As long as life goes on, there will be no final knowledge. Instead, knowledge edges forward forever, driven by various and changing needs. Under strong pressure and great anxiety, for example when confronted with psychic change and new, strange or bad situations, we all share a tendency to become concrete thinkers, who believe *final knowledge* or *primal observation* must exist. From time to time one can observe such 'solutions' also in the workshops, when confronted with a colleague whose inner template and personality is too different to be understood, which is one possible reason for the anxiety that can be elicited by the awareness of difference mentioned earlier in the chapter.

Limits

Before I come to my final remarks on how to limit constructability and how to distinguish an apt construction from an arbitrary one, I want to express the idea that to have a personal inclination and to have made up one's own mind about the different psychoanalytical schools, a decision that sometimes takes years, is not in contradiction with the aim of this project, which seeks to value each analyst as an experienced colleague. On the contrary: I think it is important to know where one stands in order to make a journey through the analytic world.

It is my personal impression that the object relations theory has become the leading concept in psychoanalysis (Hinz, 2001: 143–144). That means, statistically, that, if this impression is correct, a majority of analysts are working with a model that can in a wide sense be called object relational. Clearly there are analysts who, when speaking of an object, think of external mother and external father, as if historical truth simply were available through working analytically. These analysts do not seem to make much use of the concept of internal object representations and internal memory, which are the present result of complex transformations and of transcriptions, transcribed memories, and experiences. When I speak of an object relational model, I mean the following: object as an internal representation.

If I might be permitted to voice my own thoughts and choices on the matter, I believe that the object relational model has developed this lead because it best allows the development of what had from the start been inherent in psychoanalysis, namely that the *subject* is what manifests in the analytical situation, determined by the person's inner objects which are modified, brought into the present moment by the analyst (as the outer object of the moment), and there discovered or invented or constructed on a sure foundation by analyst and analysand alike. The radical development of this perspective has brought modern psychoanalysis in line with the most modern theory of science (cf. Reiche, 1999: 577).

This way of looking at psychoanalysis is put into practice in every clinic that sees as pivotal the micro-analysis of countertransference and transference, or the examination of the reactions of analysands to an insight of their own or to the understanding offered to them in listening to the listening. Moreover, object relations theory was able to become the leading concept because it was best able to bring together the multiple aspects of what happens (drive, object or reality, superego, ego/self, urge to repeat). These aspects appear in more isolated form in drive-, ego- and self psychology, which play a central role in French, British and American psychoanalytical trends respectively. In its full complexity, the object relations psychology can integrate many aspects, e.g. that the object is constituted by the drive, but that equally the drive is constituted by the object; or that the object is extremely important from the start, as is the ego, since it emerges in the interaction between narcissism and object relations. Object relations psychology also captures the fact that sexual and aggressive drive satisfaction can be of great significance for a sense of self, and it can conceptualize that the free association process can be restricted by an intrusively active object. As a last example, this complex form of psychoanalysis allows us to realize the idea that a feeling of security can grow through the unexpected survival of the object.

Since there can no longer be any general statements, but only statements on what becomes manifest in the analytical situation, or on what can be reconstructed or constructed in it, the situation in which the constructivist perspective places us could be called awkward, for it has dizzying dimensions through the lack of anything to hold on to and any orientation or boundaries.

We have to forgo final knowledge, for there are neither primarily given perceptions nor ultimately provable theorems.[10] On the other hand, this approach to psychoanalysis, with its double contingency,[11] challenges the fascinating dimension of openness, multiplicity, richness and freedom. It is like being greeted with a certain irony and solidarity, and, indeed, I should like to suggest a certain scientific light-heartedness that Freud himself showed in 'Constructions in Analysis' when faced with the difficulties of validating an interpretation or construction:

> Only the further course of the analysis enables us to decide whether our constructions are correct or unserviceable. We do not pretend that an individual construction is anything more than a conjecture which awaits examination, confirmation or rejection. We claim no authority for it, we require no direct agreement from the patient, nor do we argue with him if he at first denies it. In short we conduct ourselves on the model of a familiar figure in one of Nestroy's farces – the manservant who has a single answer on his lips to every question or objection: 'It will all become clear in the course of future developments'.
>
> (Freud, 1937a: 265)

Without wishing to give the impression of looking for a way out of what Nietzsche referred to as the 'gay science', I should like to touch on a few aspects that, to my mind, help in limiting total constructability. I suppose that each analytical school and each analyst in their own way has to deal with the question of how to distinguish an apt

[10] It is sometimes said of Kleinian analysts working on the micro-analysis of the current relationship that they in fact cling to a reified drive-psychological discourse, to final causes, for example inborn forms of envy, although there is in the clinical situation no way of saying that one has reached a phenomenon that cannot be explained as defence. I believe, however, that the *balancing act of combining metapsychology with constructivist openness* is possible and necessary, just as it is possible and necessary to combine psychoanalytical *knowledge* of archaic unconscious phantasy with the attitude of *not knowing* and free-floating attention.

[11] 'In logic contingency means simultaneous exclusion of necessity and impossibility' (Baraldi et al., 1998, 37 ff). Contingency means that everything which exists can exist differently (and therefore is neither impossible nor necessary)' (ibid.). The structure of the social world develops in horizons of double perspective, double contingency. The ego can observe data from the perspective of possibilities given now through an *alter ego*. These possibilities can thus become the ego's possibilities. In this way, a new systemic order emerges from the double contingency, a social system that reproduces itself (cf. ibid.). In analysis, this frequently appears as the undesirable stability of the repetition compulsion.

construction from a non-fitting one. Although there is no way instantly of distinguishing between a viable and non-viable construction, we can observe the reaction to what we say and the development of the analysis.

My own attempts to put limits on constructability naturally have to do with my personal analytical development and choices. I believe that in the analytical encounter there forms a changed social system or relationship, which tends to reproduce itself, sometimes in very repetitive ways. I think this is a central psychoanalytical experience, and one that is sometimes hard to bear. Viewed from the psychoanalytical perspective, the reproduction of a system means a system in which the reproduced elements are patterns of behaviour and experiences of conscious object relations and archaic phantasies that are related to the past in some manner that cannot exactly be defined. An action-potential in the unconscious phantasy urges the object to behave in the way that the imagination had anticipated. This unconscious urging can be called desire for identicalness (or 'pressure towards identity': Feldman, 1997: 232): it urges (the object) to reproduce the unconscious expectation isomorphically, a process that provides a paradoxical sense of safety. These thoughts refer to a level of observation beneath the manifest text of the analytical session. Thus, I believe, countless possibilities are reduced to a smaller number of patterns that can be sensed.[12] Since clearly the forces of repetition urge us towards action, it can be assumed that, beneath the various possible manifest texts of the analysand and the analyst, there are rhythms, processes, patterns of behaviour, images of relationships and experiences of object relationships repeating themselves. Very early on, analytical methodology recommended taking such phenomena

[12] Towards the end of 'Constructions in Analysis', Freud mentions that 'delusion owes its convincing power to the element of historical truth which it inserts in the place of the rejected reality' (Freud, 1937a: 268). From today's perspective one can add that the convictional power of a delusion, of phantasy, of transference, and of projective identification is constantly fed in the present by the 'action-potential' or 'intrusive action-potential' (Loch in his lectures in 1975, see Loch, 2001: 127), which these phenomena contain. In other words, they are nourished by the unconscious power that forces the object to adapt its own reality to the subject's unconscious phantasy, which means the object acts as anticipated. An assured conviction of the truth of a construction in an analytical situation must therefore spring from the description and interpretation of the experienced insight of the present-day shared reality that is of the reality of the shared (sensual and emotional) experience. This experience is presumably connected to an 'historical core of truth', but in an unknown relation (Loch, 1988: 67).

seriously; they are certainly not to be regarded as primal. This reproduction of earlier patterns and relations has been subjected to after-the-event reorderings or transcriptions and, moreover, cannot be described without reference to a particular theory.

So, here too, we meet double contingency and the formation of a changed system that reproduces itself. Such systems not infrequently appear in the analytical process as relationship-knots, as a 'knot making change impossible', and which has to be reached 'if there is to be a chance of change' (Schneider 2003: 118).

These reflections point to a level of observation that is important psychoanalytically, and which occurs particularly when the form of communication is considered along with the contents. This is not in itself new: we might for example recall Bion's thoughts on the caesura and his recommendation to examine not so much the transference but the transitions and breaks between different transferences and positions. Research by Joseph on psychical change also sees a transition as the central point for observations of the patient's reactions to an insight of his own or to an interpretation offered by the analyst. This is a process relatively close to observation and we would probably do well to study in minute detail how psychical truth is dealt with. In the next step it will, however, no longer be a question of the interpretation just given and of the theory behind it; it is solely the reaction of the patient that counts.

This short summary of my inner explicit theories or inner template might serve as an illustration of what the comparing workshop is unfolding more precisely when investigating clinical material in Step 2. Each analyst can try to describe the conscious concepts of how he or she tries to listen to and how he or she conceives to be in the centre of the analytical situation, and what aims the analyst has in facilitating transformation and psychic change. When the group discussion constructs the group's view of what the explicit theories are, and what might be the presenters' or analysts' implicit theories, this is a more or less different vertex. In the following chapters, this will be a main focus: to describe the differences through comparison. For example, I think that analysts often and for several years have actively to do much of the analytic work themselves in order to help their patient in the struggle between a hostile superego and a submissive ego. But there are also analysts who from the beginning practise much more deliberate silence than, for example, I do. They concentrate on the freedom to free associate which already exists in the ego. A further difference will be if the analytical text is mainly listened to as a story of actual happenings and external objects, or if there is a 'third ear' that listens as if to a dream. In the latter case, there is a concept that an important psychic activity is constantly going on, influencing every detail of the analytical session, even if we are unable directly to observe it. But other analysts do not believe this, work differently, and can also establish a successful analytical process. These examples should serve only as a bridge to what is examined in detail in Chapters 6 and 7.

6

Reflection and evolution
Developing the two-step method

David Tuckett (UK)

In the opening chapter I described the background to the pro-ject's inception, the early experiences of enthusiasm, the some-what unexpected emotional and conceptual difficulties we then encountered and the outlines of the way we came to approach them. Our experiences in Brussels, Prague and Sorrento have now been described in some detail. They demonstrated to us that it was no simple matter to arrange workshop groups that would be able to discuss psychoanalytical clinical material and to arrive at rigorous comparisons of different approaches. With hindsight our reflections on the difficulties we were forced into after Sorrento have turned out to be critical. They took place initially in the two meetings of the working party in Paris in September 2003 and February 2004, backed up and briefed by some exploratory qualitative research. But they were also to be ongoing as we used the new EPF working party structure to meet two or three times a year to try to analyse and compare what had been happening at the workshops themselves.

In those meetings in 2003 and 2004 we were faced with con-ceptual and emotional issues which were largely a function of the very difficulties the comparative clinical methods project had been designed to address: namely the problem of managing difference and making comparisons between psychoanalysts and within psycho-analytic institutions and the lack of easily applied frameworks to define when work is psychoanalytic (of a particular type), except via the traditional routes of appeal to charisma and authority. We came out of those 2003 and 2004 meetings with the outline of the special-ized discussion method – the two-step method – which is the main focus of this book.

In this chapter I will describe the development of the new method and also say something about how and why it has evolved sub-sequently, trying to draw out some elements of its core epistemo-logical assumptions.

I should note, however, that the two-step method was never intended to be a fixed or finished method. Its development (particu-larly in the area of Step 2) is ongoing and may well be so for as long as it is used. We continue to refine its main elements more precisely and to internalize them for the purpose of moderating the groups each year. As experience in the groups has settled we have been able to focus less on making sure the workshops were enjoyable and on task and more on the narratives about the ways analysts work that have emerged. We have begun to get some real ideas about the differences that exist and to notice they do not have a lot to do with traditional schools and this has enabled us to refine and to clarify Step 2.

The process of development and clarification has recently been greatly accelerated by the task of dividing up aspects of the project to write this book together. Those moderating and writing the book have been particularly required to reflect on their assumptions and have been considerably challenged by the process. In sum we are describing an evolving work and our understanding and appreciation of what we are doing and how it works goes forwards and backwards in time – understanding often developing après coup. Because this to and fro elaboration creates a challenge for describing what we have done, the reader's patience will be required. Detailed accounts of the experience of being in a two-step group will be found in Chapter 7; further and eventually rather surprising thoughts about it will be found in Chapters 8 and 9. An early and very limited attempt to use the method to compare three analysts will be found in Chapter 10.

The two-step method today

At the time of writing this chapter – that is in 2007 after four years of using it – the two-step method of workshop discussion is quite stable. I will introduce it as I would introduce the method to those who join

133

a group for the first time – usually providing this material ahead of time but also going through it at the beginning of each workshop.

First, we remind participants that we are aiming to provide a framework for a group of psychoanalysts from different traditions and language cultures to use their differences creatively to discuss and compare the way different psychoanalysts work. We explain that some time after we began the project we discovered that we needed to think very carefully about how to structure discussion. 'Free discussion' had significant drawbacks. We have subsequently learned that a degree of structure can be useful whenever psychoanalysts discuss clinical material – especially if the presenter comes from a 'strange' tradition. It is for them to see if it works.

Second, we emphasize that we start from the assumption that the presenter in each group is a psychoanalyst. Those who attend the groups are asked to use all the curiosity at their disposal to understand how the analyst works and to place that way of working so that they understand as precisely as possible how and why it compares to their own or others'. Quite often this is not an easy emotional task.

Third, the main general features of the discussion method are then listed:

- The moderator's task is to hold the group to the work task and to do everything possible to facilitate it. He or she needs the group's support.
- The presenter's task is to present the work and then to step back and reflect on the emerging discussion from time to time and when asked to do so. Experience suggests that no presenter, however eminent, is fully aware of the ways their working method is similar to or different from other methods and may even have misconceptions about that, as we all probably do.
- The group (the discussants) are there to try to 'construct' from the available evidence in the discussion, a picture of the presenter's work which, although it may not correspond to the presenter's own prior view and may surprise (even shock) him or her in some respects, makes the best sense of his or her account of the presented materials and discussion.
- Both presenter and discussants may find it useful to be aware that it is inevitable they will have differences and sense different issues. This is to be expected both because presenter and discussant may not share the same 'models' of working and because

134

unconscious forces specific to psychoanalytic work mean that sometimes aspects of the case not yet known to the presenter are communicated to a group of discussants. At other times what discussants think may reflect their own internal situations and have nothing to do with the presenter and the case.

- The groups are designed so that understanding arises from understanding difference. Thus, although we aim to understand the presenter's way of understanding and working, it is appropriate for discussants (provided they keep in mind their aim of finding out about the presenter's approach) to mention the way they might understand or see things differently, in order to test the relation of their understanding to the presenter's and also to provide the rest of the discussant group with a snapshot of the many other available ways of thinking and working – the more the better.

- Based on experience we also warn that sometimes differences will feel extreme or ideas about what 'the patient needs' will spill over into the emotional experience of the group – to the extent some discussants will find it difficult to keep to the starting assumption that the presenter is a psychoanalyst. All concerned should treat such phenomena as matters for curiosity.

Fourth, we state that each group will begin with a presentation of some sessions and a relatively free discussion aimed at getting to know the different viewpoints in the group. These phases will take three to four hours and are known as Steps −1 and 0, as discussed in Chapter 7.

Fifth, participants are told that the formal Step 1 discussion will then be introduced and will last a further three to four hours. It will focus directly on the presenter and his or her way of working by considering each 'intervention' in depth. What was the purpose of the remark (in the analyst's mind, so to speak)? We explain that we have found this discussion proves more interesting and rigorous if limited to deciding which of six possible purposes might make sense. Examples of each type are provided (Figure 6.1).

Finally, participants are told about Step 2. We suggest that group members keep this in mind throughout Step 1 and often assign one dimension to each member to be thinking about. Step 2 focuses on five dimensions of the analyst's 'explanatory model' of working. When we get to that stage discussion will make use of the many different ideas about how to work as a psychoanalyst (explanatory models of

Such comments apparently make the patient conscious of some observations. You will recognize them compared to 2 because they are likely to be more saturated (i.e. to have a clear and unambiguous meaning rather than more ambiguous meaning). Compared to a 4 when they concern the analytical relationship, they will be more atemporal or apersonal. The discussion why an intervention might be not 4 or 3 etc. is more important than the outcome. **Examples:** "How do you think of a wall?" "What are you thinking?" "What's going on in your mind?" "Do you think there is a pattern in the way you are here and how you are with your wife?" "You quite often seem to be irritated by your boss." "I think you feel you don't want to talk about that.' "It seems to me you get anxious when you think about coming to see me.' "There was a purpose but it collapsed." "Tell me more about that feeling." "Any associations?' 'The process of cutting yourself is happening now' (*apersonal? But not atemporal so marginal to 4*).

3

Questions, clarifications, reformulations, aimed at making matters conscious

Comments here are likely to be ambiguous, polysemic and brief – aiming to encourage more association or linking but at the unconscious rather than conscious level.

Examples: 'Walls?' 'A mouth with teeth!' 'A bedroom!' 'Not feeling hateful?'

Note: No comment can escape the conscious or unconscious but some comments are more directed at one than the other. As one participant put it: 'A certain type of wording, i.e. repeating a word that seemed to be central, is basically different from, let's say, clarification, or designation of what is happening in the here and now.'

2

Adding an element to facilitate unconscious process

1

Maintaining the basic setting

Basic behaviour creating the setting in simple ways. **Examples:** "You have forgotton your coat." "My holiday begins on Friday'. (There are circumstances where these comments might be 6 or even 3 – that's for debate!)

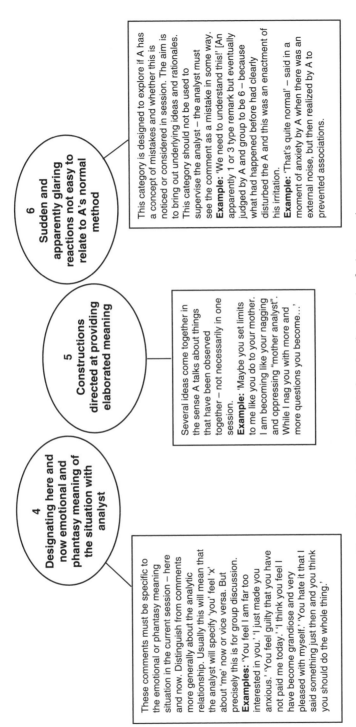

Figure 6.1 Step 1 from 2005: six functional categories for intervention

doing analysis) that exist in the group – but for the purpose of under-standing the analyst's method rather than seeking to judge or to con-vert him or her to another.

The first four instructions came out of the Prague and Sorrento experiences and the reflections I have described in Chapter 1. The Step 1 and Step 2 process is the result of our further work on the Sorrento grid-typology. The main purpose of this chapter is to set out the details of the two steps and the thinking that lies behind them. The remaining chapters will provide details about the experience of using the method.

Devising Step 1

After hearing the presentation and taking part in the earlier 'warming-up' steps, Step 1 requires the group to explore the presenter's inter-ventions one by one. The task is to consider into which of several functional categories each one belongs.

After the Prague experience 'without structure', I realized that something else was needed to provide groups with a framework for exploring dimensions of the way an analyst worked and to help them focus their attention on the way the analyst was working rather than the case itself. At that stage I reviewed the psychoanalytic research literature for something that might help, but without success: while there is a developing area of psychoanalytic process and consultation process research, none of it was at the level of specificity required to allow comparisons of psychoanalytic work of the kind we were undertaking.[1]

To try to find something that might work in the groups I turned at that stage to some clinical presentations that were easily available to me and looked at what the psychoanalysts reported saying and how they said they behaved with their patients. The thirteen categories I ended with were intended to cover the various functional intentions the various interventions the analysts made appeared to have. As we have heard in Chapter 4, this thirteen-point 'grid' definitely moved the task forward. The structure it provided allowed over a hundred

---

[1] Research uses judges who are not required to specify the elements in their judgements or investigates factors like quality of alliance, accuracy of statements made about central relatedness (CCRT) and so on (see Dahl et al., 1988, or Miller et al., 1993).

colleagues to take part in workshop groups in which sometimes there was a much more focused and critical engagement with the task than there had been in Prague. At the same time it was clear that there were too many categories and that it wasn't right.

In the months that followed the first meeting in Paris after Sorrento, I worked with a research assistant (funded by the IPA Research Advisory Board), Naama Ben Yehoyada, to try to develop the revised comparative typology we planned, namely, to arrive at a simpler revision of the thirteen-point Sorrento grid, to provide meta-rules and examples for any category points, and to try to develop an extended framework for more rigorously discussing and comparing not only psychoanalysts' interventions but also their underlying explanatory models – for example concerning listening to the unconscious or conceiving how their work created a psychoanalytic process and how that functioned.[2]

We approached the task by looking again at the published cases I had considered after Prague and also others,[3] including some of those discussed in Sorrento and more published in the *International Journal*'s 'Analyst at Work' series. Nine cases were eventually selected for detailed qualitative analysis: cases conducted by colleagues from Belgium, France, Germany, Italy, Spain, Sweden, the UK and the United States.

The analysis looked first at all the reported interventions for those cases. We had regular meetings preceded by an effort independently to classify one or two cases in terms of an agreed scheme. Where we assigned interventions to categories in a different way there was scope for discussion and so opportunity to refine or redefine them. As the thirteen points of the Sorrento scheme had clearly been too many, we looked for a simpler division; eventually settling on a five-category system, which seemed to be 'relatively' easy to recall and to define but which also seemed to result in potentially interesting discussion points. Next, we looked at each intervention in terms of other

[2] This work was supported by the Research Advisory Board of the International Psychoanalytical Association, who generously made a small grant used to pay Naama Ben Yehoyada's time.

[3] I looked at several sessions from five cases from well-known and respected psychoanalysts whose work was available to me: one presentation from Prague; one of the presentations from the Brussels meeting; one from a European-North American clinical meeting in which I participated and two published cases from the *International Journal* – one supplemented by the detailed clinical material posted in the website discussion.

distinctions discussed by the group in Paris and considered as possibly important distinctions: particularly, as to how far interventions were saturated or unsaturated or whether the 'target' of the analyst's comment tended to be engaged more with internal (unconscious?) processes or at bringing about more conscious awareness. Finally, we looked at the presented sessions and any information we had available from them and the discussion of them as to the analyst's thinking and intentions. The aim was to try to explore the different ways they seemed to think about the work they were doing and what it was that particularly seemed to catch their attention as they listened to and tried to make sense of what patients said; searching behind this for elements we might distinguish to construct comparative models. We visited and revisited the cases according to a variety of newly defined coding schemes, which we discussed and revised at regular intervals.

Table 6.1 sets out the revised intervention categories that we eventually arrived at – modifying the thirteen-category Sorrento grid to a new five-category system. Whereas thirteen categories had been too many, we thought we would all be able to hold five in mind quite easily. The five we selected were chosen because we thought they were likely to be useful to deepen the discussion of the analyst's method and to begin to tease out his or her underlying model.

Table 6.1 Preliminary ideas about Step 1 after Sorrento **(February 2004)**

---

1 Interventions directed at maintaining the basic setting.

2 Interventions directed at facilitating a psychoanalytical process:

2A Interventions aimed at *unconscious* representational process (including deliberate use of silence to further inner processes).

2B Interventions aimed more at *conscious* representational process ('getting a patient thinking').

3 Interventions directed at designating the here and now emotional and phantasy meaning of the situation with the analyst.

4 Interventions directed at providing elaborated meaning of the here and now experience of the particular session (whether linked more broadly or not).

5 Interventions directed at providing elaborated meaning of what analyst and patient are discovering but not particularly closely based on the here and now experience of the particular session.

To illustrate what we had in mind I will discuss category 3 – most of the analysts we studied said something in one of the sessions we examined that appeared to be *designating the here and now emotional and phantasy meaning of the situation with the analyst.* For example:

[The patient has arrived and said she will be attending a course and so will not come to the next session. She wonders about the tensions which exist between the sessions and the courses and eventually thinks that perhaps her decision is aggressive and in a certain sense a rejection against the sessions. At this point the analyst says]: **'An explosion against me'** [This interpretation results from the events of the session so far but also a complex chain of meaning in the analyst's mind including a recent dream *in which the patient is with her brother and her sister and they make a fire which 'explodes'*. This explosion in turn is associated to the gas chambers in which the patient's relatives have been murdered.]

I said something to comment on the change, on how – when she was talking about something lacking in the analysis and what I make the weekend like for her – it felt very real and genuine but now she is blaming not me but herself. [This example is more self-explanatory and so will not be elaborated.]

In the first example, the analyst 'chose' her words sparingly to convey a multiplicity of meanings that seemed to her to be implied by the patient's previous comments – focusing on the fact that something emotional was being described with a meaning for the situation with the analyst, in the patient's mind. In the second example, which has been summarized, the analyst used more words and with more precision to convey the idea that something had just happened in the patient's mind while talking to the analyst; sensing a resistance to direct communication perhaps because the patient feared the analyst's response. (The analyst in fact reported, 'I was not sure if this was because she thought she would offend me in talking about the analysis and so she has to go and blame herself or what.')

From the other cases we could see there might be many ways of making these kinds of comments. As the two of us discussed the possible meanings of particular comments we could see how a discussion of each intervention's meaning could be productive in eliciting ideas about the analyst's underlying models. In conventional terms this third category – involving statements that link the patient and the analyst in the room – indicates the way the analysts conceived of and managed aspects of the transference relationship.

Some analysts we studied made a remark which we judged to have a different functional purpose and so classified in a different category. This was category 4 – Interventions *directed at providing elaborated meaning of the here and now experience of the particular session* (whether linked more broadly or not). For example:

> I think you are also wondering if I still trust you enough . . . you have seen for some sessions that often nothing remains of what once had a meaning for you here . . . [you can't remember it or it feels no longer true so] what we speak about in one session is no longer alive, is somehow distorted, by the time of the next.

> You seem to feel my silence not as if I was listening, not only as if I was not interested, but as if I took pleasure to let you down alone and not to give you any help.

> I said how she wants to connect with her sister and also wants me to understand how awful it feels not to be able to be connected. I said she talked about different experiences and though she doesn't say, I understand from what she lets me know how disturbing they are – how difficult it is to amalgamate all the experiences and how she is left with unamalgamated feelings.

> Should I conclude that you keep that from me because you want to evoke in me an attitude of protection?

These examples also relate to what are often termed transference interpretations but they appeared to differ from comments in the earlier category and perhaps to have a different function. They all seemed rather clear cases of an analyst elaborating an idea to the patient and the idea itself being based on making conscious and giving meaning to some aspects of the here and now experience they have shared in that session – perhaps also over a longer time period of many sessions. We aimed to distinguish such comments (4) that elaborate the analyst's thinking about the here and now relationship somewhat from other comments that simply designated an experience between analyst and patient without explication of meaning (3). We also aimed to distinguish both types of comments from a further category (5) in which the analyst also elaborated on meaning but from other content than the direct, shared experience of the analytic relationship.

Thus, we thought some analysts offered what we considered were different sorts of elaborative comments and we separated these as category 5 – *Interventions directed at providing elaborated meaning of what the analyst and patient were discovering* but not particularly closely based on the here and now experience of the particular session. For example:

> That could be one of your beliefs. To think that you might change yet further makes you afraid of dissolving and losing your identity. Recently you thought you had to carry a gun to defend yourself. To defend your belief that analysis does not help, you often think about breaking it off and you will presumably now say you will not come to tomorrow's session.

> Maybe you are looking for the warmth in your own basement depths, where mothers come from. A woman had your blanket.

> Indeed, almost as if you had condensed a part of the road we have so far covered: in a dream in which the foreground seems dominated by the act of moving house, that is to say, by change, you seem to have described the need for belonging brought on by the analytic relationship; the fear of being abandoned, the image of the double husband/father, the loss of a warm protection – that third coat that you then find by your home and the thought that from there you can finally start anew.

These comments seemed to us to tie together (link) ideas and provide some elaborated meaning – prompting obvious questions about how the analyst arrives at these ideas and what might be the value of verbalising them to the patient in this or other ways. We thought that having to decide into which category an intervention belonged (3, 4 or 5 for instance) should stimulate the workshop discussion that needed to take place to help the groups sense an analyst's approach to listening to the patient's unconscious and to the purpose of intervening, etc. Similarly, we distinguished categories 1 and 2 – although as this distinction eventually proved inadequate and was soon modified I will not elaborate it here.[4]

Formulating Step 2

As well as enabling us to revise the Intervention Grid and so devise a Step 1, we also used our analysis of cases to explore other dimensions – starting with thinking about the theories the analysts were using. Gradually we settled on five elements of the explanatory models we thought psychoanalysts necessarily have:

- their working definition of what was psychoanalytically 'wrong' with their patient
- their working definition of a psychoanalytic process and how it might transform what was wrong
- their working definition both of the obstacles to establishing a process and how to facilitate it
- their working definition of the analytic situation (transference and countertransference)
- their working definition of the 'unconscious' by the kinds of content they seemed to 'hear' as unconscious material.

We explored other dimensions, such as the extent to which their interventions were saturated or not; or the extent to which they seemed to treat the analytic situation as mainly an intrapersonal or interpersonal situation; how far they considered infantile sexuality; whether they seemed to have a concept of regression; what theory of language and symbolization they used; and so on.

Making inferences as to these aspects of the presenting analyst's explanatory models was not really possible with the data we had: we were unable to ask the analysts more about what they had done or understood or to explore with them their ideas and try to form

---

[4] Our task at this stage was to create a new category system, define the categories and to develop rules for applying them. We did this. However, as the details have gradually changed in the further evolution of the project, as we used the schemes in the workshops and discussed them in the Paris meetings, it is mainly the rules and defining examples which eventually stabilized that are presented in this chapter.

our impressions and bounce ideas off them. We might say we had only a very limited and not interactive Step 1 process – a discussion without the analyst. The experience made me particularly aware of the special value of the group workshops. As discussed above they not only provided scope for interchange and elaboration but also would have the particular functional characteristics noted earlier – moderator, presenter and discussants with multiple orientations and explanatory models.

From the much more limited setting in which the preliminary research took place we were, however, able to notice what looked like some differences in explanatory models – in other words different points on the map of the universe of analytic practice. It seemed that some analysts (although from very different schools and perhaps with very different ideas as to whether or how to interpret it) seemed to regard everything occurring in a session as transference-generated, whereas others regarded a good deal of what happened between them and their patients as expressing what they called a 'real relationship'. Some spent a lot of time listening for infantile sexual derivatives in the material and others seemed not to notice it, and so on. At this stage, bearing in mind the limitations we were working under, we felt we could do no more than suggest what seemed to be five core areas (those mentioned above) that groups might try to explore when discussing with the presenter and also provide the groups with various questions that could be relevant under each one (see below). In effect we could specify the territory that a second step discussion might cover but little more.

Preliminary testing of the new method

The background research phase began after the post-Sorrento working party meeting in Paris in September 2004. It concluded with proposals to the working party to try out the new 'two-step method' at its February 2004 meeting. A colleague from outside the working party kindly agreed to join us and to be the presenter.

In my mind the two steps were always conceptual rather than sequential (as has become the case). But at the meeting we began with Step 1 (after the presentation and then an opportunity for group members to feel their way into the case and the analyst's way of working as well as to display to each other their different ways of understanding – Steps −1 and 0, in fact, as discussed in Chapter 7). We then proceeded to Step 2. Setting this out to the February participants and laying out our underlying methodological assumptions, I stressed that

> the method starts with, it is built on, what the presenters say – on their interventions and how we can understand the (intended) purpose or function of the intervention. We concentrate on interventions one by one because that centres the discussion on actuality and in doing so provides an opportunity to create a discussion of what the analyst's idea of doing analysis actually is . . . The approach is normative – that is to say we are trying to understand the analyst's normal intended working method – what doing psychoanalysis is for him if he can do it. This means probing what in his mind he is actually trying to do with what he says, explicitly or implicitly. We aim to find this out by using the interventions and what the analysts can tell us specifically about them. In this way we try to find out what is going on in the analyst's mind: why he does what he does; what the point of the intervention might be and perhaps his ideas of what he should try to avoid. We assume each analyst's method is implicit but that through the 2-step method it can be made more explicit. We also assume that while the analyst tries to apply his method he only imperfectly does so. So we build a normal method from instances of its application in the manner of the 'ideal type' form of analysis put forward by Max Weber and Alfred Schutz.
>
> (Letter to moderators, 13 January 2004)

I tried to stress that the Step 1 task was not to be taken 'over-seriously'. It was serious play; taken seriously enough to have a proper discussion to bring out the debate, but not likely to be overwhelmingly useful from which to draw conclusions as things in themselves. The aim was to get the discussion started and to help the group to focus away from the patient's pathology and how they would treat it (how we all think we could do it better, etc.) towards how and why the analyst was actually working as he was. As people tried to do this task and engaged with each other and argued about it, I stressed that they should think about how they would move to a second step during which the group would turn, always basing discussion on what the analyst actually did and how they understood that, to an effort to

construct the analyst's model.[5] This would be the second step mentioned earlier: to use evidence from the sessions presented and the
other things the analyst conveyed in response to the group's reactions
to identify for each analyst five (interrelated) dimensions of their
implicit explanatory model – conceived as an internal template of
linked ideas (Figure 6.2).

The first dimension (What's wrong?) concerned the analyst's ideas
about what, psychoanalytically speaking, was wrong with the patient.
In the research phase we had thought analysts have a number of more
or less worked out, more or less overlapping theories of a patient's
troubles – patients suffer from deficits, failures of empathy, premature ego development, oedipal conflicts, problems of impulse control
or representation, etc. To get the group thinking I suggested that
possible theories draw on combinations of ideas about such things as
unresolved and unconscious infantile sexual conflicts; repetitive patterns of unconscious relationships (identifications) and internal anxiety management in relationships which block current relational
movement; traumatic memories (which are not mentally represented
and so not available); unconscious and repetitively perverse

Constructing the internal template

*The five axes are related. Those on the right of the dotted line are more or less
observable through the analyst's account. The other three are not.*

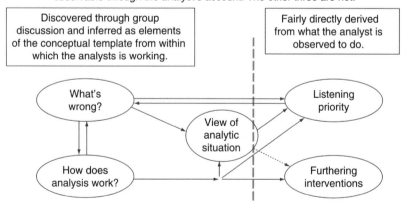

Figure 6.2 Thinking about constructing the internal template

---

[5] The group is not obliged to concur with the analyst's definition of into which category
the intervention falls. It is obliged to work out a rationale for how what the analyst said is
considered to belong to the category allocated.

addictions to pursuits of pleasure and avoidance of anxiety and other pain, which prevent learning and relational development; unconsciously maintained blocked opportunities for development caused by the consequences of problematic environmental care; and so on. This list was to be used to prompt thoughts and questions in the discussion. I thought that in practice (if not officially) analysts were likely to privilege some ideas more than others but were all also likely to work with fairly mixed models, so that it would probably be necessary to think in terms of 'mainly' one or other of the above categories, or some other.

A second dimension (How does analysis work?) concerned the transformational theories an analyst appeared to have. Each of the ideas just mentioned as to what was wrong with a patient would have more or less explicit implications in an analyst's mind for his or her theories about how psychoanalytic sessions can bring about change. We thought possible theories might draw on combinations of ideas about: providing a new object and emotional experience; making conscious and working through affective conflicts and unconscious ideational conflicts expressed in the transference relationship; facilitating representational capacity; making conscious and working through mental states and mental processes; making conscious and working through unconscious repetitions and motivations; and so on. We also wondered if we should not ask how worked out an analyst's theories were at the operational level – perhaps the extent to which transformational theories are worked out consistently and in a grounded way (i.e. linked to the actual patient and the actual material) in an analyst's mind would in itself be a very important indicator of his or her approach.

A third dimension (Listening priority) concerned the analyst's theories of listening to the unconscious. Again the research had suggested analysts have a number of more or less worked out, more or less overlapping theories about what they mean when they say they listen to the latent or unconscious content of a psychoanalytic session. There were probably distinctions between official theories and unofficial content and we thought it very likely that although an analyst's working model as to what is 'latent', 'unconscious' or 'psychoanalytic' material might be implicit, in their conduct, when they told the group about how they thought they came to say what they did, it would become apparent that certain material was privileged. Possible theories about listening might be expressed through the emphasis placed on infantile sexual fantasy and instinctual conflicts; conflicts in the mental organization; the current 'theatre' of preconscious or unconscious phantasy relations to the analyst; unconscious fantasy conflicts in current life and emotional difficulties; repressed historical memories; and so on.

A fourth dimension (Furthering interventions) concerned the analyst's theories of what had to be done session by session to further the psychoanalytic process implied within their transformational model. We supposed that interventions would be linked to implicit transformational theories – to operationalize them, so to speak. Some possibilities for exploration with each analyst might be whether they had ideas about how they facilitate an unconscious representational process; a new emotional experience; making apparent unconscious identifications so that disidentification and modification can then occur; interpreting shifts in transference affect with the idea of increasing affect and ideational tolerance; interpreting unconscious resistance; interpreting perceived unconscious themes to increase conscious ego–awareness of unconscious repetition; and so on.

The fifth dimension (View of analytic situation) has been altered somewhat by experience since the February 2004 meeting,[6] and will not be elaborated further at this point. It concerns, essentially, the analyst's theory of transference. It seemed likely that every psychoanalyst uses a theory of transference in their practice but as we had learned in Prague, there is wide variation in the meaning the term has among psychoanalysts and using the term explicitly created great confusion.

A trial case

The two–step method, as just set out, was presented to the moderators' group on the Friday evening of the Paris weekend in February 2004.[7] The next day a colleague from outside the group, Jean Pierre,

---

[6] A meeting to clarify this took place in September 2004 with the Working Party on Theoretical Issues (Jorge Canestri (chair), Werner Bohleber, Paul Denis and Peter Fonagy) followed up by a joint panel presentation discussing one of the cases analysed in a Helsinki group at the Vilamoura 2005 conference conducted by Canestri, Johan Schubert and myself.

[7] The group on this occasion was Roberto Basile, Dana Birksted-Breen, Tomas Böhm, Paul Denis, Haydée Faimberg, Helmut Hinz, Arne Jemstedt, Iréne Matthis, Roger Perron, Johan Schubert and David Tuckett. Antonino Ferro was unable to be present.

presented his work, which we tried to discuss using it. The discussion was tape-recorded and transcribed so it could be reflected upon later – a procedure that proved useful and was repeated in all further groups.

The patient (Sabina) is a 35-year-old woman, married with two children. She describes herself as imposed on by her husband but works for him at home. As a couple they are angry with each other, sexually dissatisfied and mutually frustrating. This makes her feel guilty and she is perpetually dissatisfied, impatient and irritable. She has an eating disorder. She had sought treatment previously with another analyst after recognition of the marital difficulties but left quickly as she felt that the analyst was rigid and too interventionist.

Two sessions were presented from the second year of an analysis now completed after two or three further years. The termination was in Jean Pierre's view slightly premature but at the same time he felt it important it was her decision and did not oppose it. At termination Sabina had left her husband and had begun a new and satisfying sexual relationship. In a whole variety of ways she was more outgoing and more involved in her life as well as becoming a published writer. Her eating disorder had resolved. Jean Pierre considered his work in these sessions to reflect his way of working and to be the kind of work that led this patient to change.

The first session began with a dream *in which the patient was on a river bank and caught an eel which she then put back in the water. The eel then bit her on the thigh with very sharp teeth. She was terrified, the eel did not let go and she woke feeling that if she moved her skin would be torn.* She went on to say she was thinking of another dream in which another very threatening fish appeared. *She was cooking; a river flowed through the garage of her childhood house. She was fishing with a green bean when something horrible suddenly appeared which gobbled up everything – something which also had a mouth full of teeth and a shining silver body. She was very surprised. She did not think this fish would be so nasty, or that it could have such long, pointed teeth.* She then wondered if she had drawn a dangerous catch from psychoanalysis. She also thought of her husband in this waiting phase in which she feels blocked and afraid of moving.

The analyst then asked her if she could link the eel to something male (1.1). She hesitated. Maybe, she does not know, but this big mouth makes her think more of something female. A big voracious mouth! The analyst said, 'Indeed!' (1.2). She says she has the impression of being cautious here with the analyst, of being careful about what she says, maybe she could nonetheless be surprised. She mentions that she sleeps better now that she dreams. The analyst was thinking of the dream and asked her if this fish could be like something she has no hold over (1.3). 'Absolutely', she replied. 'Even though I thought I could control it.' She said she really had the impression it hated her. 'It really is an attack', the analyst told her (1.4). She now said that she thought she has a text that would be suitable for this year's short story competition. She still thinks this although she was dismayed when she read it through again. It must be completely rewritten. She was a bit discouraged, then started on it and to her astonishment it is going well. It seems so easy to her. For once her text is too long. She must cut it and it is much easier. She also wants to simplify her style, whereas before she always tried to complicate it on purpose. Basically, things are as usual for her at the moment! She goes on to mention there is another short story that she is probably also going to rework. It is a short story about battered babies. She had forgotten about it as it was hard for her, but as things are going well with her children, she can now cope with it.

A second session presented contained three interventions. In the second session the patient began by thinking about the summer holidays, eventually associating to a story about holidays when she was 11 or 12. She says she will no longer go on holiday alone with her husband and talks about various plans which give the impression they live very separately. She says she knows this is what she has wanted but it seems strange. She goes on to say that on Sunday they had made love for the first time in several weeks and that all of this astounded her – as to how far they were now apart. She had thought they only needed to come together for everything to be as it was before but now had some doubts. At this point the analyst asked her if she means 'to have things the same as before or to evaluate her present choices and wishes' (2.1).

She responds that in any case it seems strange. Her husband was different, much less needy and greedy, whereas before she had always had the impression he wanted to devour her. It flattered but repelled her at the same time. In the same way, when he shows too much physical desire to her taste, she does not feel anything any more. She does not know why. It is as if there were no more place for it. But this time he seemed more passive, waiting for something. She felt better but, at the same time, it was rather worrying, she felt less loved. She then remembers a discussion she had with a girlfriend who asked her whether she did not risk harming herself by living like that. She did not really understand, but it worried her.

However, she went on, it was a good morning, then her husband went out on his motorbike in the afternoon. And things were fine with the children. Her analyst now intervened again: asking whether 'you can link what you say about these devouring experiences to the dream you told the day before' (2.2). 'Indeed', she said, there is a kind of oppression and love that she sees as devouring in her husband. Something that holds, grasps, constricts her when he squeezes, catches her. She then thinks of *The Naked Ape* by Desmond Morris and to the connection he makes between a kiss and a bite. She sometimes feels attacked by her husband's marks of love. Why did she choose to get married? Why did she rush into it? Now her analyst reminds her she told him she had had the dream before the weekend. So could these be aspects of herself she had just discovered in psychoanalysis? (2.3). She says that for the other dream it was very clear, obvious, even if everything was formless – as for this one, she had not thought about it.

In considering into which of the five preconceived intervention categories each of Jean Pierre's various comments might fit, working at Step 1, the working party group in Paris had a lengthy and intriguing discussion which seemed much more naturally than usual to focus on the analyst's approach rather than their own ideas. (We did all have all sorts of very different ideas as to what we would have understood and said but we cleared that out of the way in a warm-up phase.)

In the group we were aware that each of the interpretations might be described as 'unsaturated' – i.e. as opening meaning via introducing ambiguity and so prompting in the patient, as in the group, many different possible thoughts about the underlying meaning (and therefore uncertainty as into which intervention category each one would fit). In such a diverse and articulate group many meanings could be 'read in' to the comments, so to speak. Discussion, therefore, ranged at various times across the whole range of intervention categories. We could eventually see, however, how this analyst might be differentiated from others – including others among us, based on various suggestions we each made at various points. From this perspective we could see how it made sense to consider all but the last interpretation properly rated as (2) – interventions apparently aimed directly at facilitating an unconscious representational process. The last interpretation (2.3) might also be a 2 but it could also be a 5 – as it was somewhat more saturated than the others, linking ideas together in a more direct way. The interpretation also refers to the analytic relationship although not specifically to the *hic et nunc* of the relationship in that session.

The discussion also began to clarify many issues that would come up time and time again in the workshop groups and which are explored in Chapter 7 – such as how to recognize when an analyst might be using silence as an intervention as opposed to the more ordinary situation when he or she was just quiet; or exactly when a comment was in the 3 or 4 category rather than the others. Such discussion showed us how having to classify interventions in that way made us inquire into the analyst's approach.

As we transferred our attention from discussing interventions towards trying to explore Jean Pierre's explanatory model via the five dimensions of Step 2 it was interesting that, despite the groups' initial relief that Step 2 would allow a broader and perhaps more congenial discussion than the slightly rigid consideration of interventions, it did not immediately come easily. There was a tendency for Step 2 discussion to get abstract and then evaluative and so to reproduce all the old difficulties. There were also problems linking the detailed discussion of Step 1 – with which people became increasingly comfortable – to Step 2. For the time being, however, we were satisfied that we had a much improved way of organizing the workshop discussion groups and this was the method we took to Helsinki in April 2004 and have, essentially, used in the following meetings.

The group discussions in Helsinki using the two-step method were generally considered to work and took us forward. The experience was incomparable to Sorrento. The groups were well mixed with members from six or more societies in every group and each case and every assumption was therefore questioned from many points of view. Several hundred people attended a plenary review afterwards and despite initial scepticism, it was felt that the two steps had facilitated a sharp and rigorous debate about the detail of what an analyst was actually doing from which the analyst's thoughts, feelings and conceptualizations could be discerned at some depth (Foresti, 2005).[8]

---

[8] A well-known and appreciated colleague from Geneva, Danielle Quinodoz, has summarized with a couple of phrases her ideas about the working party group method. 'At the beginning of this experience,' she said,

> I was convinced that the method being utilized was too artificial and would not work. But after taking part in one of the groups using it I have changed my opinion and now believe this grid is really useful and makes possible an interesting and far from artificial work.

> (Foresti, 2005, translated from the Italian)

The tape-recording of the groups produced a great deal of data, which has allowed us to share each other's experiences better and to work at comparisons subsequently.

Refining Step 1

Following the first use of the two-step method in the Helsinki workshops and having reviewed the reports from the various groups, the three Swedish co-authors of this book met to discuss their unease with some aspects of the Step 1 categories. Having five categories (Table 6.1) rather than thirteen was welcome and had worked well but the categories themselves seemed in need of refinement.

They felt that category 1 (Table 6.1) was not controversial; it dealt, so to speak, with housekeeping and was relatively clear. It allowed the group to see how those kinds of issues were dealt with in the presenter's way of working and where a presenter or people in the group saw a housekeeping type comment as having more complex functions or unforeseen unconscious consequences, this would come up in the discussion. Category 2 was also relatively clear, even though its two subtypes (2A and 2B) were quite different. In general we could all see that Category 2 was about facilitating remarks of different kinds, with the message, 'Go on, I'm listening!' but stated according to the particular presenter's underlying ideas about process. Discussion about what was facilitating would bring such ideas 'to light'.

The Swedish moderators group thought, however, that categories 3, 4 and, to some extent, 5 (in Table 6.1) were more difficult to differentiate and also, to their minds, put a disproportionate emphasis on differentiating interventions about the transference relationship rather than others. I thought this very possibly reflected my internalized British model. As analysts we are perhaps more interested in and more sensitive to small differences in the area familiar to us and less able to perceive the complexity in ways of working that are more foreign. Very likely my interest in different ways of intervening had perhaps skewed the differentiations towards a preoccupation with different approaches to transference interpretation, rather than subtle differences elsewhere.

Setting out his views on behalf of his colleagues, Tomas Böhm wrote: 'We have tried to notice what kind of interventions we are doing ourselves, and what we hear in peer supervision groups from colleagues.' The category scheme

> becomes somewhat of a Procrustean bed, where some real life interventions don't seem to fit in. If we want to describe what really goes on in the analytic offices, we have to adapt the model more to real life, so it doesn't become a mixture of a transference focused ideal and a description of what really goes on. What do these analysts, including ourselves, do beside type 1 as described above – and different transference interventions?

Reflecting on these points, they suggested that when they were work-ing they might put questions to their patients, make remarks about life, make remarks about relationship dynamics, make empathic state-ments, try to confront their patients with ego–syntonic symptoms, try to clarify conflicts, aim to contain emotional pain, and make various constructions and so on. But not much of that seemed to fit into the category scheme so far, as they understood it. They suggested a somewhat revised scheme – designed to pick a wider range of ways of working and provoke discussion about them. Their main additions were, first, to revise category 3 so that it would include: '*Interventions of different kinds concerning external relationships, inner world, emotional states and conflicts but without drawing attention to the relationship between patient and analyst.*' (These interventions might take the form of questions, clarifications, comments, constructions, confirmations, confrontations, or explicit empathic remarks.) The second change was to category 5, which was now widened to include remarks beyond the here and now or transference context. It became: '*Elaborated constructions, inter-ventions directed at providing elaborated meaning of what analyst and analy-sand are discovering, with or without reference to the relationship between analysand and analyst, as well as "analytic wisdom".*'

Finally, the Swedish moderators group also suggested an entirely new category – 6. This would be for: '*Interventions difficult to relate to the psychoanalytic process being described by the analysts, e.g. sudden counter-transference reactions.*' They made the comment that even if we are supposing that the analyst does good analytic work in the sessions, there still needs to be a category for the analyst's 'mistakes'. 'Mistakes', they suggested, might be wonderful 'gold mines' enabling us really to see how the analyst is working and useful for drawing out Step 2 dimensions. They might prompt more awareness because they might indicate the analyst's deeper convictions compared to more super-ficially 'correct' ones that he consciously endorses. 'Of course there are also more personal, idiosyncratic countertransference mistakes', Böhm added, 'but it would be interesting to see if such a category could catch hidden ideological conflicts in the presenter.'

The whole group discussed these ideas in February 2005. The main point – that the existing categories were too 'one-model' dom-inated – was accepted but it was felt one of the categories (4) should be restricted not only to broad comments about the relationship between patient and analyst but also to specific comments related to the here and now of that session. As it happens, the debate around when comments are and are not of this type has gone on proving very useful as some analysts like to be highly specific (saturated) in their remarks about fantasies and feelings in the here and now and others wish to be more allusive (unsaturated) choosing to interpret 'in' the transference. These distinctions have often come out in discussions in recent work-shops, thus justifying the feeling that one category was restricted.

However, the main discussion surrounded whether or not to intro-duce the proposed sixth category – 'mistakes'. My main anxiety was that it could easily reintroduce an atmosphere of supervising and judging the analyst and was of a very different order. A mistake could hardly be an intentional part of a model of practice, I thought, and, since, as set out above, the aim was to picture and map 'typical' models of intended practice, I was not greatly interested in inevitable tempor-ary aberrations in analytic 'performance', unless in some way we could see them as linked to or consequent upon the model of working. However, against this over-simplistic view we did have examples of small-scale enactments or mistakes in the clinical material from Helsinki and these we looked at. They included one case where, at the beginning of the third session presented, the analyst had 'reassured' the patient about a 'worrying' noise outside the consulting room and then spent the whole session having to 'make up for it'. It was clear in that and other examples that the way analysts might come to realize and then think about and use (or not) their 'mistakes' might well be a very important indicator of their approach.

After extensive discussion, therefore, category 6 was included but also carefully defined; it was necessary for workshop groups to be cautious and to establish before deciding on this category that the analyst saw the particular intervention as 'outside the usual run of their approach'.

The introduction of category 6 has in fact been particularly successful. When carefully moderated it has allowed groups to retain their focus on the analyst's thinking rather than their own but at the same time has facilitated their exploration of how far being sensitive to and reflecting on the effect of their interventions or enactments, is in fact part of a particular analyst's way of working. In general the new categorization (set out above as Figure 6.1) has proved effective in creating the kinds of discussions we were looking for.

Developing Step 2: epistemology

Step 2 was more conceptual than Step 1 and it has taken several more years to become more comfortable with it. While the general idea behind it undoubtedly worked right away, in the sense of focusing the project on the analyst's way of working, it was to take several more meetings, much more discussion and even the writing of this book before we were able to refine it enough to provide the right kind of template to begin to make rigorous comparisons between ways of working. Over this time we have gone on struggling with two kinds of issues – one more philosophical and one more practical. In this section I deal with the philosophical issues.

In more philosophical terms, now that participants were focused on trying to understand the presenters' way of working, they were asking very significant questions about the focus of that inquiry. Was it how group members thought the presenter worked or was it how the presenter thought he or she did? Did we want to know how the presenter 'really' works or how he or she 'tries' to work? Still more difficult, did we want to know only about the conscious way group members thought the presenter worked or the unconscious ways as well?

Since the beginning of the project we had been concerned with the relatively obvious point that most psychoanalysts enact their theories of practice rather than thinking them cognitively, at least in any simple way. Psychoanalytic work brings together a combination of personal, emotional and cognitive components, which are both conscious and unconscious and sometimes even include somatic levels of experience.

Many analysts are not necessarily either comfortable with or convinced of the value of spelling out the principles of their practice.

Although in practice a given session can be rationalized in a post-hoc account, very little of what even a highly articulate analyst does in a session is explicit in the sense that he or she can easily outline it or answer direct questions about it. They feel they have internalized their clinical method and feel their way with a patient, so to speak. While there are many psychoanalytic books describing ideas and theories in the field, there are few modern ones that describe technique in any systematic way.

On some occasions some group members felt unconvinced about the way the presenter thought he or she was working and mentioned other implicit ways the presenter worked, which the presenter did not agree with at all. These difficulties tended to come up when the group was having difficulty understanding the presenter's approach and what the presenter was saying seemed inconsistent to them, but sometimes it happened when the presenter or some members of the group had rather strong views. Thus there were occasions when this part of the discussion returned us to the familiar situation of judging what the analysts were doing rather than being interested in seeking to understand their clinical method from their point of view. This indicated the need for ongoing clarification as to the level of analysis we wanted to use. We had decided that we wanted to infer the 'rules' of conduct that analysts follow in their enacted clinical practice – the underlying ideas about procedure which differentiate one method from another – but if these are implicit rather than explicit what really did we mean if we said we would try to discover an analyst's implicit working model?[9]

Joseph Sandler's (1983) seminal notion of implicit theories in psychoanalysis has been taken up widely. Sandler wrote:

> With increasing experience the analyst, as he grows more competent, will pre-consciously (descriptively speaking, unconsciously) construct a whole variety of theoretical segments which relate directly to his clinical work. They are the products of unconscious thinking, very partial theories, models or schemata, which have a quality of being available in reserve, so to speak, to be called upon

---

[9] Paola Mariotti was the first in the group of authors to concern herself with the exposition of the role of implicit theories in the project in any detail, when collaborating on the writing of Chapter 7. For clarity of exposition and the avoidance of repetition, some of her ideas have been moved here.

whenever necessary. That they contradict one another is no problem. They coexist happily as long as they are unconscious.

(Sandler, 1983: 38)

Canestri et al. (2006) have been collaborating on a parallel EPF Working Party on Theoretical Issues; the project is concerned with developing novel and useful theory from practice in just the way Sandler
(1983) hoped would prove possible. For the 2003 Sorrento meeting they created what they called a map of private (implicit, preconscious) theories driving everyday clinical practice and this has
developed since.

Canestri et al. (2006) take the view that the psychoanalytic theories
used in clinical practice are based on both public theory-based thinking and private theoretical thinking, which interact with one another
to create individual instances in which there is implicit use of public
theory. We might say there are official public theories, private theories and an implicit and only partly conscious mixture of the two. The
theories may have all kinds of issues as their target – for example a
theory of psychic change or a theory of what it is reasonable to expect
of a patient and analyst – and among the theories which go into the
mix are not only official psychoanalytic thinking about the unconscious, the transference, the drives, free association and so on but also
assumptions about such things as the role of language, what might be
reasonable cultural achievements for a patient of this age and background, ideas about relationships, world views and common sense
psychology. Moreover, individuals have more or less conscious knowledge of and relationships with these theories – holding them for a
variety of reasons, including deeply unconscious ones.

To map the range of possibilities and so to allow a more formal
exploration of the way psychoanalytic theories are used in the consulting room, Canestri et al. (2006: 30–43) elucidate and then list six
vectors, along which the theories that analysts can be seen using
in descriptions of their work can be plotted. They are represented
frugally in Figure 6.3.

For our purposes, the crucial point about Canestri et al.'s (2006)
way of thinking, following Sandler (1983), is that implicit theories and
the specific combinations of partial theories contained in them are
mostly unknown to the analyst holding the theory; because they are
unconscious. In this respect some of their ideas are unconscious
because preconscious but more usually they are *dynamically unconscious*

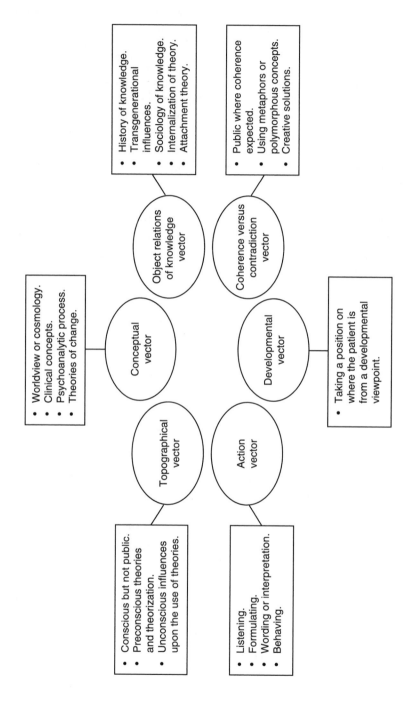

Figure 6.3 Six vectors for analysing private theories (Canestri 2006)

so that there will be resistance to knowing; because the repressed theories are at variance with the public theories to which the analyst is expected to subscribe and so likely to create emotional consequences when known. Contradictory theories can exist happily in the unconscious but produce difficulties when made conscious.

These ideas and the analysis of cases using the six-vector 'grid' demonstrate how psychoanalytic clinicians operate with theories built up implicitly and illuminate the basis on which they do it. Insofar as the implicit theories they bring are ones to which they are emotionally attached and in unconscious conflict with the official theories they adhere to, it is not difficult to see how our workshop discussions could become emotionally challenging and this must be one reason why they did.

Thinking along these lines clarifies that the clinical methods project is not concerned with establishing implicit theories as such. It is a subtle difference but our primary aim was not to understand an individual presenter's use of theory but to identify and map the range of practice in the psychoanalytic community as a whole. This has caused us to be interested in establishing the main underlying rules of practice enacted by different groups of presenting analysts (all of whom are reputedly respected as highly competent) in their accounts of the work. In that project we have not wanted to second-guess, supervise or judge presenters but to try to understand their method, their 'explanatory model' in their own words.

The explanatory models, as used here, therefore, are not implicit in the sense of Sandler's (1983) implicit theories; that is mainly dynamically unconscious. Rather, they are implicit because they are an evolving and routine part of the analyst's everyday experience. They are not immediately known to the analyst, not because they are dynamically unconscious (i.e. repressed) but because they are taken-for-granted or familiar. The level of analysis, in this sense, is more superficial.

Thus, when within a group or as observers we seek to construct an analyst's explanatory model, as we try to do in Step 2, we must always be asking ourselves how, if the analyst were offered the chance to reflect on the matter rather than to take it for granted, and given his or her psychoanalytic context, would the analyst explain this conduct to him- or herself. The very special opportunity provided by the workshop groups, made up as they were by psychoanalysts from many different traditions, was that they could draw on each participant's sense of shock based on their everyday knowledge and skill from their own traditions (and the opportunities presented by discussion with others from other traditions) to sense the 'foreign' rules of conduct and more widely the explanatory models used by the presenting analyst in the analytic sessions.

Explanatory models, it will be recalled, were introduced in Chapter 1 as a device based on the proposition that most things that do not make sense from the outside do make sense if understood from the inside – in this instance the idea was to make sense of differences in analytic practice by understanding the rules and rationales we can discover in the presenting analyst's essentially conscious mind.

Ideal types were also introduced in Chapter 1 as a device to reduce many complex instances of practice to a small number of instances typified by a number of selected characteristics. Empirically, no two human situations are ever the same in all respects. To treat several situations as belonging to the same category and to compare them as different from others, therefore, means that we abstract certain aspects of a human situation and ignore others. Psychoanalysts have a disposition towards sensing and showing almost infinite patience and curiosity towards complex and subtle *individual* meaning. We need that capacity in clinical work. Comparing and typing, on the other hand, although required for the project, means placing individuals together in collections defined in terms of one or more common attributes, necessarily ignoring those individual attributes not covered. Typing, therefore, can be felt to entail a loss of complexity and individuality.

A related issue concerns the question of how to recognize what in an ordinary session is an individual's typical or invariant conduct and what is situational or temporary. Although presenting analysts who are observed doing psychoanalysis 'choose' what they hear as the patient's unconscious communication and otherwise how to understand the situation and their options in their own individual way, it does not follow that every aspect of what is observed is typical of their work nor that the presenting analysts can easily specify their type. Several principles are required to move on from this point.

First, it is useful to regard particular examples of regular and repeated human conduct (for instance an approach to being a psychoanalyst in the consulting room) as normative – that is, as an observable representative of a 'typical' way of conducting oneself according to the norms and values in that colleagues' reference group or socio-cultural setting as mediated by their individual personality. In a psychoanalytic session the normative framework is provided by the particular public psycho-analytic socio-cultural tradition internalized in training and modified thereafter by experience. A public tradition of work in, say, the Berlin Institute, or perhaps a subgroup within it, lays down and leads to the internalization of appropriate conduct – perhaps to an extent where alternatives are not even glimpsed. The shock that we all noticed in Prague and elsewhere at how such traditions vary is evidence of how norms vary.[10]

However, normative conduct is routine and implicit. We act in ways we take to be 'normal' without reflecting on this. In psychoanalysis the psychoanalyst's implicit conceptions of how psychoanalysis works derive from his training and personal experience. These form the foundations of his or her 'explanatory model' – not all of which is apparent to the participant.

Explanatory models are necessarily put into practice through con-duct. What psychoanalysts are trying to do in sessions, what they take the patient's unconscious to mean, the ways they assume their words have unconscious meaning, what they consider the basic rules of psychoanalytic practice, and all the other ways they con-duct themselves, are enactments of their explanatory models. Actual 'knowledge' of the rules being followed in conduct is not gener-ally explicit, although the aim of training or subsequent continuing development might be to make it explicit enough to reflect on and modify. The rules of everyday life are routine and do not need to be thought about to be followed.

All this has important implications for the methodology of Step 2; the aim is to discover the rules and routines governing analysts' work and to do so by construction; by obtaining and fitting together what analysts do (their routines) along with how analysts explain the prin-ciples governing what they do (their rules of conduct).

Psychoanalysts, like other ordinarily functioning social individuals, are not necessarily explicitly aware of the normative framework informing what they are doing or why they do it (their explanatory model), and thus observers cannot simply ask them – which was a source of confusion in Prague and Sorrento. Rather observers must construct what normative conduct is implicit from all the material

---

[10] Mundane examples included details given about ways to pay (cash is absolutely correct in one place and highly suspect in another) or ways to end the session.

available – much as we do as psychoanalysts in constructing salient aspects of a patient's history and internal world (Freud, 1937a). We more or less hypothesize an internal unconscious understanding driving current experience. To be valid, the construction arrived at about his explanatory model and its links to his way of working, must, in principle, make sense to presenting analysts, even if they would not have put it that way themselves, did not particularly like to see themselves that way or, perhaps, thought of their way of working differently.

We might have started such a comparative project by creating our own list of criteria for psychoanalytic work – using existing theory to define a list of parameters, such as how the analyst used 'free floating attention' or transference interpretation of a certain type (etc.) – and then asking participants to work out what exactly the presenter was doing. This would have been a simpler and from that point of view more attractive approach – but the obvious objection from early on was that in that way we would have created a comparative clinical method determined by the viewpoint of the designer of the instrument.[11] Each analyst's work would be being evaluated against a master plan.

Instead, from the outset we have aimed to find a method to describe all the ways of working we encountered *in their own terms* rather than in ours, while at the same time making terms comprehensible and comparable. Thus, after establishing the key elements of each person's declared type of working we hoped to draw up a map of actual practice, placing those whose type is similar (as we understood the way they worked) nearer together on the map. On the one hand the method we envisaged involved trying to elucidate how the presenters think about and describe their work in a context where that can emerge rather than be told directly. On the other hand we try to fit those presenters with methods that seem similar, once understood, together.

Developing Step 2: refining the dimensions

In practical terms the remaining issue with Step 2 was how to abstract what really matters from the long discussions and then use it to

---

[11] See the discussion in the Appendix of the attempt to ask each Prague group to explore a list of common questions. To this day and despite many efforts to the contrary the Step 1 or Step 2 categories are easily felt as imposed from a referred theoretical orientation.

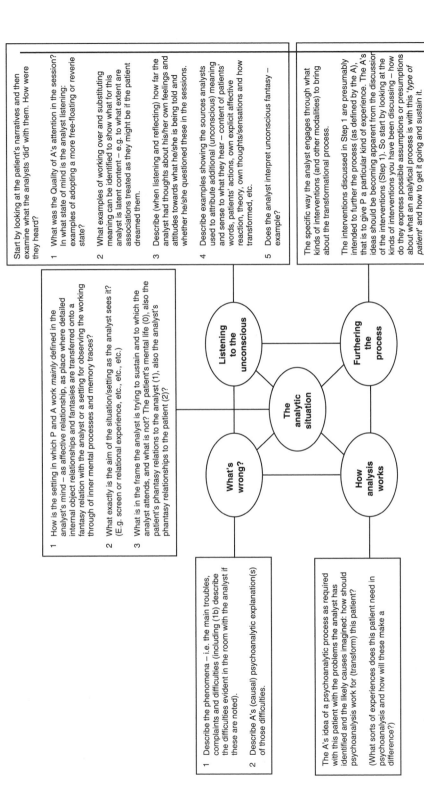

Start by looking at the patient's narratives and then examine what the analysts 'did' with them. How were they heard?

1 What was the Quality of A's attention in the session? In what state of mind is the analyst listening: examples of adopting a more free-floating or reverie state?

2 What examples of working over and substituting meaning can be identified to show what for this analyst is latent content – e.g. to what extent are associations treated as they might be if the patient dreamed them.

3 Describe (when listening and reflecting) how far the analyst had thoughts about his/her own feelings and attitudes towards what he/she is being told and whether he/she questioned these in the sessions.

4 Describe examples showing the sources analysts used to attribute additional (unconscious) meaning and sense to what they hear – content of patients' words, patients' actions, own explicit affective reaction, theory, own thoughts/sensations and how transformed, etc.

5 Does the analyst interpret unconscious fantasy – example?

The specific way the analyst engages through what kinds of interventions (and other modalities) to bring about the transformational process.

The interventions discussed in Step 1 are presumably intended to further the process (as defined by the A), that is to give P a particular kind of experience. The A's ideas should be becoming apparent from the discussion of the interventions (Step 1). So start by looking at the kinds of interventions you have been discussing – how do they express possible assumptions or presumptions about what an analytical process is with this 'type of patient' and how to get it going and sustain it.

1 How is the setting in which P and A work *mainly* defined in the analyst's mind – as affective relationship, as place where detailed internal object relationships and fantasies are transferred onto a fantasy relation with the analyst or a setting for observing the working through of inner mental processes and memory traces?

2 What exactly is the aim of the situation/setting as the analyst sees it? (E.g. screen or relational experience, etc., etc.)

3 What is in the frame the analyst is trying to sustain and to which the patient's phantasy relations to the analyst (1), also the analyst attends, and what is not? The patient's mental life (0), also the analyst's phantasy relationships to the patient (2)?

1 Describe the phenomena – i.e. the main troubles, complaints and difficulties (including (1b) describe the difficulties evident in the room with the analyst if these are noted).

2 Describe A's (causal) psychoanalytic explanation(s) of those difficulties.

The A's idea of a psychoanalytic process as required with this patient with the problems the analyst has identified and the likely causes imagined: how should psychoanalysis work for (transform) this patient?

(What sorts of experiences does this patient need in psychoanalysis and how will these make a difference?)

Listening to the unconscious

Furthering the process

The analytic situation

What's wrong?

How analysis works

Figure 6.4 Step 2 today

compare different practices – which in turn meant how we could maintain our focus in the groups rather than getting carried away in other details. Over a number of years, therefore, we have made a succession of attempts to reach a suitably frugal and illuminating definition of the main elements in each of the five step dimensions. The process of doing this was necessarily incremental. In fact, we could only begin to do it as we managed to conduct and report the work of the groups sufficiently to accumulate examples of work that we could organize well enough to keep in mind when we discussed it. This was difficult and we have tried several schemes.

Figure 6.4 is a somewhat simplified representation of the scheme we now have. Each of the five axes is associated with a relatively small and relatively clear number of questions for the workshop groups to explore. These questions derive from important issues that differentiate public theory in psychoanalysis and have been developed by trying to make actual comparisons across the approximately thirty cases we have now assembled. Each workshop group now attempts to cover those questions and to produce a report describing the presenter's method using that format. Examples of discussion using this framework come in Chapter 7 and some preliminary descriptions of several cases compared using the new format are presented in Chapter 9.

7

Work in progress

Using the two-step method

Dana Birksted-Breen (UK), Antonino Ferro (Italy) and Paola Mariotti (UK)

We assemble in a small group of around ten to fifteen people. We have come from many different European countries, and sometimes from outside of Europe – a heterogeneous group of people who mainly have never met before. We are going to be working intensively together for about twelve and a half hours. It is a group experience within the context of a research project.

We start with introductions. Some have been in these groups before and others are starting afresh, not knowing what to expect. Perhaps their friends and colleagues have told them it is a worthwhile experience. This is how it all starts in what we would come to call 'Step −2' (minus two), which is the preparation before the 'Step −1' (minus one) meeting, the presentation of the case history, and 'Step 0' (zero), the free clinical discussion.

Step −2: the stork

Everything that precedes the meeting – its history – is relevant. We are psychoanalysts, after all. There are the parents and the grand-parents, those present at the inception of the ideas; the EPF, David Tuckett, the selection of the presenters, the formation of the group, the participants who got in and those who were too late to register, those who have been before and the newcomers. It is an unusual situation when psychoanalysts who have not met before come together for two days from different European countries for a very detailed and focused clinical and theoretical discussion.

A group identity begins to form in the exchange of emails and information between David Tuckett and the participants. To this, we can add the fantasies based on rumours about past experiences, and the anticipation of the current one. The meeting starts with each participant briefly introducing him or herself and this gives shape to more structured fantasies, based on supposed models relative to the nationality or reputation of a participating colleague.

A group identity settles into place even before we begin the appointed task, with the impact of the conference room and the acclimatization problems that may arise (room, light and temperature). These are a focus for the anxieties generated by the first contact between members of the group, which the new organization (the group itself) entails.

The seating arrangements often reveal that the participants prefer to sit next to their 'schoolmates' – if they have any in their group. The brief introduction of every group member generally breaks the ice and effectively constitutes the Big Bang of the birth of the group.

Step −1: the case history

The moderator reminds the group of the strict confidentiality rules. The presentation of the case is obviously very detailed, and, even though a degree of disguise is often possible, the moderator empha- sizes that making the patient unrecognizable to others is a prerequisite of working in the group and that neither the presenter's name nor anything of the clinical material should be repeated outside of the meetings. The report on the group's work is subsequently discussed in the working party, under the same conditions of confidentiality. (The original presenters have approved all the examples reported in this chapter.) The moderator also explains that the discussions are being recorded.

Step −1 consists of the presentation of the clinical case history. It is brief – usually around one to one and a half typewritten pages in length. Some presenters prefer not to distribute this to the group for reasons of confidentiality.

As explained in earlier chapters, moderators of these comparative clinical groups were not at first given much guidance on how to lead or facilitate them, for they are entirely new. It has been interesting to realize during the moderators' meetings how much variation there has been in the style of the different moderators and how this has obviously impacted on the groups. Common to all, however, is the aim of facilitating fruitful work, and different moderators will implement this aim in very different ways. One of us presents the work more as 'play', a sort of board game for psychoanalysts which goes on for many happy hours like Monopoly. Others feel that the notion of a 'task' can offer a fruitful backdrop to creative developments.

In any case, the moderator, in the stages that we here call Steps −1 and 0, needs to keep in mind that there is always at least some ambivalence about the method, and that they need to create an atmosphere in which negative thoughts can be voiced if necessary but in which the work itself can, as it evolves, come to dispel doubts at least sufficiently not to impede the work. For this to happen, the moderator needs to perceive and be enthusiastic about the value of the project.

These groups, at least as they have been run so far, are open groups with newcomers and a different membership each time; the preliminary phases are needed to build up trust between group members, an acceptance of novice members and the possibility of working within this newly formed group.

Even at these initial stages, a non-judgemental attitude towards other people's theoretical and clinical approaches will need to be fostered or even taught. Different contributions from group members can then be seen as reflecting different perspectives on a clinical situation, and it concomitantly becomes possible to differentiate between various ways of working.

Step −1 immediately points to different modes of listening: most groups require many precise details about the history, but one group felt that they were listening to the presentation of the patient's history almost with 'evenly suspended attention' − not as facts, but as though the presenter were saying, 'I had a dream about my patient.' The mode of listening of course is linked to the group's response to the style of presentation, and to the analytic situation between the presenting analyst and her patient. Different ways of listening, indicated by the participants' comments and questions, can be picked up by the moderator, thus setting the tone for the task ahead. The moderator of one group likes to think of the group's response to the presentation of the clinical history as *the dream of the group* about the analyst's dream.

In this context, the moderator brings into focus the *patient's* response to the analyst's interventions. For instance, to an interpretation which moved him, the patient replies, 'I think I love Liz [his girlfriend], she is so sweet and innocent', while at a moment of the session where the analyst is felt to be less receptive, the patient speaks of a 'black man' who betrayed all his expectations. The group wonders if these characters, Liz and the black man, continue an unconscious discourse independent of the analyst, or if they have been generated by the relational situation of patient and analyst in the *hic et nunc*. We shall present a more detailed discussion of this group's work shortly.

Step −1, the presentation of the history, is an opportunity for an exchange that gives life to various points of view and contributes to a warmer and more hospitable atmosphere. For instance, in one case the patient presented has an ill brother, affected by a genetic illness. This leads to many points of view, from a literal understanding of the brother as a character in the patient's history, to a view that sees the brother as the carrier of the patient's psychic functions. From another point of view, one can look at the functioning or malfunctioning of the group itself as expressing the way of functioning of the analytic couple at the time of the presentation.

Interesting as they are, these phenomena are not the main focus of the task, which is to construct the implicit (explanatory) psychoanalytic model of the presenting analyst in such a way that it can be compared to that of other analysts. At this early Step −1 the moderator already needs to be building up a sense of the group's task.

Step 0: free discussion

In the previous phases, the moderator is conveying the aims of the group's work, while enabling the spirit of free and collaborative exploration. The presenter has prepared two or three consecutive sessions from an analysis where a psychoanalytic process can be seen to be taking place. The analyst now distributes a copy of the verbatim report of these sessions to each participant and reads out the sessions.

To begin with there is a free discussion of the sessions. The free discussion is necessary for the group; it hoists the collective sails, allowing the group to head out to sea. At this time, the moderator may want to point out the different ways of listening to the case, the different aspects that interest different participants.

The more anxieties and prejudices there are regarding the 'grid', the more important is the clinical discussion. The mere word 'grid' makes people anxious, though interestingly enough it is hard to say where the word came from; it was not the name given by David Tuckett, but perhaps arises on account of his belonging to the same British Society that conjured Bion's 'grid' (Bion, 1962). In fact, as it has developed it has looked less and less like a grid, even if one of its aims is to produce a representation of what is being looked at and discovered.

The free discussion enables the group to start from something more familiar, which helps to alleviate the anxieties aroused by a relatively unknown tool. At the same time, it also allows the moderator to begin to formulate hypotheses and to organize clinical material. We have come to realize that the free discussion constitutes a productive segment of the group activity, especially with regard to the development of themes addressed in Step −2. The first half-day's work is usually dedicated to the exposition of the case history, the presentation of the sessions and the free discussion of this material. In the free discussion, various theoretical orientations emerge, and the group begins to formulate generic perspectives on the reading of the case.

The moderator aims to render the atmosphere agreeable and to modulate the tensions that may arise between supporters of different psychoanalytic models. In general, it has been possible to avoid anything resembling 'supervision' or notions of correct and incorrect interpretations. However, as we saw in Chapter 1, the group does sometimes descend into a 'basic assumption' mode (Bion, 1952), and it is the responsibility of the moderator to steer the group back to the task.

There have been cases, characteristically towards the end of the work, when the group is tired and 'turns' on the presenter or on the moderator – who is told that he or she has not understood the negative transference, not valued the patient's positive traits, has overlooked the severe pathology, or, conversely, has concentrated too much on the pathology. While the points raised by the group at that moment have often a considerable kernel of truth, the emotional strength with which the arguments are conveyed, and a peculiar feeling of unanimity – as if the group members had suddenly found a way to sing in unison, eliminating differences and conflicts among themselves – suggests that basic assumption group phenomena are at

171

work. In these circumstances it is the task of the moderator to steer the group back to the task, although he or she should avoid taking on the superego function of *enforcing* the task, but rather should try to facilitate a spontaneous 'playing' with the theme.

In some groups occasional remarks about the tape-recorder indicate the difficulty of eliminating all persecutory feelings. Enabling participants to feel free to participate with their thoughts is important for the creative outcome. With this freedom comes the discovery of very different ways of doing things, which analysts usually do not appreciate. For instance, there were interesting discussions about different ways of handling the structure of the setting, such as the beginning and ending of sessions or issues around fees. Other topics come up incidentally during the presentation and highlight assumptions, which can then be questioned.

Introducing the formal method

At some stage, usually at the very beginning of the meeting or after the clinical discussion, the moderator reviews the general aim of the two-step method with the group. The aim is to identify different 'implicit models' and eventually to place the model used by the presenter metaphorically on a map of all of the implicit models that potentially exist. It is important to distinguish these implicit models from the stereotypical and 'known' official models of practice. Often these official models exist in outline form only and contain a variety of implicit models, some of which may be quite different from the official model. For this reason the moderator does not mention which school of thought a presenter belongs to and, interestingly enough, it is never something the group asks about. The two-step method steers interest away from these labels and proceeds empirically to build up an understanding of the presenting analyst's particular model.

The group does not aim to establish which model is best or 'more psychoanalytic'. The premise is that each presenter is working psychoanalytically. The task is to try to understand what a psychoanalyst does when he or she is 'doing psychoanalysis', considering both similarities and differences with other ways. As set out in Chapter 6, the two-step method was developed over a number of years to facilitate the discovery of the implicit working model (or the explanatory model) of an analyst, starting from the detailed presentation of two or three sessions with a patient. Some analysts seem to have quite a well-formed model, while others have more of a set of ideas that we combine into an approximation.

The task may at first seem simple but it soon becomes evident that it is much more difficult and complex than it appears. One reason for this is that it involves listening in a quite different way from the way we are used to in clinical groups. Usually in clinical groups, we try to bring our own ideas and interpretations to the material. Here, on the contrary, we put our own ideas in parentheses, and we try instead to understand the way in which this particular analyst is thinking. Why does this analyst say the things he or she does, how does this analyst think this will lead to the development of the analysis, and how does this analyst think this will lead to transformation in the patient? Of course the analyst will not be thinking about these questions while doing analysis, but the group is there to abstract the analyst's preconscious ideas, which lead to his or her particular way of working.

Because the method involves going into the minutiae of every single intervention, we just about manage to get through the two sessions in twelve hours! Going into such detailed thinking in a group of colleagues with different perspectives leads to very interesting discussions, and it soon becomes apparent that there is little consensus and common ground on even such basic phenomena as 'unconscious' or 'transference'. It is in part through this process that the group gets an idea both of the presenter's model and of the universe of possibilities from which it is drawn.

Step 1

Step 1 involves thinking about the function of what the analyst is doing and/or saying when he or she intervenes in sessions. This involves giving a number from 1 to 6 for each interpretation (see Figure 6.1, pp. 136–137). This can feel quite constraining to psychoanalysts who are used to letting their imagination float freely, and just the thought of putting numbers to interpretations can seem anathema to some. The task is to have a discussion about the analyst's technique, focusing first on the interventions made and then on what was in the analyst's mind when making them. To make this process rigorous, the group debates into which of the six categories the intervention might be placed. In Step 2, this process of deconstruction will be used to construct the analyst's particular way of working compared to various alternative types of working.

Moderators have found different ways of presenting the value of this first step. Some introduce it not as an assignment but as an amusing form of play. Although it may look like the least creative part of the group work, Step 1 can in fact lead to some surprising discussions. When one doesn't have to worry about whether the interpretation is 'right' or 'wrong', 'suitable' or 'imprecise', or 'correct' or not, the evaluation of Step 1 grants an unusual perspective on the formal nature of interventions. For example, there are interesting discussions about what is meant by a 'here and now' (*hic et nunc*) interpretation (this seems obvious until one has to decide whether an interpretation is 'here and now' or not), or about the difference between an 'interpretation *of* the transference', where the connection of the patient's material to the analyst is made explicit, and an 'interpretation *in* the transference', where the possible link is present in the mind of the analyst, but not put explicitly into words within the interpretation. The discussion that takes place in Step 1 brings out the complex thought processes that lie, if only implicitly, behind an interpretation.

As described in the previous chapters, the categories have evolved over the years, becoming both more sophisticated and simpler in order to construct a framework that facilitates a rigorous discussion of what an analyst is doing, investigating the various concepts used by different analysts from different schools. The categories were developed from the session reports. For instance, category 6 is 'sudden and [at least at first] apparently glaring [countertransference] reactions not easy to relate to the analyst's normal method'. This category was added at a late stage, following suggestions from some of the moderators, in order to account for situations when an analyst says: 'I don't know why I said that, it just came out and I'm not altogether happy about that.'

The use of a meaningful classification obstructs the subjective element. We tend to assume that we share with the presenter a theoretical and personal, subjective, understanding of psychoanalytic work. In the group, we challenge the existence of common ground – we expect it to be there as we are all well-trained analysts, but as we come from different traditions, it is often not immediately evident. For instance, an analyst trained in one tradition will tend to offer several interpretations in every session, each one made up of several sentences. Perhaps that analyst will often refer directly to the here and now of the relationship between patient and analyst. Another analyst who has been trained in another tradition, by contrast, will tend to make few interpretations, each consisting of only a few carefully chosen, sometimes ambiguous, words. In one group there were two such presenters. The initial feeling of incomprehension, and perhaps even doubt, about those working with a different model was often dispelled very successfully through a vigorous discussion in which it transpired that the other was in fact working psychoanalytically. In that instance it lead to an interesting conversation about the different ways in which narcissism is understood in different psychoanalytic societies, such as on different sides of the English Channel.

In looking at the interpretations in detail, in some cases the presenter is able to give some background to the interpretations but as the discussion progresses the group realizes that there are guiding principles of which the analyst is only partially aware, but which affect his or her comments. We speak of 'implicit models' because often the analyst (at least at first) does not articulate his or her assumptions beyond some vague notions – about transference, for instance. But it becomes clear that even the notions being used (transference as a common example) can be understood to mean different things. What may sometimes appear as a simple interpretation may lead to quite a lot of disagreement.

The use of this classification of the interpretations is paradoxical. On the one hand, it needs to be done with great care, and the group often gets into an animated discussion in trying to establish to which category one of the analyst's comments belongs; on the other hand, the assignation of categories *as such* is not that important for the following stage. In fact, the moderator might play 'devil's advocate' by suggesting reasons for a different category than the one suggested in order to push the discussion.

The classification is a *tool* to be used in order to proceed in our work. At the end of Step 1, the tool can be laid down. The three examples that follow are taken from different presentations.

Step 1 – Example 1

The patient, who lives in a different village from the analyst, starts the session by commenting on the weather: he says with surprise that it is snowing. The analyst says: 'It isn't snowing in X [the village where the patient lives].'

In the group discussion, someone thinks this might constitute a category 6 comment – a kind of enactment from the analyst, who has been somewhat wrongfooted into expressing a non-analytic thought. But the group has some difficulties with category 6: some find it badly formulated, worded judgementally, and too negative. Could the comment be assigned to category 3 – a simple question on the conscious level? On the other hand, the comment could also be seen as belonging to category 2: a spontaneous, unsaturated comment on the emotional climate that facilitates the unconscious process (implying that the patient is in a different mood now from when he was at home). The intervention probably works simultaneously on both the conscious and unconscious levels. Finally, the group agrees that it is a category 2 intervention – or maybe a category 6. This discussion has brought out specific ideas about the psychoanalytic process and different ways of furthering it. They will be used later as we try to think about Step 2.

Step 1 – Example 2

The analyst and the patient have been talking about the patient's actual move to a new house in terms of the patient finding herself and allowing different parts of herself to develop, some of which were opposed to her mother's wishes for her. The patient says that her current house is too small for herself and her new partner, but she does not feel at home in the new one. The analyst says: 'You are telling me that with analysis you have found a larger space, in which you can make a place for yourself and for someone else, and in which you can develop a relationship.'

There was some difficulty in giving this response a rating because when it was discussed in terms of the relationship of the patient in the outside world, the analyst said that she was thinking of this interpretation in terms of the here and now. It is a reference to 'the analysis as a mental container which is now larger'. Eventually it was decided that this is a here and now interpretation, but not an explicit one. It was therefore given a category 4 (we might say a 4 with a quality of 2).[1]

---

[1] This example illustrates the paradox: we had to have a frugal number of grid categories (see Chapter 6), but as we are not in a research project trying to achieve reliable ratings we can improvise as much as we like, provided we do so to serve the task of getting as rigorous an idea of what the presenter is doing as we can.

Usually, this analyst's interpretations are hinting at the patient's experience here and now, but are worded in an ambiguous way. Furthermore, the 'here and now' that this analyst has in mind is about the mental functioning of the patient more than the unconscious phantasy relationship with the analyst, even though she mentions that relationship. One could say it is not a 'strong' here and now interpretation, even if it is explicit.

This can be contrasted with the next interpretation.

> The patient mentions that she can find meaning in her new sexual relationship, but that she couldn't find meaning in the relationship with her husband whom she is leaving. She says that this is why she finds it difficult to leave her husband and has to think that there is nothing she can do to change it. The analyst says: 'This means that there is still work to do in analysis.'

It was difficult to know how to rate this statement. Some felt it was simply a 'supportive' interpretation. Again, the analyst said it was a 'here and now interpretation', and that the patient claims not to understand why she and the analyst must separate. Discussion in the group led to the conclusion that, while it was certainly a comment on the task between analyst and patient, it was more a clarification about that than an interpretation of the situation between them as such; therefore, it is a category 3 statement. Again, the issue is not whether it was fundamentally in one of the categories or not; the discussion brought out the analyst's thinking and, in the context of the group's ideas, showed how her way of addressing the here and now and what she considered it to be was different to others' ways.

Step 1 – Example 3

The analyst makes a very long interpretation (not reproduced here). The group finds it rather difficult to get to grips with it, because it seems to be saying and doing many things. It is easier to see what it is not: it isn't obviously directed at maintaining the basic setting (category 1); it isn't clearly facilitating an unconscious representational process (category 2); it isn't simply a question (category 3); and it isn't here and now (category 4). So it seems it must be a construction directed at providing elaborated meaning of what analyst and analysand are discovering (category 5). In trying to make sense of this long interpretation, someone points out that the analyst feels that what is missing for the patient is the linking function, and so, at this moment, she has to provide all the links for the patient who lacks this function. This would not necessarily be consciously articulated, but more of a preconscious idea on the part of the analyst. Here we see the value of the Step 1 discussion in bringing out ideas: anticipating several dimensions of the next step by illustrating something about how the analyst understands the psychoanalytic process with this kind of patient and what her aims are.

In fact, the analyst intervenes here and says that she has been 'a spectator of this construction [which just] appeared' in her mind when she made the interpretation. Again this tells us something about the way the analyst thinks about the process and what she responds to in the sessions.

Because this Step 1 phase goes into the minutiae of interpretations, the discussion at times tends to digress to some aspects which are not directly relevant to the specific task at hand, even though interesting. For instance, people pointed out that, with regard to Example 3, countertransference elements have unconsciously motivated the analyst to make an extra long interpretation. The interpretation was made in the context of the patient talking about separation (from her husband). Perhaps, the group suggested, the analyst wanted to respond to all the demands of the patient, to be an idealized mother rather than the one who deprives. It was pointed out that while the analyst is saying to the patient that the patient is moving towards separateness, in fact 'oneness' is 'acted in' via the structure of the interpretation (its length and comprehensiveness).

There is a narrow line here. Such comments may help the analyst to articulate more of her theory – in which case they work. They might also be experienced as supervision and so dampen the process. Or they might just be diversionary. The group needs to be reminded that, while such ideas are very interesting, our task is to discover and draw out the analyst's implicit rules and procedures for working, not her or his countertransference enactments. Comments about countertransference are helpful only insofar as they provide an opportunity to see how far this analyst considers her feelings as relevant to understand what might be happening unconsciously or more generally listens to her countertransference as part of her psychoanalytic model.

Step 2

We have now shared around seven hours of concentrated discussions and exchanges. We understand each other better and the deeper differences between us begin to emerge more clearly. The fact that there are clearly many points of view within the group means that nothing can be taken for granted and that there is great opportunity for the material under discussion to be scrutinized under the microscope. This may lead to heated moments of frustration and confrontation within the group, particularly during discussions about what constitutes psychoanalysis. Again it is the task of the moderator to steer the group away from value judgements and group enactments towards curiosity about a very different approach that can also be seen to be based on a solid psychoanalytic understanding and thought-out technique.

An important aspect of Step 2 (which can help to focus participants within the group) is that moderators have an opportunity to give each participant a task to accomplish. At the beginning of the meeting each group member, with the exception of course of the presenter, is asked to keep in mind one of the five axes in Step 2 (see Figure 6.4, p. 164), and to pick up relevant things which are said all the way through. When we formally begin the Step 2 discussion, the participants help the group to focus on their particular question. This makes people participate more actively in the game and feel that they are vested with an enzymatic function that vitalizes the development of the group.

The five axes of Step 2, which can be put in the form of questions, help to probe deeper into the analyst's approach. Trying to address the questions leads the group to identify the analyst's guiding principles in the session she has presented.

The five axes are interrelated, and different moderators approach them in a different order in each workshop, depending on which question they feel will speak more immediately to the participants. There can also be a to and fro between questions as the discussion deepens. Sometimes the participants themselves suggest starting with a particular question like 'What is wrong with the patient?' because they see this as coming first historically. But it is important to remember that the question is not what is wrong with the patient but what *this analyst thinks is wrong with this patient*. In that shift of perspective lies the whole interest of the method.

So if we start with the question 'What does the analyst think is wrong with his/her patient', we aim, psychoanalytically speaking, to understand the analyst's model of how the mind functions and what can go wrong with its development. We think this is likely to have a bearing on other aspects of his or her model – such as how he or she thinks psychoanalysis works and how to make it work ('furthering'). Analysts certainly differ in terms of what they emphasize. For instance, simplifying greatly, in the presentation of an analyst whom we shall call John, the group felt that John saw his patient's problem in terms of conflicts between internal objects where an internal aspect of the patient, identified with an internalized neglectful mother, was preventing a creative hard-working aspect of herself from growing. Another analyst, Mary, on the other hand, felt that her patient's tendency to withdraw from relationships had originated in her history with an overbearing mother who hadn't allowed her to grow. Mary's emphasis is on the external historical mother, while John's is on the patient's internal world. Neither analyst is thinking in the same terms as other members of the group, for instance in terms of psychotic or perverse areas of psychopathology.

Discussion of the analysts' models can lead on to the axis 'What does the analyst listen to in the session?' In other words, what is unconscious in the session as far as these analysts are concerned? For instance, John was particularly attentive to unspoken connections in the material. Through careful attention, he thought he could detect signs that his patient was struggling with depression. Mary, on the other hand, was listening out for details of how her patient seemed to connect with other people; for example, whether she has to preserve her isolation or can make space for another person, and what that experience is like for her.

The group may then want to discuss the axis 'How is the analytic situation conceived?' by this analyst. For example, John conceives the analytic situation as a setting where internal processes and phantasies express themselves in the transferential affective relationship between patient and analyst and can be seen to provoke enactments by the analyst. Mary sees the analysis as creating a potentially good space that is free from intrusion and in which she helps the patient to explore aspects of herself and to build her own identity boundaries. In these very simplified examples, we surmise that both analysts focus their attention on the patient's psychic life; the analyst provides the setting but does not enter directly into a relationship with the patient. Both cases veer toward a one-person psychology, a conception that is very different from others in the groups.

We now move on to the question of 'What is the analyst's transformational model?' John saw his patient's problems in terms of unconscious conflict around dependency. In John's case, therefore, he thought he needed to increase the capacity for experiencing internal conflict by diminishing the splitting of the object into good and bad. In this way, he aimed to foster in the patient a more positive experience of independence. Mary, on the other hand, saw her patient's problems in terms of an overbearing maternal environment, which, through fostering a constant sense of guilt about her responses, had diminished her capacity to grow and enjoy her life. She sees the positive transference (being able to feel good with her analyst and that her analyst feels good with her) as necessary for developing the patient's ego and diminishing her sense of persecutory guilt. She puts forward an image of a good and even idealized mother who provides a holding space and frame for the fragmented parts of the patient.

We come now to the final axis, which concerns the specific ways in which 'the analyst furthers the process'. John, who thinks that his patient will improve if he can diminish splitting off conflicts from dependency, is keen to support what he sees as genuine independence in his patient and to distinguish this from the manic independence of which the patient has often made use. John would not interpret the patient's attack as being specifically against himself, but rather as a consequence of other attacks on the patient's internal world. John proceeds with small steps, offering as much as he feels the patient can take at any given time and no more. Mary aims to foster her patient's good feelings about being with her analyst by providing 'holding', but she does not put herself on the scene too much. She emphasizes the positive rather than the perverse or negative meanings potentially available in the material. She is also sensitive to information in the material about how the analysis is working, and uses this to adjust her behaviour, although she often doesn't spell it out.

These accounts are highly summarized and basic, but even in this very partial account of two analysts' implicit models of practice, it can be seen that the discussion has brought out both the similarities and the differences between John and Mary. For instance, they both make some 'transference' interpretations, though only rarely, especially regarding negative feelings toward the analyst. On the other hand there are substantial differences between them, for example over the recognition and handling of conflicts. Perhaps this provides clues to underlying models.

We will now give some more extensive excerpts from another group's Step 2 meetings, to give a more extended flavour of the kinds of discussions taking place in Step 2. We will describe separately the issues raised in relation to each of the five axes, although as will readily be seen the discussion itself naturally obeys no such tight categorization.

A Step 2 group discussion

To what does the analyst listen?

In one particular group, after the period of free discussion and then Step 1, the first aspect to be discussed in Step 2 was the analyst's way of listening – involving such matters as what state of mind did the analyst seem to think it appropriate to adopt when listening to the patient, what kind of material did she draw on, and in what sorts of ways did she transform the meaning of the manifest discourse into something latent and dynamically unconscious from which to talk to the patient.

Although analysts do this on a daily basis we usually find that pausing formally to ask such questions makes it apparent they are not easy to answer; practice is implicit rather than explicit and perhaps, like the presenter, each participant just does it. So each participant of course has his or her own particular way of listening to what has been presented and comes with his or her own implicit models of how material is heard. It can be very difficult to move from the way we each hear the material to think about the underlying processes causing someone else to hear it as they do.

This particular group had been discussing three sessions from the analysis of a young woman Nadia, who after coming to analysis in part because of difficulties with her marriage, had finally decided to leave her husband and live with her also married lover with whom she had previously had a secret relationship – for a while secret from the analyst too. The analyst (Mary, mentioned above) had told the group that when the patient was very young, her parents split up and she lived with her mother and her elder brother but always felt she had a secret relationship with her father. The manifest content of the sessions concerned this change in the patient's life but the analyst believed the latent content concerned changes in the way the patient was relating to the analyst and the anxieties being stirred up by change.

The group heard the analyst describe three sessions containing various manifest narratives. In the first, the patient was describing the details of the separation which was now taking place that day, concerns about the financial effects, the successful end of an academic course, and moving into her lover's house. About the latter she wondered what a young male relative would think and also whether or not to take her motorbike which she had not been using but which she views as male. She also volunteered she would also like to start skiing – also seen as a male activity.

The narratives were quite long and the analyst listened for a long time before eventually sensing what it seems she thought was the meaning enough to talk to her patient about what she took to be the underlying unconscious conflicts – divisions or splits in the patient's mind about what she was doing, whether she felt like a little girl inside an adult woman, and her anxieties about her mother's wish for her to be 'brave' like a boy. After the analyst said something along these lines the patient responded that her present house is too small for two but that the new house into which she will move with her boyfriend may be too large. This is heard by her analyst as a reference to her ambivalence about the increased space the analysis is taking up in the patient's mind, there and then.

Asked to explain her interpretations and so reveal more about what she was hearing as the latent content, the analyst said: 'If you ask me, in this case I had in mind to stress the difficulty of separation.' She also suggested that her long interpretation about the change in the patient's mind just 'appeared' in her mind. – suggesting a relaxed reverie-type way of thinking.

There were clearly many ways of hearing all this which had become apparent in the group during the free discussion. We will not summarize them here but when the group turned formally to try to think about this aspect of the analyst's method, someone started by suggesting that, when listening to the patient, this analyst is implicitly thinking of how the mind of the patient is built and pays special attention to evidence of splitting (between infantile and adult; male and female) and to the feeling she has that there is beginning to be a developmental integration of the split parts. Group members thus suggest that this is why patient and analyst, metaphorically, speak in terms of the patient moving into her partner's larger apartment and leaving her own small flat, albeit with anxiety. For example, should she take her motorbike to the new place?

At this point there was a discussion about the level at which the analyst and the patient were hearing each other. The analyst, it was suggested, was hearing a latent meaning and then speaking metaphorically to her patient in a way influenced by it. But the patient might be hearing it in different ways; either metaphorically or concretely, depending on what stage one thought the patient was at. Different participants wondered if the analyst might have supposed the patient took it more concretely and so less symbolically than the analyst had in mind; but the analyst maintained her view, consistent with the sequence of her interventions, helping the group to see her approach.

How does this analyst see the analytic situation?

The next Step 2 task concerns trying to explore the way the analyst sees the analytic situation – how is it defined in the analyst's mind, what is its main role in bringing about a psychoanalytic process and how much of the potential field of conscious and unconscious relations between patient and analyst are considered in the frame.

Some participants are struck by the fact that patient and analyst seemed always to be in agreement with each other. Someone describes this as the analyst being 'the double of the patient, not identical but just slightly different'. This commentator goes on to suggest that perhaps this analyst feels that being in this 'double' position is the condition necessary for analysis to start, and that only then is it possible to make more direct interpretations of the patient's unconscious phantasies about the analyst and also to interpret the sexual material more directly. Influenced by this thinking, the group discussion eventually centres upon the analyst's belief that, when analyst and patient are in the room together, they are able to come together and tolerate differentiation. People wonder whether, as this analyst seems to avoid picking up on the patient's hatred towards her, she feels her patient to be too vulnerable at the moment to face such a question. It is then suggested that the way the analyst looks at the setting is mainly as a mental space – 'the space of the analysis' – rather than as an actual relationship to the person of the analyst driven by particular unconscious wishes or enactments.

These ideas then lead to a discussion about space. The analyst sees the consulting room as a potentially good (facilitating) space, and looks at whether the patient is able to use what is potentially a good space or not. At this point the group members become pre-occupied with whether the analyst had a 'claustrum' in mind, that is more an environment than a well-defined object; in which case would this correspond to the sense of needing to be the same and in agreement.

The group feels that the analyst is very aware of the strength of the patient's relationship to her (the transference), but not of the detailed phantasy ideas or wishes about it. She has a place in the patient's mental space, which is now more secure: the work so far has created a situation where analyst and patient are feeling safer in the analytic space, and not so worried that separation means an explosion. It is pointed out that analyst and patient seem to have the same idea about space, that it is a space for growing, not a space between them. We notice that the analyst tends to emphasize the togetherness rather than the separateness. She focuses on a primitive need for fusion by putting forward the positive and even idealized mother. This may be stage-dependent, the group members surmise; the patient's vulnerability indicates the need for holding and not challenging. Mary responds to the patient's preconscious need for a positive atmosphere, and this is what Nadia can tolerate at this point.

This analyst's transformational model

The third component of Step 2 requires the group to try to draw out how the analyst thinks psychoanalysis works or should work for this patient. Some participants think that the analyst is using a develop-mental model of achieving change through internal maturation: hold-ing is necessary at this stage, but later a differentiated relationship could develop that could include taking up the influence of the patient's internal 'bad mother' and the black hole of which she spoke in the second session. One of the patient's complaints, we are told, has been: 'I am guilty of not loving my mother.' There is debate but some think that it seems the analyst believes it is not necessary now for the patient to consider that perhaps her experience is of having a 'bad

185

mother' (her analyst) in the session. Certainly, in these sessions the analyst is not concerned with love or hate, and does not concern herself with any problems the patient has in loving or hating another person. The implication is that with her view of how psychoanalysis works it is not necessary to interpret transference directly by seeking to make the patient conscious of how she is relating to or thinking about her analyst.

There follows a long discussion about the theory of 'interpretation of' the transference versus the theory of 'working in' the transference, and about what kind of transference the analyst needs to interpret and with what effects. On the whole it is felt that this analyst works with what some call the positive transference (i.e. is prepared to be experienced in a more or less idealized way), despite the fact the analyst said she had perceived a negative transference when she said to the patient: 'You are telling me that this emptiness, this black hole is what it means to you to be female.'

This highlighted how different analysts have very different ideas about transference and why it is so easy to get into a debate about which is better. Some participants do not think that a comment about the black hole the patient has as a woman can be considered as a negative transference interpretation – it not being at all clear to them that the analyst had been inviting the patient to think about her negative feelings towards her. However, from the analyst's point of view, it was clear that she was suggesting to the patient that she, the patient, had experienced being in the room with someone who was an infinite and dangerous black hole – and which she now felt was the analyst and also herself. We do not establish how this emptiness came about. We see here again a view of a non-differentiation of analyst and patient rather than a relationship. The exchange clearly brings out in the group how very different meanings are attached to apparently clear concepts, such as transference and also highlights that whomever wishes to capture the term and impose one meaning on it, there are clearly two very different conceptions (linked to very different underlying models) around.

Because in her interpretations the analyst does not make a direct reference to herself, she can be said to be working 'in the transference'. This led on to a discussion that by making interpretations 'in the transference' and not 'of the transference', that is, by not using 'you' and 'me' or discussing motives, feelings and wishes in the relationship, the analyst is being consistent; she is in her view protecting the new safe space that has recently been acquired with her patient and which she feels shouldn't be challenged too openly in the patient, because she believes this space to be necessary for the patient's development.

What does this analyst think will further the psychoanalytic process?

The group now moves to the specific way the analyst furthers the process – linking up all the interventions discussed at length in Step 1 to the analyst's underlying ideas about how to make analysis work. Soon, someone points out that they think it would be a good thing for the analytic process if the image of the 'bad mother' came in and was interpreted, and then the patient could work on it. This gives the analyst the opportunity to say she does not agree and to show that she believes that providing a good object in the treatment will allow a good object in the patient to grow without that recourse.

Someone else suggests that maybe at this point the analyst is most concerned not to act in as the overwhelming mother: she lets her patient play; she doesn't put herself in the scene too much; she gathers the material and shows the patient some of what she has collected. This is her way of working with this patient: not to be too much, nor too overwhelming, nor to force her into confrontation. The various things she says make sense with this idea. In particular the analyst tells us that Nadia's mother is a well-known figure who has taken up too much space and crushed her daughter, and it is with this in mind that the analyst feels it is important to refrain from being in any way intrusive and to help her patient to build up her own boundaries. It is for this reason that she tells Nadia that it is all right for her to have secrets from the analyst. At this point in the analysis, the analyst believes that her patient has started to build up her own boundaries and so it is time and possible to expand those boundaries (her move to living with the boyfriend). Her anxiety about whether this move to being with another person is premature or not is the theme of these sessions in the analyst's mind. She appears to take the material as a description of Nadia's ability to expand her boundaries and have stronger boundaries, rather than as a reflection of being able to make a relationship. To further the process she takes up these issues in a way which addresses the external situation but by 'larger space' she is meaning a larger mental space.

What according to this analyst is wrong with the patient

Finally, the group comes to what this analyst thinks, from a psycho-analytic perspective, is wrong with the patient. Someone suggests that the analyst is listening to a fragile patient with a weak ego structure and that this is why she is careful not to intrude or say distressing things. It is this conception of the patient which guides the interpret-ations. Someone else again points out what has come up often in the discussion in one way or another – the analyst doesn't understand or interpret the patient's experience of the void as a here and now or transference experience; she doesn't take it up as something between them, but she rather conveys that it is all right for the patient just to experience it, to know about the experience. Just experiencing it becomes part of having a bigger mental space. There is no interest by the analyst as to how things got to be this way for the patient.

Gradually we return to the analyst's interest in the split between the patient's child and adult self and the split between her male and female self, and the analyst's efforts to further the psychoanalytic pro-cess by pointing out these splits. This leads to a discussion about what is meant by splits: what is split off? The analyst appears to be working specifically around bringing to consciousness the image of a woman as a devalued object, as a dissociated split aspect of the patient. Now it seems the analytic work can be understood as helping the patient to enlarge her mental space, to allow herself to be someone other than this devalued person.

It now makes sense that by confirming what the patient is feeling, by verbalizing the feeling of emptiness, for instance, and by letting her be (by not being intrusive, by saying she can have her secrets), the analyst is aiming to help the patient to overcome this devaluation, to encourage her not to feel guilty and to help her to think for herself. The patient can then take in parts of herself: the 'masculine' motor-bike part, etc., and be much more herself – a development which is set in train and which lies behind, perhaps, why the analyst selected these sessions as examples of a live and ongoing psychoanalytic process.

We had asked the analyst to take a back seat during most of these discussions, but at the end of the last session she gave us her own view. On the whole, she was in agreement with the group, except for the above-mentioned issue of the understanding of negative transference, where she did think she was trying to address it.

188

Attempting to explore and construct implicit models: some group phenomena

We have just identified a small instance in which the analyst present-ing the material held an opinion of his or her approach which did not entirely fit the group's assessment of it. The group's task is to con-struct a model of the analyst's approach by using the five axes – but sometimes the group and/or the presenter seem reluctant to discover what is going on in the analyst's mind. Alternatively, at times during the discussion at this stage, there can be a suggestion that the group knows what the presenter is doing 'better' than he or she does, or that the analyst has 'blind spots' that need to be looked into. In our experi-ence this is often about the interpretation of the negative transference which seems to be one area where the analysts who present and the analysts who are in the groups may be considered to hold strong but implicit theories of the kind first discussed by Sandler (1983).

We have also noticed in a number of groups that participants can get angry when they feel that angry, frightening or bizarre aspects of the patient are not being interpreted. In these instances, the anger, which is thought not to be interpreted by the analyst or presenter, gets enacted by the group. Sometimes the participants express con-cern about the patient, who, they feel, is not receiving proper treat-ment – to the point, even, of being seriously damaged. This tends to happen especially when the theoretical model used by the presenting analyst is different from the one used by the concerned participants. It is possible that the group feels that *their own model is under attack*, and they feel emotionally shaken by the experience. For example, in the case of one presenter, the group felt that he had not interpreted the negative transference and argued that the analyst 'really' was unable to deal with conflicts. Even though in our clinical groups the aim is to understand what the analyst *does* and then to draw out the analyst's explanatory model in terms that everyone can recog-nize, there are moments when the group members cannot refrain from discussing what they believe the presenter *should have done* – according to a different model. In these situations the group is no longer curious about the presenter's model. Instead it is attempting to reconcile the participants' own theoretical approach with the analyst's behaviour in the session; if their own model includes a robust interpretation of the negative transference, why has the analyst not interpreted it?

It can happen that a group expresses near unanimous conviction around a point of theory or technique, but that the emotional atmosphere surrounding the discussion indicates that the issue is not about a theoretical principle, and that the participants are clustering around a model of their own in an emotional way. The words used are not about theory. Group members '*feel*' that the presenter is '*not in touch*' with the patient, that she is '*talking too much*', or that the patient's anxiety is '*not contained*'. There is a sense that the presenter has not said or done what the group members would have done and that this makes them angry. The group coalesces around a vague dissatisfaction. Now the group verges on forming a basic assumption group – perhaps a fight or flight group. To understand this development it is essential to reflect on the emotional challenges faced by the group members. In order to be open to the presenter's model, they have to put into perspective their own approach, an approach that each member has arrived at through study and research but especially through personal conviction. Personal (not only theoretical) beliefs about psychoanalysis are at stake, and one's own identification and narcissistic value as a psychoanalyst may feel threatened by being confronted by other, different approaches. The participants' *curiosity and imagination* may falter and it may seem impossible to conceptualize a model substantially different to one's own – and so the group momentarily takes solace in the certainty of a more or less implicit personal model instead of facing the challenge of uncertainty, difference and separation.

At such times, the moderator needs to bring the group back to the task in hand, and the use of an instrument, namely the five axes, can help the group to regain its neutral position and to focus on the presenter's way of understanding psychoanalysis.

The discussion of course requires a great deal of openness on the part of the presenter. She is confronted not only by the group's different points of view, but also by her own theoretical and technical models, which may well prove more complex and inconsistent than expected. The discussion reported above is a good example of the work necessary to arrive at a mutual understanding. The presenter was felt to be fostering the positive transference and not taking up the negative transference. When this was mentioned, the analyst did not agree at all and believed that she was taking up the negative transference. She reported the following interpretation as an example of taking up the negative transference with the patient:

You are telling me that over the last three years of analytical work we have built a house that you like, you like being there, and it's a valid image of yourself. Now you have to leave it because there isn't room for two and you are sorry, you don't know if you can modulate your times with those of the other person so as to be in sufficient tune with one another. But you've found your own system of freeing yourself from the anxiety of emptiness, of being a woman like a black hole: the washing-machine analysis, where you put these anxieties to get rid of them.

This shows that the notion of 'taking up the negative transference' itself can have different meanings for different analysts. In this case the disagreement was about what constituted 'taking up the negative transference'. If the group is to understand the analyst rather than simply feel a sense of disjunction attention needs to be given at this point to the potential role of implicit theories in influencing group discussion.

How implicit or private theories can overwhelm discussion

In the heat of the session an analyst uses not only a well-integrated theoretical context but also bits of theoretical models of which she may or may not be aware. Sandler (1983: 43) advocated that 'research should be directed toward making explicit the implicit concepts of practising psychoanalysts, and it is suggested that this process will result in an accelerated development of psychoanalytic theory'. What we have inadvertently discovered in these groups is that finding out more about implicit theories in Sandler's terms is quite challenging. They are often unknown to the analyst and subjective in nature and as a consequence they are difficult for an observer to identify. In that sense implicit theories are unconscious. Sandler (1983) thought that sometimes they are unconscious in the sense of preconscious but more often they are dynamically unconscious or in other words, repressed, because felt at variance with official theories. Insofar as they are dynamically unconscious, the analyst herself may well feel uncomfortable if aspects of her private theories, which are in conflict with the theoretical approach publicly held by herself or at least the society or subgroup to which she belongs, get revealed. Sandler himself suggested:

191

One of the difficulties in undertaking such research is that posed by the conscious or unconscious conviction of many analysts that they do not do 'proper' analysis (even though such a conviction may exist alongside the belief that they are better analysts than most of their colleagues).

(Sandler 1983: 38)

Even if there are potential links, it is important to distinguish the analyst's unconscious or implicit theories in Sandler's (1983) sense from the implicit working models (explanatory models) that are the focus of this project, as well as from a third important aspect; the analyst's unconscious response to unconscious aspects of the patient's communication, to which the analyst inevitably responds (enacts) but which he or she cannot yet represent – let alone use to interpret – in the analytic work at the stage of analysis when presentation takes place.

As discussed in Chapter 1, it is a feature of clinical discussion that some of what the analyst does not (yet) see will be 'seen' in the group. Analysts regularly present cases to a clinical group that promptly recognizes all manners of negative transference, and/or psychotic pathology, which the presenter, even an experienced and skilled analyst, seems either to have overlooked completely, or, contrary to the group, regards as not particularly important.

When we work as analysts we use a different (highly specialized) part of our mind, a function or capacity or skill which we use less when we are listening to a presentation. Freud's 'evenly suspended attention' requires openness to one's own free associative processes and to one's unconscious communications, which sometimes supersede the functioning of logic and keep our theoretical understanding of the material firmly in the background. When we hear a presentation on the other hand, we still are able to use intuition but perhaps we can more easily make use of our theoretical knowledge. If so, it would seem that as an audience we can use our explicit working models: we can evaluate the patient's mental state, we can keep in mind whatever we have heard about the history and we can draw intuitively a valid and well-supported conclusion. In the consulting room the analyst is in a very different and more challenging predicament. The analyst will draw together various elements in order to make an interpretation and will construct, or be guided by, his or her own theoretical context. Sometimes the theoretical context will be consistent, but at other times it will be Sandler's *variety of theoretical segments that relate directly to [the] clinical work*. These segments, writes Sandler, *are the product of unconscious thinking*. They are implicit theories that inform the analyst's implicit working model and that direct the analyst's attention and the course of his or her interpretative work. They may sometimes contradict each other and the analyst's explicit beliefs, with important consequences for clinical discussion.

Psychoanalytic theories of therapeutic action have tended to be quite abstract and are also usually somewhat distant from the clinical situation. Therefore, the analyst's transformational theory, the part of an explanatory model dealing with how the psychoanalytic process works, the specific ways in which it affects the patient, the limits of psychoanalysis, what can be treated and what can't, may be an area where there is plenty of scope for personal and/or implicit theories to become particularly influential. Insofar as the implicit theories an analyst holds are dynamically unconscious and conflicting then the process of a clinical discussion in which they become apparent is very likely to become emotionally complex.

For example, perhaps an analyst is unaware of holding certain general opinions like 'psychosis (or sexual perversions, or mental retardation, etc) cannot really be treated' or 'all patients can benefit from psychoanalysis'. In such cases, particularly if the analyst has not thought a great deal about the way he or she thinks change works in psychoanalysis, underlying beliefs can both have a strong effect on one's practice and on the discussion of one's practice in a group, particularly if other colleagues in the group respond from their own also potentially conflicting implicit theories; such as that psychoanalysis can help all patients, or that it can cure only the neuroses.

An example that occurred in one workshop group concerned an analyst who reported that a patient had cancelled a session but did not report any thoughts about whether or not this could be an attack against herself and the treatment – although this idea was not foreign to her in other examples of her work. When this possibility that she had avoided discussing the attack was discussed by the particular group, it emerged that the analyst's (pre)conscious doubts about how much that patient could be helped by treatment seemed to have led her unconsciously to avoid either noticing or interpreting the conflict the patient felt with the analyst. Implicitly the analyst thought it would not be useful to take up anyway.

Another example of how unconscious implicit theories can power-fully influence an explanatory model is suggested by the case of another analyst who did not consider the possibility that her patient might be at risk of a psychotic breakdown, in spite of the whole group being concerned that this was the case. Her explicit transformational model included the importance of preventing the patient's psycho-logical withdrawal from the analysis. One could surmise that this position implies a model where primacy is given to establishing meaningful contact with the patient (strengthening defences) as opposed to exposing the relationship to potentially overwhelming and/or frightening thoughts and feelings. This situation is similar to those (background/foreground) optical illusions where the same drawing can be seen either as two human profiles facing each other, or as a Greek vase. The profile is not better or worse, more or less appropriate, than the vase, and if you see one configuration you may have difficulties in seeing the other, even though both perspectives are valid. Analysts tend to prefer one perspective over the others, however, and a preference is indeed essential for providing one with an orienta-tion in listening to the patient. The analyst who, in his or her trans-formational theory, appears to feel that good contact with the patient is a priority may privilege good contact even when this could mean strengthening some reality-syntonic defences; while the analyst who regards the acknowledgement of frightening psychotic anxieties and ideas as essential to the development of the analysis, will orientate her attention to those aspects of the material, even when this may for a while provoke opposition and anxiety in the patient. *In theory* the two analysts may agree that both aspects are important, but *in practice* their work will be very different.

These examples illustrate how when discussing clinical material presented to a group it is very easy to find one has unearthed aspects of a presenter's explanatory model which rest on unconsciously repressed implicit theories, which may conflict with the way the ana-lyst likes to think about his or her work more consciously. An explanatory model based on implicit theories may be quite frequent, particularly in those cases where the analyst's more conscious model is not particularly well articulated or linked to the details of the work. But if such unconscious models spill out into group discussion, great care needs to be taken that the moderator ensures that the task of constructing explanatory models, which was the main focus in this project, is prioritised and conceptually separated from any wish to explore their unconscious determinants and the judgemental complexities to which they can give rise.

One final point we have noticed concerns the fact that implicit theories have the potential to be intrinsically variable. They may shift between patients and between various stages of treatment or they may be a more stable part of the analyst's approach. The analyst may react strongly, to an extent, or not at all when the efforts of the group bring hitherto repressed theories to view. Sometimes implicit theories are congruent with explicit models, and sometimes there is a glaring contradiction. But if there is a very considerable degree of flexibility over even glaring contradictions it may allow the analyst to give space to the patient and not to try to 'fit' the patient into the specific theoretical model that he may usually rely on. This was the case in some of the examples given above. In each case, however, the group was, at some point in the discussion, troubled by what was perceived as a lack of awareness in the analyst. One interesting possibility is that this apparent 'lack of awareness' is an essential aspect of the analyst's attitude at a particular point in some treatments, an attitude that may be supported by a multitude of implicit models expressing the message 'not yet' or even 'not ever'. For instance, the apparent 'lack of awareness' of a patient's psychotic propensity might not be something that could be thought through consistently at that moment by that analyst but which may function as an unconscious attunement to the patient's need to find a connection with his inner life in such a way that it does not trigger an unbearable explosion. As Sandler (1983) suggested, the study of such contradictions, carefully modulated, could lead back to the eventual modification and strengthening of the official theory – whether the analyst's own model or more widely.

A new form of clinical discussion – two examples

So far the focus in this chapter has been on the workshop discussions as part of a method for comparing differences. An unexpected bonus of these comparative clinical workshops is the breadth and depth of the clinical discussions that the two-step method actually generates. The focused approach paradoxically generates creativity. The very detailed attention to the material and the length of the meetings enhances the multidimensional perspectives and the possibility of an evolution in ordinary clinical understanding.

195

People, objects, characters

Different psychoanalysts discuss characters from their sessions according to their theoretical model: that is, depending on the analyst's own approach, the characters can be seen either as a part of external reality, or as internal objects, or as a representation of the ongoing process between the patient and the analyst.

Characters, therefore, can predominantly be understood as animated beings. An example of this would be the character of the black man described by one patient who was in the United States to investigate a deal:

> He knows so many people. He is so active and full of energy. I admired him, I liked him a lot. He is a true entrepreneur, full of enthusiasm, so successful and rich. He made me feel a pal. I felt sure that we would make the deal. And then, a few days later, he just sends an email to say that he gave the deal to someone else. I felt such a fool. I somehow trusted him and even showed him that I liked him. It makes me feel so bad.

This character could be seen either as a real person in the patient's life, as an internal object, or even as a representation of a frustrating and disappointing aspect of the analyst.

However, while a character is predominantly to be understood as an animated being, a character may, as per narratology, also be inanimate. In one of the groups, an analyst presented a case where one of the main characters was represented by a foot and its sock. The patient tells the story of his sister's suicide, before explaining that he worked on his computer from an early age, and then revealing that he had 'a special preoccupation with feet': he refused to show his feet and wore socks both day and night. During the Step 1 discussion groups, the sister, the computer and the socks were seen by some as forming part of a concrete reality, while others understood these three to lie beyond actual reality (for example, the loss of the sister expressed a loss of his capacity to experience alive and tender emotions; the use of the computer was understood as a mechanism by which each emotion was reduced to an autistic modality; and the socks were understood in a range of ways, from the fetishism of the foot with all its semantic shades to the need of a cover by a condom or a protective shell against emotions or contact with others).

Other interpretations of the sock came up during the free discussion of the clinical history of the foot/sock 'character': it was seen at first as a fetish-foot, then as an erotized object, and subsequently as a prophylactic shell (that is to say, as an illustration of the defence from contagious emotions and also an illustration of the need to protect the other from contact with aspects of the self experienced as inadequate). Eventually the sock was reconceived as a metaphor created/dreamt by the group in order to illustrate some aspects of the mental functioning of the patient. The patient at the age of 17 had had to undergo a surgical intervention on his foreskin. It was at this point that someone in the group commented that it seemed again like the problem of the sock – being too tight a sock/foreskin/hypercontainer, and creating a kind of claustrum.

During the discussion of the first session, the sock is interpreted both as a partial exciting object and at the same time as a metaphor for the mechanisms of depression and masochism at work in this patient. One participant said that the material made him think about

> the double levels of persecution and masochism present in this patient, which on the one hand work as a protection against his depression, and on the other work as a kind of sock, because the patient is terrified of having an authentic relationship in depth with anyone.

During the discussion of the second session, the socks are deconstructed into the yarn with which they are knitted, and subsequently interpreted as the price to pay for getting in naked touch with pain and suffering.

Finally in Step 2, in the discussion of the so-called analytic situation the argument becomes more abstract and complex. Here, the analyst shows that the goal of the analysis is, so to speak, to show the foot without a sock. The analyst says that 'she tends *to show* the patient, through her verbal interventions, what he is doing, how he can wipe out warm feelings from his mind, twist things and how he can cut himself off from his feelings.'

Understanding in evolution

A number of the presenters who have taken part in the project have reported back that the work of the group over two intensive days has been a transformative experience for them. There were many hours of discussion and so it is difficult to give a full flavour, but we shall here summarize one of the presentations, before presenting and discussing the analyst's working models.

Jennifer is a middle-aged paediatrician, divorced and with a 12-year-old child. She is currently in a relationship with Leonard, who has recently moved in with her. She comes to analysis because of her sense of loneliness and isolation. She is the first-born of a teenage mother and it is probably her paternal grandmother who looked after her in infancy. This paternal grandmother, who is reported to have had a sadistic relationship with Jennifer's mother, died when Jennifer was 3 or 4 years old. A brother was born a few years later and, because the boy had a disability, Jennifer was sent to a boarding school. There she was beaten regularly by a teacher, which the parents never knew about. After a year at the school she was expelled for her bad behaviour. Jennifer's mother would speak about how Jennifer always would go and eat the neighbours' apples while refusing to eat her mother's own. Jennifer has the habit of trying to seduce people; in that way she is said to resemble her father, with whom she formed an alliance. Jennifer helped to look after her disabled brother when she was older.

At a time when analysis is about to be put on hold owing to the May Bank Holiday and an approaching conference, the patient explains that she wants to have plastic surgery on her breasts and that she wants the approval of her analyst. The two have previously discussed this matter – at almost exactly the same time of year for the past two years, just before a similar break in analysis; the analyst explains that the first time the plan came up was two years ago following a longer and unexpected break due to a bereavement of the analyst.

The analyst understands the plastic surgery as a wish for 'false breasts'. By this she means Jennifer's wish to believe in something false, namely that she has an ideal analyst and ideal analysis. In so doing she refuses to know anything about the more 'real' feelings that her analyst lets her down and leaves her. She understands the surgery as a false solution to a problem which cannot be worked through in the analysis.

The three sessions

During a *Monday session*, the analyst talks to Jennifer about her desire for the analyst to decide for or against the operation, together with her determination to stick to her own interpretation of the situation, as opposed to the analyst's. Jennifer says that she won't go into the sea when she can't touch the bottom and that she won't ever learn to swim. This is said more in a defiant than in a hopeless tone. The analyst asks Jennifer about why she has to do things on her own [meaning without the analyst] and resort to the false breasts, and refers to how this same issue has in the past been raised at around the time of the May Bank Holiday break. What she has in mind is that to get in touch with her feelings about the break would mean to Jennifer going into the sea when she can't swim and hence Jennifer prefers a solution which bypasses getting in touch with her feelings.

In the *Tuesday session*, the patient says she is depressed and she tells a long story about how she was going to get up early to buy food for her son for his picnic as there was no food in the house but that she overslept and then rang her own patient to say she would be late for the appointment. But she got the day wrong and rang the wrong patient. Then another long story about a former patient who contacted her about her anorexic daughter who is not getting better in a clinic and the clinic is blaming the mother and she had to phone another colleague and therefore move another patient's appointment. The analyst understands these stories as expressions of Jennifer's unconscious idea that she has an analyst 'with nothing in her fridge' who experiences her as a daughter who refuses her offers of love and food, and is anorexic. Jennifer's analyst also links all this with the issue of the plastic surgery and what she considers the patient's fear of going mad if the analyst does not agree to what the analyst believes Jennifer knows is a false and idealized solution to her much deeper feeling which she can't put into words, that something is not right.

The *Wednesday session* is different in tone. Things had been good at home with Leonard and with her son. Jennifer had been able to ask Leonard to buy meat, and her son, a fussy eater, had been happy to eat it. The analyst asks Jennifer whether all of her concerns had been addressed in Tuesday's session, to which Jennifer responds in the negative. Jennifer also talks about how she can see how her son took advantage of his having to go to the picnic without food to get compensation from her. The analyst takes up the internal propaganda for a victim position (she is thinking that the breast surgery is meant to be a compensation for a grievance). The patient says that Leonard had said that her dissatisfaction with herself was offensive and he couldn't see why she wasn't satisfied with her body and the way she is. The patient adds that it was good with Leonard yesterday, that she knows Leonard is right, that she can look at it this way and that it was as if the analyst was holding her hand.

Free discussion

In the open discussion, there was interest in the fact that the analyst had not expressed openly any position in relation to the operation despite considerable pressure from the patient to get her agreement. It seemed Jennifer was reacting against this, feeling that the analyst's refusal to agree was a real deprivation. The analyst interpreted this in terms of an oedipal situation: the patient could not stand her experience of not being able to feed/interpret to herself when the analyst was able to have new ideas of her own (to stay neutral, to analyse), rather than to be bullied by the patient into agreement or disagreement. There was also a discussion about whether there was evidence of an analytic process taking place at all, since, for some group members, this would require more explicit transformation of meaning by the analyst and more mentalization on the part of the patient, than was being shown in these sessions.

The history was discussed. The analyst said that she has two pictures: one is that the patient doesn't put much hope in the analysis because her mother didn't put much hope in her; the other is that the patient is alive, intelligent, she has resources and is not psychotic, and so she must have received something from someone at some point.

During Steps 1 and 2, we repeatedly came back to the question of whether the analyst thought that Jennifer was suffering from trauma and deficit (it seemed from the presenter's account that Jennifer's mother was in reality very young and quite immature, coupled with early separations), or from conflict (her envy of the fabulous mother, which depleted her and made her just an empty 'fridge', or her split-off jealousy and need encapsulated in a split between mother and grandmother, etc.). Was it the mother who, according to the analyst, had nothing in the fridge? Was she a phantasy or a reality? The analyst seemed to oscillate between the two and could not make a clear choice. Theoretically, she may have felt that Jennifer embodied a conflict model, but implicitly she also saw a model of trauma. The two seemed to be able to coexist in her mind, but the group could not find an overarching theory to which she subscribed even implicitly that linked them – a developmental theory of how trauma can create conflict, for example.

In conclusion, therefore, we said that the analyst saw in Jennifer a narcissistic structure in which the patient fears being dependent on account of past traumas (the teenage mother who has nothing in her fridge, the death of the grandmother, the abuse in the convent school). She also sees Jennifer as a borderline patient who deals with her problems by using concrete solutions:

> If I don't agree to the operation you are afraid you will go mad, you are afraid that my treatment will hurt you and that you will get too close to the mother who has nothing to give her child to eat, and the anorexic girl who doesn't eat and holds herself together with her own will.

The patient uses splitting, denial and idealization, and resorts to magical thinking ('different breasts will be a solution'). This extends to the relationship with the analyst, which Jennifer cannot use: she denies her own needs by attacking interpretations with the phrase 'Yes, but ...' – apparently accepting the interpretations, but then rejecting them. She sees this mental anorexia as protection from knowing there is no food available rather than as an oral, anal or sexual problem. The analyst also feels that Jennifer has 'virtual relationships' idealized and unreal (previous to this new phase of living with him, Leonard had been talked about in a way that didn't sound real to the analyst, and as if he wasn't a real person).

The ambiguity of the two models of what is wrong seems to be held by the analyst without contradiction because of her mode of interpreting. She functions in what has been termed 'transitionality' – a transitional space in which there is no specific attribution of intent to either patient or analyst (so that there is an unsaturated or ambiguous flavour to what would otherwise be very direct or saturated interpretations). For example, when addressing the anorexic strategy to avoid being in contact with a mother who has nothing to give she says: 'today we have not only the mother who has nothing to give her child to eat, but also the anorexic girl, and also the problem of different psychotherapists in conflict as to who can treat who.' She also addresses how the patient feels and states that because her needs weren't met, she feels that she has the right permanently to recriminate others.

The analyst never says directly to the patient that the mother in reality had nothing to give, although this seems to be in her mind. However, the analyst tells us that, following our discussion, she has been thinking about the question of trauma. Trauma is certainly the patient's theory, she says, but she doesn't know if she, the analyst, thinks this. On the whole the analyst works in the here and now, but often also relates her interpretation to the patient's past or to an outside situation. The following interpretation is an example:

> I comment that I know analysis helps her, but it helps her to get in contact with the mother who has nothing to give her child to eat and with the anorexic girl – and we remember how not long ago you spoke for the first time of your experience with your newborn baby when you brought him home and how having nothing for him to eat now was a repeat of that anxiety – and one can see also how having a different psychotherapy from mine (the plastic surgery) is relevant here and that there is a conflict as to who is treating the anorexic girl and how you want to find your own solution.

Alternatively:

> you are afraid that I can't help you with that, that I have nothing available to help you with those things which make you angry and despairing, afraid of those things which disturb you so much, just as you told me you are feeling today, mixed up, frightened and alarmed at feeling like this.

In the comments brought out by the group discussion, the analyst believes that her task is to address the patient's defences in the here and now, and in particular the narcissistic structure created by the patient to prevent the catastrophic knowledge that the maternal provisions were insufficient. In so doing, she hopes to help the patient to be more able to rely on and take from the analyst and from her external objects. If this happens, she will be able to make use of her own capacities and to develop her ego functions rather than 'not see', idealize and act rather than think. This is evident in two interpretations. First, 'I tell her that she resorts to her own remedy – false breasts, pretence, doing things for herself'. And also:

> you are telling me now that you realize many things and that you are happy but you are very afraid because deceit is behind the door, just yesterday we were talking about the dates of the May Bank Holiday break, and because of your fear of being deceived, there is still a lot of propaganda in favour of idealization, of not seeing things as they are because 'blindly' is safer than seeing.

Her theory seems to be one in which there is repetition of conflicts and experiences in the analytic situation, rather than corrective experience. When interpreted, this repetition is integrated, and so helps to develop Jennifer's capacity to contain. In so doing the analyst also shows the patient that she is not the mother from the past and that her other relationships need not be either. The analyst also addresses the external relationships of the patient in order to help her to have real relationships rather than 'virtual' relationships.

In line with her transformational theory, this analyst, therefore, listens to what she thinks of as unconscious fantasy, in particular as it reflects issues of dependency and the state of the patient's objects. She listens to how it connects with the objects and relationships and traumas in the past. The analyst does not listen to the negative transference specifically (and does not hear the patient as hating her, complaining at her, or having the operation to spite her), but she does address what she perceives as being instances of false idealization. The group considers the possibility that the analyst is concerned with not repeating the trauma, in that she seems to believe that if she more directly interpreted the aggression behind the operation, it would cause defensive splitting.

Reflection

The lengthy discussions in these groups bring in multiple perspectives that throw the presenter's model into relief. For instance, on the first day some people were puzzled as to why the analyst felt that the breast augmentation should be seen as an alternative to the analysis and why the analyst should think of it as the end of analysis. Wasn't it a good thing that this woman wanted to make herself more attractive? Someone suggested that the analyst maybe thought middle-aged women should not be concerned with their looks. Someone else wondered if the analyst would feel the same if the plastic surgery was related to another part of the body like the nose, and there was talk of social norms of beauty. To the analyst's despair also came the voice of hope: this could be a good thing, someone suggested, a new beginning for the patient. Still, there was something puzzling as to the meaning of the operation. The patient claimed that the difference would be minimal and wouldn't even be noticeable. But especially, Jennifer reported that her new partner could not see why she wasn't satisfied with the way she is and even called the plan for surgery 'offensive' – an offence against his love and her body as it is and running instead after a non-existing ideal.

This also brought out more clearly the analyst's implicit model in particular around two issues: first, that the patient was acting out rather than symbolizing her problem, and that this was consequent on a trauma in the analysis, which repeated an earlier trauma, and second that, for analysis to take place, the patient needs to be able to symbolize, this is why she thought that having the plastic surgery meant the end of analysis. Furthermore, within the analysis, talking about 'breasts' was a reference to the maternal breast and mothering. In talking about 'breasts', the analyst is thinking symbolically of the maternal feeding breast, which Jennifer now identifies as her own in a melancholic way, and which the patient now hates and thinks needs changing; talking in this way in her sessions is understood as a concrete solution which doesn't address the psychic problem which could be modified only by understanding her dissatisfaction with the analyst's maternal provisions as representative of the original lack of provisions by the mother.

One could say that the impasse presented at this moment of the analysis rested on the fact that the analyst and the patient had two different models: the analyst was thinking symbolically while the patient was thinking concretely. In fact the patient was, she said, happy with the analysis and thought it was helping her, but the analyst felt despairing because Jennifer was unable to move to a symbolic mode of functioning.

When we speak of implicit models we are talking about something which the analyst has not necessarily thought about. We are not speaking of something which is unconscious, but of preconscious guiding principles, even maybe contradictory ones, which the analyst may not have articulated to herself.

The group discussions enable a more conscious level to be reached. On the second day, the analyst told us that she had woken up in the night and thought to herself: what is it about the May Bank Holiday that inspires the patient to think about breast surgery? She thought that, were she a Winnicottian, she would say that Jennifer's grandmother had died when she was 3. Now that Jennifer has been in analysis for three years, perhaps the analyst's unplanned absence in May two years previously could explain some of Jennifer's behaviour: the analyst herself has had an impact on her through her unplanned absence. It is interesting that the analyst attributes these thoughts to a (Winnicottian) perspective other than her own in order to be able to make use of it,[2] presumably because it doesn't fit her conscious model, and because she needs an interlocutor with a different perspective (a 'third') to help make sense of a worrying situation. She links the loss of the grandmother, a failure to mourn her, and a failure to deal with the analyst's unplanned break two years ago. She tells us that she has finally, and for the first time, 'found a place' for this grandmother (a lost good object) in the analysis. The analyst therefore thinks that now, instead of being able to mourn, the patient resorts to a 'concrete' solution: she rejects the inadequate breast/mother, with whom she identifies (her dislike of her own breasts) and turns to surgery for the wished-for ideal breast.

Interpretations in the sessions presented had addressed the 'propaganda' surrounding the surgery and not the surgery itself as a concrete solution to the patient's fear of being let down, deceived and/or abandoned. The analyst speaks of 'false breasts' as a representation of a false solution to a problem that is not being faced, the belief that changing her breasts literally will provide an internal feeling of being cared for. However, it turns out that Jennifer, in spite of these seemingly productive sessions, missed the next session and went ahead with the operation – causing the analyst to feel deceived. The analyst did not interpret this move as a direct attack on the treatment, but she was well aware of her angry and resentful countertransference, which from the beginning she had conveyed to us.

As the meeting went on, it increasingly emerged that the analyst had been unconsciously feeling herself to be Jennifer's abandoning mother, and that she was imprisoned in this role.[3] She felt that she had let Jennifer down two years previously because of the cancellation, and because, when she came back, she was preoccupied with her own bereavement and not as sensitive to Jennifer's reaction to her absence as she normally would be. Herein lies the trauma in this particular analysis, which we discussed during our sessions. The analyst said that the discussions helped her to realize that she was afraid that indeed she

---

[2] In reply to a question on this point the moderator commented: 'I never ask a presenter their theoretical orientation so I do not know which theory she officially recognizes as her own.'

[3] Jennifer's analyst later reported to the moderator: 'I have realized in the course of the group that unconsciously I have assumed in this analysis that really I am an empty analyst/mother/fridge'.

had nothing to offer Jennifer (that she was an inadequate 'breast'), and that the patient's defence was stronger ('false' solutions) than the solutions that the analyst could offer.

Thanks to the discussion, the analyst began to come to the conclusion that she had, in her own mind anyway, taken an opposing position to the plastic surgery because it might signal that the analysis was over and had nothing to offer Jennifer. Through these discussions, however, she came to feel less worried that this was the case. Her experience in the group made her aware she could take the patient's wish as a message, as mourning; and that there were various ways of thinking about it. She realized that her frustration resulted from thinking that Jennifer's decision to have the operation meant irrevocably that she could not help her and that she *was* now the mother with the empty fridge, even though she did not mention this to Jennifer in her interpretations: 'It's the projection of an enormous desperation which froze me.' The analyst feels that the group helped her to see her own countertransference and how the new trauma that the analyst's own bereavement had imposed on Jennifer was a projection on Jennifer's part. From this realization reached in her own mind the analyst now felt that she could go back to her patient with more hope and a sense that analysis could go on. We can see that the analyst's despair connected to an essentially unconscious feeling that she had done irreversible damage to Jennifer through her absence and subsequent self-preoccupation, and that Jennifer was now not allowing her to make up for the damage by doing something irreversible and taking 'a surgeon's knife' to her analysis.

By searching for the analyst's own model in detail, we had not imposed a different model but had helped the analyst to come to her own understanding of what was happening with her patient.

It also emerged from reflecting on the discussions that the group itself had sometimes been driven to defend against despair by arguing that there is nothing wrong with plastic surgery, and that it is a question of aesthetics which hinges on cultural notions of beauty, and did not in this instance mean that the analysis was spoilt. It was also pointed out that the group had sunk into concrete thinking by taking the story quite literally. Perhaps we had similarly wanted the analyst to remain the perfect breast, not depleted and irreparable.

We might also add, finally, that in these workshop groups, we were also facing our own depressive anxieties about our resources as analysts (i.e. looking inside our own 'fridge'), and about whether we can help patients through a method based on symbolization rather than on concrete action. Indeed this case brings out that which is at the heart of the psychoanalytic project.

And do we also turn to 'false breasts', or can we tolerate anxiety when we think in such detail about what we do and about our differences?

8

Experiences of participating
Group processes and group dynamics

Johan Schubert (Sweden)

The experiences and impressions that I describe in this chapter derive chiefly from the groups in which I have been working as a moderator. These groups have been very different and accordingly the group processes have developed in divergent ways, forming the basis for an ample description of various group phenomena. However, in order to prevent the following presentation from being limited to my own experiences or from running the risk of it being biased only to a moderator's perspective, I have supplemented the description with comments and commentaries made by many of the participants in a questionnaire about the workshop and how it worked out.

Preconditions for the group work

Group processes and group dynamics have determined how the workshop groups have functioned in interesting ways; as they have been influenced by several specific preconditions concerning the setting, the frame and the task. The changes that have been introduced year by year as we have tried to learn from experience have had a great impact on work with the group task, how it has developed and how it has been managed. Some of the more important will, therefore, be briefly outlined.

The composition of groups has been decided on in advance with some of the participants being selected for certain functions. Each group had a moderator who was responsible for leading the group work. This involved introducing the task and the working model and making the group work with the task and stick to it. Initially, none of the moderators was prepared in any special way for this job, and each had to work out his or her own understanding of what was expected and needed as well as his or her own style. But from the beginning of the project a permanent group of moderators have met regularly and exchanged their experiences; these meetings (the meetings in Paris described in Chapter 6) have had a supporting function.

The recruitment of participants to the groups was strictly regulated. Those who wanted to take part in the group work had to apply for participation. The working party chair reviewed applications in terms of experience, linguistic ability, reputation (if known), past experience of the task, stated preferences (where known), potential confidentiality problems and psychoanalytic society of origin. In good time before the workshop, he divided them into groups which were made as heterogeneous as possible. After the first year or two late applicants were usually turned down. Each moderator was informed about the members of his or her group and who would be the presenter(s). Then it was up to the moderators to prepare the group participants for the work (Step −2: see Chapter 7). This was done in different ways: some moderators sent out a great deal of information in advance, asking group members to study the material thoroughly before the meeting. Others were less ambitious in this respect and relied on the members' ability to learn about the group work at the conference. All the participants were told that it was important to attend all group meetings, during the entire group process.

In Prague and Sorrento the groups had two presenters, but this was changed to one presenter in the groups that met in Helsinki, Vilamoura and Athens. They were asked to present in writing a short background account of the patient in question, followed by a detailed description of two or three sessions.

As described in Chapter 3, in the first groups in Prague two members were chosen beforehand to function as discussants of the two presentations. The reason for this was to stimulate the following group discussion and to initiate the process of describing the two analysts' work and how they differed. Although these contributions were interesting and valuable they were found to be too time-consuming and insufficient in regard to the task. The idea of having discussants was therefore given up.

In order to collect information about the results of the work of the groups and what group processes were developed, some members were commissioned as reporters. This function was defined rather differently in the groups, and it has also changed considerably during the course of the project. To begin with, one group member was pre-elected as reporter and this person was to gather as much information as possible from the proceedings. This model did not work out well and in subsequent meetings the moderators, who were responsible for leading the group work, took over the reporting function. Gradually, as the project developed, group members were asked to help the moderator to focus attention on certain issues during the group sessions and in this way were helpful in producing a comprehensive report of the groups' work and what was achieved. Since the Helsinki meeting tape-recorders have also been used.

After Sorrento (see Chapter 4) up to twelve hours was eventually allocated for group work, an unusually long time compared to that of most other clinical groups. However, this was considered necessary to allow the groups to accomplish their task. Since these groups were meeting during the EPF conference, the group members found it difficult to take part in some of the other items on the conference programme and complaints were made. However, at the later conferences this problem was handled by planning part of the group work outside the ordinary conference programme.

A detailed schedule was suggested for the proceedings with a timetable consisting of different steps. As the project developed, this timetable gradually changed, but a few main parts remained. The first was the presentation of the clinical material followed by a relatively free discussion of it in the group (Step −1 and Step 0). In the second part the grid-typology was introduced, and the work concentrated on scoring the analyst's interventions according to Step I. The third part was devoted to Step 2, which was introduced and gradually elaborated in recent group meetings, as described in Chapters 6 and 7.

The groups' task as presented at the outset involves three main sub-tasks, which have been subject to constant development. First is to study and discuss the clinical work of qualified psychoanalysts in a thorough way. Second is to establish a professional language and conceptual tools that could facilitate description and characterization of this clinical work in a consistent way. Third is to make comparisons between different ways of carrying out psychoanalysis and between different psychoanalysts' ways of working and thinking psychoanalytically.

Thus, the task was quite specific and clearly defined. However, this did not prevent the groups from finding their own informal ways of understanding the task and putting their ideas into practice. In fact, an incentive to make the groups search for possible models to set about achieving the overall tasks was actually implicit in the project.

Initial problems

The project aimed to introduce a new method for working with clinical material. The fact that this was an untried method presented a challenge to the group members. Despite a genuine interest in the aim of the project, the change of procedure in the handling of psychoanalytic case material raised many questions, not to say suspicions, about what the result would be. Psychoanalysts as well as psychoanalytic institutions are known to be often very resistant to changes and innovations. Defending strict rules for exercising the profession has always been an advantage in maintaining its basic standards, but reluctance even to try new ideas entails the risk of stasis and lack of development.

There was an inherent, conscious as well as unconscious, hesitation or opposition among many participants to the group task and to the new way of working. This was evidenced in various ways from the very beginning. Some group members did not prioritize taking in the information they had received in advance, while others seemed to find it too complicated to study the information or just neglected it. A few applicants simply didn't turn up. Others were present only part of the time, some came late and some were absent part of the time. Some participants left the group for good early in the proceedings, most without giving any reason, although a few were quite outspoken in their opinions.

Participants had been asked to respect the timeframe and stay in the group for the entire process. The fact that people entered and left the group caused worry and uneasiness among its members and disrupted the work. However, this problem was temporary; the more the project progressed and became well known, the more people tended to meet the attendance requirement. Many group participants returned to subsequent group meetings, and often demanded to be placed in the

211

same group as they had been in before. When the special timeframe had been accepted it was increasingly appreciated, illustrated by the following two comments:

> There was enough time to elaborate, to study detail and to develop thoughts, which is uniquely positive. It promotes understanding, reflection, learning, integration and internalization.

> The extended time permits a better accumulation of associative evidence on behalf of or against different interpretive approaches and clinical orientations.

Another problem had to do with the constellation of participants from different countries who could not speak their mother tongue in the group work. The majority had a fair or good knowledge of English or French and could be placed in groups where these languages were spoken. However, their proficiency varied considerably, and this caused problems in some of the groups. People left the group because they were not able to follow the proceedings. For others it was difficult to understand part of what was said in the discussions and they felt left out. This was commonly cited as an explanation for their silence and for not taking part in the discussion.

However, this was probably not always the whole truth. The language difficulties could easily disguise problems in taking initiative and finding space to articulate personal views about the matters being discussed. Another factor was the dynamics of the group, how generous the atmosphere was felt to be and if the expression of vague ideas or uncertain observations was permitted. When the moderator was attentive to such phenomena, this was sometimes helpful.

Confidentiality was another issue. Initially firm instructions – both written and oral – were given to all participants about the careful managing of case material and about restrictions on discussion of such material outside the groups. Despite these precautionary measures, a few presenters were anxious not to give certain details about their cases and this tended to have a hampering effect on the discussion. For instance, in one group the leaving out of detail was done on the surface to protect confidentiality about what appeared to be very sensitive issues in the patient's previous experiences, and the organization she was involved in. At the same time the presenter's non-verbal communication conveyed her reluctance to allow the group members to gain insight into her work. This relative restriction on the part of the presenter flowed into the group and led to many muted responses. However, such obstacles were rare. On the whole, questions about confidentiality were not a big issue in the groups. One obvious reason for this was that that the focus of attention was on the analyst and not on the patient. When confidentiality became an issue, other related problems, such as countertransference reactions to the patient or anxiety about being exposed to the group, could not be ruled out.

At the beginning of the project, before the grid-typology (Chapter 6) had been developed as a structuring tool for the group work, great difficulties appeared in the understanding and use of concepts. Many basic psychoanalytical concepts have multiple implications and gave rise to vivid discussions without any resolution. It became obvious that within separate psychoanalytical cultures these concepts are defined very differently. Much time was devoted to this problem, and the work on the case material sometimes tended to recede into the background. Many participants felt that this was a major obstacle to progress, and the need for auxiliary measures was urgent at this stage.

The objective of the group's task – to study and categorize the analyst's interventions – was to find a common language for this purpose. For many analysts the narcissistic investment in theory is difficult to overcome. By introducing a specific theoretical frame of reference as a starting point, which happened a few times, the ensuing discussion was restricted to a certain perspective, and the assessment of the analyst's interventions tended to verify what he or she had intended to do rather than questioning what was actually done. For this reason it was recommended that theoretical discussions and statements should be avoided during the scoring procedure. Later in the project, learning what the analyst's theoretical orientation was and how this could be specified was the intended result and aim of an exhaustive description of the analyst's way of working. In fact, discussions about concepts and conceptual definitions tended to be less pronounced as the project developed.

General group processes

A special situation arises when psychoanalysts come together in a group and are tasked with studying each other's clinical work. It is not like meetings among engineers or dentists, where professional skills and workmanship or the practice of various aspects of the profession can be discussed objectively and neutrally. Because analysts are extremely involved personally, the discussions are often characterized by a confrontation between subjective attitudes and value judgements of what is presented. The issues in question may be related to what is apprehended or how this is understood and may also involve personal ideas about how an issue should be thought about and managed. In fact, a non-judgemental stance is quite uncommon among psychoanalysts discussing clinical material – as discussed in relation to journal and conference discussions in Chapters 1 and 2.

There are many reasons for this. The practice of the psychoanalytic profession is based on the analyst being the main instrument in the clinical situation. Not only his or her theoretical knowledge and technical skills, but also the analyst's personality and individual characteristics are involved. Because of this, analysts can be sensitive and vulnerable to being questioned and criticized when their own work is studied, but this doesn't prevent them from being critical of the professional performance of others.

Contributing to this rather complicated situation is the existing insecurity regarding many theoretical and technical matters. Most psychoanalytical concepts are unclear and ambiguous, and the great number of theories makes it difficult to reach a mutual understanding of clinical phenomena. What happens in the individual clinical situation is always subject to different interpretations. Against this background the overall aim of finding out what we really do as psychoanalysts is challenging, and realizing one's own shortcomings and limitations in the practice of psychoanalysis may be anxiety provoking.

All this is mentioned as a background to the study of the processes and dynamics in the workshop groups. There are, of course, basic similarities between these groups and most other groups with psychoanalysts designed for working on clinical material. Moreover, some of the group dynamics that occurred should be common to most groups, such as competition, rivalry, sibling manifestations, clique formations, sympathies, antipathies, etc. What makes the workshop groups different, however, are the previously mentioned preconditions regarding the setting, frame and task, which strongly influenced the group work and made the groups develop in rather unexpected ways.

Special group processes

There was much curiosity and great expectations among the participants at the beginning of the group work. Of course, this was especially pronounced at the start of the project, in Prague, but also in subsequent group meetings people seemed to be on tenterhooks when the group was assembled. This was easy to understand. To meet with new colleagues from different countries and psychoanalytical societies who represented other analytical cultures and traditions was interesting and challenging. The fact that they had all been pre-selected to a group contributed to a feeling of having been chosen, and this was reinforced by the experience of taking part in a new and much discussed project. However, a few participants were hesitant and anxious about being placed in a predetermined structure, of which they knew nothing.

The group members were usually presented to each other at the beginning of each workshop group; this procedure was more or less comprehensive in different groups. Some groups gave much attention to the group and time was devoted to its members' thoughts and feelings. They were asked about their expectations about the work and why they had chosen to participate in this project. These preparatory measures obviously influence the group climate from the very beginning. In many cases they were helpful in creating a more relaxed atmosphere during the subsequent group work. However, the importance of this element was probably secondary to many other issues decisive for the development of group dynamics, which will be discussed further on.

The presentation of the case and its initial discussion undoubtedly had great importance. We learned that, in order to bring about a good working atmosphere in the groups, it was essential to begin by allowing space for a free discussion of the clinical material. Everybody felt at ease with this familiar procedure. It gave participants the chance to become acquainted with the material and get a general view of the case, with the aim of approaching a personal understanding of it. The importance of this phase was highlighted by the comment: 'It is very useful, the brain-storming phase and the active presence of the analyst'. Without such a preparatory element in the proceedings the next task – to study the analyst's interventions – would probably have been more difficult.

This initial phase of the work also affected what came to the fore in

215

listening to the case material. Some discussions were focused on very literal and concrete details such as anamnestic data, matters about the frame or the series of events in the analysis. Others were performed in a more free associative way with contributions of the group members' fantasies about what was being presented. The outcome of these ways of treating the material could differ a lot; the former led to a detailed history of the patient with much emphasis on the manifest interaction with the analyst, whereas in the latter interest tended to focus on more unconscious contents with the emergence of modalities of the patient's mental functioning.

When the grid-typology was introduced, initially, everyone approached this energetically, but activity soon slowed as people realized how difficult it was to decide on the scoring and to reach agreement about it in the group. The contrast between the previous free discussion and this rather structured way of working was striking. A few participants started to grumble about the difficulties and question how meaningful the work was. They found the task 'boring', and someone compared the group to 'a school-class, having to do its lesson'. Another negative attitude is illustrated by the following comment: 'How could we come to terms with the personality of the analyst, the analyst's sensibility, style and way of approaching the other's mind? It is a variable which is impossible to grasp.'

As discussed in earlier chapters, the instrument was initially over-complicated, incomplete and not really workable. Thus such negative reactions were not inappropriate. Nevertheless, the work in the groups helped us to find out what the problems were and what needed to be changed in the grid-typology to improve it. Opinions in the groups were absolutely essential for this purpose. Some of the group members found it difficult to understand this aim alongside the task of classifying the analyst's interventions. They expected the grid to be a finished product and were disappointed when it was found to be deficient.

This underlines the importance of the information and instructions given to the group members at the beginning and the different ways people worked them through. In retrospect, there were probably shortcomings in these respects. This was commented on in the following way:

I think it would be helpful the next time to explain very clearly why it is important to apply the categories, why it makes sense to learn about the presenter's implicit mental template, and how this should be done. This should be explained to the moderators first, who should then forward this information to the groups.

Because of this deficiency, too much stress was laid on the classification procedure in some groups with the result that people felt it was almost obsessional. This was probably one of the reasons for some participants' prejudice against the project in Sorrento especially and why some of them tried to stir up opposition to it.

Another important lesson had to do with the task of making comparisons. In the first group meetings in Prague and Sorrento, two analysts were asked to present clinical material and the groups tried to compare their respective ways of working. It soon became evident that this was too difficult. Since any type of comparison runs the risk of being implicitly charged with value judgements, it gives rise to much anxiety that someone might be offended or upset. The result is that most statements tend to be guarded and cautious, which obstructs an open and unprejudiced discussion. This was the reason for giving up the setting with two presenters. Nevertheless, we should not forget that in discussions of clinical material comparisons are always made, though mostly in less explicit ways. In the study of somebody else's work one inevitably draws on one's own experiences and opinions, based on one's own frame of reference.

There were important differences in the degree to which the presenter was expected to be active and take part in the group discussion. One extreme was represented in groups where the presenter was asked to sit back and listen to the discussion and, if spoken to, he or she was asked only about matters of vital importance for understanding the case and what had occurred in the sessions. At the end of group sessions the presenter was invited to comment on how the group had dealt with the material and what it had accomplished.

The other extreme occurred in groups where the presenting analyst was constantly engaged in the group discussion. This could mean that the analyst was asked to present additional material, provide special information and give explanations of various kinds. The analyst occasionally got into fierce arguments with the rest of the group as a result of trying to justify his or her analytic style, understanding of the material and way of handling the patient. This sometimes involved declarations of affiliation with certain analytical schools or cultures as well as rendering an account of the theoretical frame of reference used. Sometimes when this happened the presenter either got into a very exposed position of being vulnerable and defensive or got out of touch with the group, being isolated and feeling misunderstood. In such cases group members expressed the view that the presenter should give fewer 'rationalizations' of the interventions and that the group should work more on the presented material and the presenter's implicit views and less on his or her conscious comments.

It is obvious that the different directions in which these things developed had a great impact on the outcome of the group work and on the dynamics of the group. All the groups had been asked to use the analyst's written interventions as the basis for the investigation. When there was too much additional information of various kinds, there was a risk that the analysis of these interventions became indistinct and out of focus. In fact, however, even written interventions constitute a mix of what the analyst actually did during the session and how that was rationalized in the reporting afterwards. One group used verbatim notes from the sessions. Perhaps this is the best way to study how the chain of verbal interventions is made.

There is, of course, much more to an analytic intervention than its verbal content. In some written reports from the sessions, material was provided about what the analyst thought and felt before the interventions and also what reactions the analysand's responses created, constituting a sort of listening to the listening. Sometimes the group was told about this during the oral presentation. Such additional information undoubtedly had an impact on how the interventions were understood and scored, and this reflects the complexity that is inherent in every intervention, with both manifest and latent content. It was as a result of discussing this issue in the moderators' group that the grid was later extended to include the type of interventions which are not explicit or consciously thought out or might be the result of countertransference reactions (Chapter 6). Eventually this contributed to vivid discussions in the scoring procedure.

The requirement to assume that the clinical material being presented represented decent analysis was not easily accepted by some group members and could become the subject of much controversy. (From Helsinki onwards, all presenters were training analysts or had equivalent experience and reputation.) Sometimes the analytical work seemed to many participants to be incomprehensible or of low quality with the analyst apparently sometimes out of focus in certain respects. Where this happened it created strain. Group members sometimes found it difficult to go on being curious and wanted to point out what they thought or, alternatively, became passive and avoided real engagement with the analyst's work. Many of the presenters were able to handle such questioning in a positive way and could accept and even appreciate the points made. However, sometimes the presenter felt criticized and misunderstood. He or she then became defensive, and in a few cases and despite all the precautions the group discussion tended to develop into a 'trial'. Another negative outcome was when the analyst's problems were not made clear or not even mentioned. In such cases, the situation tended to become unreal and a pseudo-dialogue was developed to which people reacted by feeling uneasy or irritated. The discussion then became vague and insignificant, and the group struggled to accomplish its task.

The moderator's role

The role of the moderator became a focus early in the proceedings. Since the group's task initially was only vaguely understood by the participants it was important at the outset to carefully inform everyone about this task and to give clear instructions about how the work would be carried out. Some group members found it difficult to understand the task, others easily forgot what the task was, and one or two participants were against it or simply neglected it. The moderator had to repeatedly remind the group of what was expected of them, but without being authoritarian. According to one of the participants the ideal moderator should function as a 'benign superego'. In other words, the challenge was to find a balance between activity and passivity, between taking the lead and staying in the background.

Thus, the moderator's demanding responsibility was to watch the aims and timetables and to get and keep everyone on track. However, this was not sufficient: the moderator also needed to create a working atmosphere for combining the group task with a free and open discussion in which everyone could take part, keeping the focus and at the same time maintaining a level of creative exchange. This was not always an easy matter because of the questioning of various elements of the proceedings. If it happened that the group coalesced around some vague dissatisfaction, such as a complaint that the task was too detailed and extensive or, on the contrary, that the instructions for the work were incomplete and vague, the moderator's invitation to the group members to try to find their own way of handling these difficulties was not always met with enthusiasm.

In most groups the moderator's role was respected and appreciated. However, it has happened that group members have objected to the moderator's management of the situation and tried to compete as informal leaders. Some even tried to take over the role of the moderator by developing a dominating role in the discussions, by giving advice about how the case in question should be handled or by exposing authority regarding certain theoretical matters. In one group it was pointed out that there were 'too many moderators', after which the situation tended to become chaotic.

The moderator also had another important issue to look after: the situation for the presenter, who had to be protected from being too much drawn into the group, being asked too many questions, and being called into question or criticized by the group members. There was also a permanent risk that the work with the clinical material would turn into supervision of the presenter. This tended to happen now and then, sometimes in subtle ways and at other times more explicitly. The moderator had to be very attentive to these situations, since the presenter was easily troubled or took offence. No matter how interesting the discussion, if it was beyond the group task the moderator needed to point that out and sometimes stop the process rather firmly.

The presenter's role

The analysts who functioned as presenters had each been asked in advance to present clinical material from his or her own practice. Most were experienced analysts who were expected to guarantee a certain quality of work. However, these prerequisites did not alter the fact that many presenters were quite anxious about having their work discussed in the group.

One might expect that an opportunity to have one's own clinical work with a patient discussed at length among colleagues, all focusing their attention on understanding and describing this work, would be a rewarding experience. However, this was not always the case. To all presenters it meant taking the risk of being exposed. In addition to the possibility of being scrutinized in a negative way by the group members, it might also be a challenge to re-evaluate one's own work. Being forced to reconsider an established method of thinking and working is not an easy thing.

In spite of this, most of the presenters seem to have had a good experience of being in the group. The following statement is probably representative: 'I did feel respected and I did not feel unduly pushed, persecuted or unhelpfully intruded upon'. This promoted an open attitude in the group, and the dialogue between the presenter and the group members developed into a constructive and creative dialogue. When everything worked out well, new views and perspectives were added and this was much appreciated. One of the presenters made the following remark: 'I had not been able to anticipate how much I would be benefiting', and another: 'I appreciated the feel for detail and nuance which the group members gave to my work'.

However, some presenters tended to be somewhat restrained or defensive from the very beginning. In one case the presented clinical material was pre-elaborated to such an extent that it was difficult to discuss. This also happened when the analysis was concluded a long time ago or when the material had been discussed at length on previous occasions, even being published. In some of these cases the analyst's work was found to be 'impermeable'. The discussion was also limited when presenters didn't take notice of the group, were reluctant to accept comments from the group or actively criticized or objected to what was suggested. In such cases the result of the group work was quite meagre.

A different problem arose when the clinical material was an especially difficult patient or when it became evident that the analyst was in trouble or perhaps engaged in some kind of less than conscious enactment. This invited the group members to become engaged and involved. The outcome of this was dependent on whether the presenter was open to having the material seriously discussed. If not, the atmosphere gradually became tense and the group members became guarded and overcautious. The method of investigation and the grid-typology did not seem to alleviate the difficulty of these more extreme situations. One presenter had the following experience: 'I left this seminar with the feeling of being happy to have survived.'

However, if the presenter was implicitly asking for help, the group quickly complied with the request. This came about in an interesting way compared to conventional clinical groups, and it benefited greatly from the use of the grid. Instead of directly addressing the analyst, the group concentrated on the task of trying to find out and describing how the analyst was working. The analyst was sometimes spoken of in the third person, which emphasized the focus on the material. The presenter was free to reflect on what resulted from this work and often declared afterwards that the efforts had been helpful. One of the presenters expressed this in the following way:

> In some ways I felt that the experience went beyond my expectations. I was very impressed with how some of the group members stayed on task, and continually tried to understand what it was I was doing. Much of the time I felt they got how I was working and this matched my understanding of how I work.

The choice of case material and how it was presented varied considerably. Some analysts presented material from work with patients who were considered to function well in the analytic situation and the analysis with them was thought to be representative of their way of working. A few analysts brought material from work with very difficult patients or with patients belonging to the close professional environment. Members of the group thought that this was problematic or inadequate and that attention was directed away from the task: 'There was just too much about the patient'.

Further developments

The participants reacted in various ways to the different parts of the group work. Almost everyone was happy with the presentation of the case material and the free discussion of it, but when it came to the central task of assessing the analyst's interventions with the help of the grid opinions varied considerably. In fact, there were as many attitudes to this task as there were participants. Nonetheless the great majority of the group participants declared their interest in this part of the project and, in spite of difficulties with the grid–typology, they remained expectant and positive to various degrees. Many colleagues have returned year after year. Some participants (especially in Sorrento) were frustrated with the scoring procedure, and as a result sometimes became rather silent. One or two members of each group found the efforts tedious and meaningless and clearly conveyed their view that the grid was simply too blunt and not adequate for psychoanalysis.

Comments were made such as: 'I don't want to spend two days listening to such crap'. However, those who stayed with the group in spite of this and were able to be specific about their criticisms often made considerable contributions to developing the procedure and the instrument.

Notably, quite a few group members who were critical at the outset gradually changed their minds – either at the individual group meetings or in the long term – and became positive and even enthusiastic about the project. There were many reasons for this development. The special procedure for treating the presenter and his or her work was found to be grist to the mill in finding new ways of working with clinical material without exposing value judgements or having supervisory pretensions. It was gradually understood that the group procedure could be instrumental in a creative way in getting to grips with what the analyst was actually doing and thinking and at the same time avoiding the common pitfalls of ordinary clinical groups.

Another motive for the change of attitude was the experience that the development of the grid had advanced considerably and – although not fully developed – it was found helpful for a more systematic study of what was going on in a psychoanalytic session. Step I of the grid, which was developed initially and focused exclusively on classifying the analyst's interventions, was considered essential, but was soon found to be limited and to leave out important parts of the analyst's work. The addition of Step 2 meant an important extension of the instrument, but if the scoring of Step I had been difficult, the work with Step 2 was found to be even more exacting. Moreover, it was felt that in the work with Step 2 'certain members' biases came to the fore'. One participant expressed this dilemma in the following way:

> I think that, while drawing inferences about the presenter's implicit theory, the group members' own working models are evoked and claim their space: they are to be voiced. This results in the tendency for supervision and competitiveness to come to the fore.

However, on the whole, the motivation among the participants to tackle difficulties was quite strong and the problems occurring functioned at times as a motor to drive the process forward.

Group dynamics

The development of the group climate was essential to facilitate the work. It is no exaggeration to say that the atmosphere in the room and the relationships between the participants were the most important factors to ensure that the group worked in a constructive and creative way. One significant comment about the relationship between the specific discussion method and the task of understanding and comparing ways of work was: 'It depends more on the group than on the method'. However, the opposite is of course also true: a creative method is a means of enabling a good working atmosphere.

Being together for so many hours put heavy demands on the group members but was soon found to be reassuring. The long sessions were sometimes felt to be trying and energy consuming. The vigour of the group declined considerably during certain periods, as did the level of activity. In spite of this, most of the participants were positive about the timeframe and found that many advantages could be derived from it. It was recognized that 'the difficulties in gaining understanding while preserving differences and disagreements require quite a lot of patient working together over time'. The extended time was also found to 'promote understanding, reflection, learning, integration and internalization' and permit 'a better accumulation of associative evidence on behalf of or against different interpretive approaches and clinical orientations'. There were actually very few complaints about the long sessions and, when someone was critical, this was rather about matters for which there was not enough time. For instance, one participant found it 'difficult to catch the psychoanalytic process' because of lack of time. Another point made was that 'it's too complex for a medium sized group such as this to grapple with, and in the time available'. Thus, in achieving the group task the size of the group was obviously negatively correlated to the time at their disposal.

Along with interested and expectant attitudes to the work in the groups there was a streak of anxiety among its members, which was most pronounced at the outset. The unfamiliarity of the colleagues, the setting and the task all contributed to this. There was a fear of not being respected, of difficulties in maintaining differences, of not being able to articulate arguments, and of being criticized or let down. Another concern was how the group would function: would it be able to contain contradiction and differences, would there be a risk of serious confrontations or would the work in the group be experienced as just empty and uninteresting?

Group dynamics depended on several elements; such as the combination of participants, who was the moderator, the choice of presenter and what case material was presented. The various personalities of the group members, their nationalities, and the psychoanalytical cultures and traditions they represented constituted a network of interactions that gave every group unique characteristics. It is impossible to present a general picture of the course of events in the groups and what was enacted. Rather, I summarize the major dynamic issues and the challenge of achieving an adjustment between certain aspects of the group process.

Balancing activity

The structure of the group could be superficially compared to that of a symphony orchestra, with a conductor, a soloist and orchestra musicians. To create a harmonious piece of music it is necessary to find a good match between the different members of the orchestra and the musicians must respect each other's parts and way of playing. The same is true of the clinical groups, whose members were chosen to work together and expected to respect the presenter as well as being attentive to and accepting each other cooperating in a constructive way in trying to achieve the set objective.

A question of great importance for the group dynamics, which needed careful attention, was the adjustment of activity between the moderator, the presenter and the individual group members. In some groups the moderator was found to be too passive, giving too much space to free associative discussion among the members. This tended to be anxiety-provoking and to cause the work to lose focus. Interestingly enough, there were no complaints that the moderator was too active, and this seems to point to the need for a moderator as a driving force. One participant, probably quite representative, had the firm opinion that 'in the end, it is the leader who influences the group'.

As mentioned above, the activity of the presenter had to be carefully monitored by the moderator. The presenter's experience of the group greatly influenced the group dynamics and there was a constant watchfulness regarding the well-being of the presenter. Many participants felt that it was an advantage for the group ambiance if the presenting analyst was experienced and had an authoritative stance. Someone said: 'It is easier if the analyst is older and more self-confident'. If the presenter appeared to be unsure or anxious, this immediately made the group atmosphere more tense and the majority of members felt that they had to watch their tongue. Quite often one or two of them took on the role of defence counsel, which resulted in an unfortunate splitting of the group. These developments effectively inhibited a sincere exchange of ideas regarding the analyst's work, and the focus was instead gradually moved to discussing the patient. Another outcome could be 'the participants' spontaneous response of turning the discussion to a supervisory occasion'.

The activity among the group members had to be well balanced to achieve a good working atmosphere. The ideal situation, of everyone taking part in the group discussions, seldom materialized, although many groups functioned fairly well in this respect. However, due to language problems and varying degrees of clinical experience, the individual group members took and required different amounts of space. The important thing was to prevent this inequality from being too pronounced. If anyone became too dominant, this created uneasiness and irritation among the others and if anyone showed signs of lack of activity or was too silent this also had a disturbing effect.

One or two members in almost every group were well-known analysts. This affected the group dynamics from the start. There is always respect for colleagues who have created a distinct image for themselves and, depending on the extent to which such individuals emphasized their status, the group reacted accordingly. If the analyst was low key and respected the group task, the other members gradually took less notice of the situation and the analyst would be considered as on an equal footing with the others. In a few cases somebody wanted to be 'best in the class' and didn't listen to or take notice of the arguments of others. When this occurred it had a deleterious effect on the group atmosphere and seriously hindered the group from fulfilling its mission.

Curiosity and defensiveness

I will now provide an example to illustrate a main precondition of the groups' effective work is that presenters be open to possibilities and have some capacity to be curious about what may be discovered.

226

In one group the presenter was an elderly female analyst known to work according to a certain distinctive tradition and to have published a lot. She started her presentation by telling the group that the analysis was going well, but that it had come to a standstill and that the analysand did not take in her interventions.

It emerged in the workshop group that the analyst seemed mostly to follow her working model but occasionally she used theories that did not quite fit with it. In the discussion the group members tried to understand why the patient did not take any interest in the interventions. It was pointed out that the analysand was talking indirectly about somebody who does not understand what is said. However, the analyst rejected this idea and found it wrong and irrelevant. She just didn't agree with the group members.

In this situation the moderator strove to understand how the model is affecting the patient and the group members. The presenter then became increasingly defensive and unwilling to accomplish the task of finding out what inner models she actually was using in relation to which interventions she made. The situation developed into a battle in which the group members became frustrated and provocative in their arguments. The moderator had difficulties in intervening and protecting the presenter from the group's attacks.

At the end the presenter declared that she was not interested in what the group had to say and that she considered herself to be the expert on the case. Somebody pointed out that initially she had said that she was concerned about the development of the analysis, but now the presenter denied this. It was difficult to finish the group task and the session ended with much dissatisfaction.

Presenters' sensitivities also showed themselves when group members were silent for long periods. The presenters were especially attentive to this, since they could not exclude that suspicion that the silence was a sign of criticism or negative reactions. One of the presenting analysts noted: 'I realized it was only one-half of the group members that were regularly participating in the formulation of what I was doing'. Other remarks from presenters included: 'The silent people were stewing' and 'I remember people being totally silent; it worried me'.

The emotional climate

The emotional climate affected the group dynamics more than the intellectual atmosphere. This was manifested in several ways and originated either in the participants' emotional involvement or in the clinical material and the way it was being handled and presented. One group member reflected upon this:

> I think any group has a problem if one or more members have not enough affect-control in discussing such sensible work. We all know how sad/disappointed/disturbed/angry one can feel if one has the impression that the analyst does not really meet the unconscious level of the patient or the underlying sub-text of the communication between them.

Most of the groups had obvious problems in working with clinical material containing manifestations of aggression, destructiveness and despair. When confronted with such emotionally charged material the groups' reactions went in one of two directions. At one extreme people got terribly involved, the temperature in the discussion was raised, and the group lost sight of the task of studying and understanding the analyst's intervention. At the other extreme the group members experienced the material as so charged with emotions and affects that they felt it was impossible to discuss or that special consideration had to be shown towards the presenting analyst. There were, of course, many examples of cases in between. Cases where the analytic process was considered to be stagnant or interminable usually caused much involvement and turned out to be difficult to handle.

In one of the groups great emotions were stirred up because they did not understand and could not elucidate how the presenter made her interpretations. There were also problems in the efforts to find out what was wrong with the patient. Work in the group was made especially difficult by the presenter's declaration that categorization according to the grid-typology did not correspond to her idea of the analytic process. According to her there are no rules for making interventions and psychic change occurs spontaneously or through enactment and liveliness in the intense and sometimes even violent emotional contact between analyst and analysand. To most of the group members the analyst's interventions appeared to be countertransference reactions, the use of which the majority of the colleagues in the group believed to be adequate.

The group tried hard to understand the analyst's way of thinking and of conceiving the analytic situation. Many group members had difficulties in accepting the presenter's view that understanding is not a primary aim of psychoanalysis and that coming to insight is mainly an internal process. Moreover, the presenter evoked irritation because she didn't seem to be interested in making herself understood by the group. Possibly there was a parallel in what was going on in the group of chaotic movements and lack of understanding, and what the group members experienced of the intense interaction between the analyst and the patient. The group was simply not able to contain the anxiety (probably with psychotic elements) that was evoked by the material and by the way the presenter seemed to have handled it.

In many cases parallel processes seemed to be going on, and what was happening in the group mirrored that in the consulting room. One participant made the comment: 'It seems as if the groups may at times enact the process between the patient and the analyst'. Such a resonance seemed obvious in one of the groups. Early in the presentation, there was a complaint from a number of people that the room was too cold, and indeed, it was on the chilly side, but not unbearable. Shortly after this incident there was a comment by the patient in the session that was being reported, that he felt cold. In several groups, the flow of issues in the transference–countertransference interaction being transformed into the group interaction was more or less actively pursued in the efforts to enhance understanding.

Unanimity and disagreement

It was important for the group dynamics to find a balance between free discussion in the group and purposeful work with the task. It was essential to have both ingredients: free discussion alone did not allow for working with the grid-typology, and remaining strictly task-oriented tended to seriously impair the creative part of the work. The more successful groups were able to establish a good balance between freedom and structure, which resulted in a pleasant working atmosphere – with both seriousness and playfulness – that obviously helped them to do a decent job and accomplish the task.

A closely related issue, which seemed to be on nearly everyone's

229

mind, was the conflict between striving for consensus and similarities on the one hand and, on the other hand, allowing differences and diverging opinions to be developed and expressed in the groups. One impression is that in several groups people felt that there was too much understanding and agreement and too little confrontation and contradictions. This comes out clearly in several statements made by group members: 'The need for cohesion prevents people from confronting more different approaches', 'It got a little too cosy', 'The group agreement did not allow enough room for criticism', 'The existing differences stayed more or less in the background'.

Some participants were overtly critical or hostile towards this phenomenon in statements like: 'It would be unreal and unhelpful for members who have strong convictions on some point of theory and clinical technique to deny them expression by means of some dead-pan pseudo-polite inauthentic expression' or 'I expected more of a challenging clinical discussion with other participants voicing differ-ent points of view'. Such critical reactions to the structure and the rules under which the workshop was conducted often gradually disappeared when the task was better understood.

To give the full picture, most members appreciated the lack of confrontation in the groups and found this both reassuring and con-structive. This was evident in comments such as 'the lack of rivalry and open conflict lessened anxiety', 'I liked the friendly atmosphere' and 'it's good to translate different psychoanalytic jargons'. Many members stated that they greatly enjoyed working together: they appreciated the group cohesion and liked the tolerance and feeling of trust in the familiarity that was developed. The members in question felt that the group cohesion allowed the work to be serious, product-ive and focused on the task. This was probably true to some extent but, at the same time, many of the very positive and polite attitudes seem to reflect a strong idealization of the group.

In summary, there was obviously a dilemma in the working groups: they tried to find a balance in the discussions between unanimity and divergence of opinion. The problem with the appearance of criticism and conflicting ideas is that the discussion can quickly move from being interesting and constructive to becoming scathing and unhelp-ful. In the latter case people easily take offence, which prevents the dialogue from being fruitful and creative. However, without diverg-ing opinions and a lively discussion there is a risk that the group atmosphere becomes empty and the exchange of ideas loses vitality.

Connected to this is the fear of legitimizing clinical work of doubtful validity – allowing that 'anything goes'.

However, it seems that this problem has diminished slightly during the development of the project and with the improvement of the method of study. With a better instrument to categorize interventions and to describe the analyst's inner template there is perhaps less need to create a personal image for oneself and it may be easier to attain a better mutual understanding. In one of the recent groups such a development seemed to be under way: 'We succeeded in finding a respectful but authentic and passionate confrontation between very different models'.

The efforts to make the group concentrate on the task of studying the presenting analyst's work were supported by making the members responsible for reporting on how this analyst was functioning according to the categories describing the analyst's inner template, i.e. Step 2 of the grid. In addition to the advantages dependent on the improvement of the instrument, the introduction of this working order had a marked effect on the group, which became calmer and more task-oriented.

Doubts about the aim

One important contributory factor influencing the group dynamics was the existence of a certain element of insecurity about the overall aim of the entire project – a point touched on by Helmut Hinz and Manuel Fernández Criado in reporting their survey of criticisms in Chapter 5. In spite of all the declarations made both orally and in written documents there seems to have remained in some participants a slight uncertainty about whether there was an implicit, perhaps more profound and devious purpose within the project. Most group members didn't ponder over this: they didn't bother, or reacted by pursuing a wait-and-see policy. However, when the question of the aim was mentioned and singled out, it tended to cause an element of suspicion and there was a breeding ground for persecutory as well as paranoid reactions.

Everybody perceived that the group work might be part of a research project. The use of tape-recorders during the group work substantiated this notion. Some made an issue of it being an 'empirical research project': they were quite prejudiced about this and found it incompatible with psychoanalytical objectives. There were also worries about the project being 'academic' or 'experimental' or that it might be used for unknown or unwanted purposes. In connection with this, the initiator of the project, David Tuckett (DT), came into focus, both as project leader and in person. A lot of difficult matters occurring in the group were projected onto him and what he was thought to represent and what he aimed at. Moreover, there was also oedipal content: DT and his wife, who was taking part in the project as a moderator, were subject to various fantasies. What were his (their) motives and intentions for bringing about the project idea, and what was he (were they) supposed to do with the results? 'We surely are DT's guinea-pigs', one of the group members exclaimed with a mixture of approval and disgust, and no one seemed to be totally immune to such fantasies.

The effect on the group dynamics was easy to see. The notion that the project might have suspect or unknown aims made people want to rebel, and there were quite a few jokes, such as: 'We are put in the situation of being teenagers' and 'Let's do something else than what DT suggested'. When this happened there was a tendency of more or less of regression in the whole group. In some cases this resulted in efforts to create a split between the moderator and the research leader (DT), the former being considered 'the good guy' and the latter 'the bad guy'. The moderator had to watch for these situations since it was tempting to refer all problems to DT and thereby avoid the responsibility of making the group work with what was at stake.

Post-group opinions

Some aspects of the experience of participating in the groups were sparsely expressed or articulated during the group sessions, but were mentioned after the group work had been finished. Some of them were communicated via email. The opinions presented on these occasions were often a summing up of what each participant felt they had gained from taking part in the group work. Thus, the following remarks are important in contributing to a comprehensive picture of the experiences of participating in the workshop groups.

Some comments focused on the importance the project might have for the psychoanalytical profession due to the 'de-idealization of psychoanalysis', 'the working on the gap between theory and technique' and 'translating different psychoanalytical jargons', 'improving clinical expertise', 'the instrument being developed was of great value for clinical understanding and in clinical seminars, however probably questionable for research'.

Other comments concerned the positive experience of having participated in the groups: 'the brain-storming was exceptionally useful', 'the benign interventions were of benefit for members and presenters', 'a work without the usual quarrel between different schools', 'the group having had a supervisory function without being supervisory', 'the coming together as foreigners to work for a common purpose', 'afterwards being friendly foreigners again without further discussion and gossiping'.

A third category of comments were about the more personal gains: 'it's given me a better self-observation', 'it has made me think over my clinical technique', 'it may have contributed to improving my analytical skill and promoted my personal growth', 'it has been an exercise in psychoanalytic listening', 'it has given me the possibility of sharing the lonely and often arduous work with patients'.

After having taken part in the comparative clinical methods project and learned about the work done there, some group members tried to experiment with the same approach in their clinical practice at home. Those who did so had personal experience of how working with the grid-typology had initiated a serious scrutiny of their own work and influenced them to a new understanding of their practice. Some participants also expressed the belief that the grid could be introduced as 'an excellent educational tool' and could be used in training seminars: 'I came home with new ideas for my clinical seminars with students'. Some of these ideas are taken up in Chapter 9.

9

Some surprises
A new style for case discussion?

Roberto Basile and Antonino Ferro (Italy)

From the very beginning, we have been struck by the high number of people willing to participate in the workshops organized by the Working Party on Comparative Clinical Methods. Demand has consistently outstripped availability of places. Many colleagues return either every year or at least when practical circumstances permit. Where does the special appeal of the experience of the working groups lie?

It is as if the groups had answered a hidden demand within the psychoanalytic community. Their success has been far greater than expected. Not only have they enriched research in psychoanalysis, but also the many colleagues who were participants in the groups have been enthusiastic about their experience.

Among other comments on the special qualities of the groups' experience we would like to quote the following about the Athens meeting in 2006:

> My expectation was to find something helpful for the task of teaching clinical psychoanalysis to the students, and the experience was very rich in this way. In this group the position of the presenter was respected and protected, all the participants worked hard to think about the analytical situation, and to think about psycho-analytical means, each in his theoretical way. A real comparing method was used in the workshop, helped by the lines traced in the 'method'. Particularly useful was the task of selecting a place for every analytic intervention; this task revealed the internal model of

234

every participant, in very cooperative, friendly way We had the feeling of the unity of psychoanalysis, beyond our difference of theory . . . I came home with new ideas for my clinical seminars with the students.

A difference with the ordinary supervision group

The difference of these groups from a group supervision carried out with an acknowledged supervisor may help to explain the enthusiasm for this work. No matter how tactful and discreet supervisors try to be, their own approach remains inevitably present. There is a line of strong thought, people know more or less what to expect and the group is formed around this. A follower of Klein or Kohut will tend to choose an analyst who will confirm his basic theoretical assumptions. Some psychoanalytic schools, such as the British one, have made this into a theoretical principle, taking the view that continuity between analysis and supervision should be retained so as not to engender confusion. Unfortunately this practice has sometimes resulted in the establishment of schools of thought of a sectarian type, leading to a hierarchy of power within psychoanalytic institutes. It has also made it difficult to question or investigate the supervisor's knowledge.

By contrast, in the groups you never know who is going to be working by your side, you have no idea of the identity of the analyst and limited influence over who will be the chairman. In our opinion, this minimizes the danger to group work which sometimes comes when participants idealize the supervisor-conductor of the group.

It is fascinating to work with people whose culture, technique and emotionality are very different. There is also a pluralism of tongues which – although the official language is usually English – becomes a pluralism of psychoanalytic tongues. Participants seem to feel freer out of their usual geographical and cultural borders. The relative lack of idealization and the reduced concern about orthodoxy increases the democratic circulation of ideas and the symmetry of the colleagues at work. We may say that it facilitates the constitution of what Bion (1952) would call a 'work group' and it also reduces the chance of creating groups built on 'basic assumptions'.

Normally, in group supervision, it is considered sufficient to work for an hour and a half. The difference with these longer meetings is

235

quite remarkable. Participants work for up to twelve hours on two or three sessions, and tend to end up spending a lot of free time together where communication continues informally. The interval between the first and the second day of work often allows the budding of new thoughts. Working for so many hours together seems to us to create a collective mentality – perhaps a group orientated towards what Bion would call K (knowledge). Coffee breaks, mealtimes and evenings are sometimes used to continue the talk in small subgroups that later bring their comments back to the big group. Conviviality and digestive pauses become, so to speak, fully entitled elements of the setting.

Another element that contributes to the groups' success is the structural organization. The chairing of the groups is firm, but control is exerted over the procedure rather than the content of ideas. The moderators are like traffic controllers. They do not decide about the final destination of people's thoughts, but limit themselves to regulating the flux.

The introduction of the two levels of the grid (the various steps) has opened up new perspectives. An analogy might be the passage from macroscopic anatomy to a study made with the help of an optical or even an electronic microscope. Participants have often reported that sometimes the group comes up with surprising and enlightening answers to the questions being posed. The grid seems to us to be an instrument that makes 'play' possible. It affords the pleasure of playing a game with many rules that seem to facilitate rather than preventing unpredictable developments.

Another unusual aspect of the groups is the fact that in supervision the supervisee is under observation as a junior, but in the case of the groups the presenter is often a very experienced colleague. The usual modalities of participation are reversed. Participants do not tell the presenter what to do but try to learn about how he or she works. This affords an opportunity to deepen some aspects of theory which are normally well known by hearsay but which may not constitute an aspect of our actual praxis. The groups are not just a chance to learn about other people's models: they also enable the participants to come to know their own models better, because the definition of the limits of others' models also clarifies the limits of one's own. Moreover, they help us to uncover the common ground among various therapies versus their specific characteristics, along the lines – we could say – of the article by Wallerstein (1988) entitled 'One psychoanalysis or many?'

The experience for presenters

Obviously this can be true also for the presenter. Here is a sample of a presenter's commentary on her participation in a group:

> The experience was new, and different from other experiences I have encountered in the past while presenting clinical material. It was quite an exceptional event for me.
>
> The first stage is a feeling of immense narcissistic pleasure. A large group of people, my colleagues, brilliant, experienced, and estimated, is perusing 'my' material. All are busy in an attempt to get inside my head. I see myself reflected in the eyes of some other persons – reflected in the eyes of someone else. The reflection is in the eyes of colleagues – brothers walking together, that is, on a peer level, on the same eye level. The reflections come back to me and as I see myself reflected in the thought of the others; my image feels familiar to me. I feel known, recognized and understood. It is like being in a bath of mirrors. The reflections are realistic, not idealistic, and not enlarged, so the experience has credibility. Although I am presenting an analysis in which I am stuck and lost, the experience is pleasant. It is so satisfying, that for a moment I want to stay in this bath of mirrors, simultaneously, however the thought processes are working. I am alert. My work is seen from both a close up and distant perspective, concurrently from the interior and from the exterior. New ideas came to my mind.
>
> This method enabled us to test out and observe how a particular analyst does psychoanalytic work. Differences became an interesting, intriguing question that enabled the participants to ponder each one for himself about his own work. Out of the meticulous observation of my work, the participants in the workshop started checking the validity and accuracy of their theory of technique. Criticism certainly was present in the discussion, although it served as a tool that assisted in thinking and examination, and not as part of condemnation of the different other.

Rights to citizenship

The decision made at the inception of the project to treat every theoretical and technical position within the IPA as worthy of respect was very important. It helped to engender a working atmosphere that was free of subtle moral or pedagogical condemnation. Rights to citizenship have been conferred in a really precious way.

The working method in these groups is democratic but rigorous. Nobody is thought to hold the ultimate key to a case. The method allows interest and curiosity in other points of view but does not attempt to gloss over differences: one is there to hear and understand various points of view. We may say that the only truth to be sought is to understand the way one works and the reasons for it. All participants contribute to the development of this understanding.

Training supervision and the new method

Traditional supervision is part of analytic training. The candidate needs to be taught what the analytical tools are and to learn how to use them. It has didactic elements. But the need to convey basic tools is not among the goals of the groups. They begin rather with an enquiry into what tools are being used and how they might work. While inexperienced candidates do of course need to learn, we have sometimes wondered if the method of the clinical groups might have a role to play in traditional supervision as well. The aim of supervision is to create a learning process for the candidate and one way this can happen is by learning about what one is doing just as much as from learning what one is not. In this respect both traditional supervision and the comparative groups have aims in common; it is worth reflecting on how the former might learn from the latter.

Very schematically, in traditional supervision there is a tendency to believe that the one who knows teaches something to the one who doesn't know. The dynamics are, so to speak, those of transferring knowledge from the container of the teacher into that of the student. From that viewpoint the student is in a fairly passive position.

Curiously enough, this position is similar to the model of what we might call one-person psychoanalysis or the idea of analysis by saturated interpretations. It may have its place but one of us (Ferro, 2002) has called attention to the fact that we shouldn't assume the only strategy available to the analyst is to make saturated interpretations, which is to say interpretations of the transference or of the patient's history. Ferro believes that in addition to the value such interpretations can have, there is a further and essential value to be gained from interpretations made 'within' the transference; open, unsaturated, narrative; all those sometimes called 'weak' or narrative interpretations which can contribute to mental functioning. For long periods, or during certain periods of an analysis, sharing the experience can be more important than elucidating/decoding the content of associations or the transference phantasies. It is the capacity for unison, together with the negative capacities of the analyst, which allow the development of containment.

Just as saturated interpretations have often been focused on as problematic because of their intrusive characteristics, also in traditional supervision there is a risk of intrusiveness; which may turn the potential knowledge of the supervision into '−K' as Bion would call it. We might think this is the case when we have a very saturated supervision, that is to say, when the supervisor essentially talks in terms of what the supervisee should do or say. We think that these are the occasions where humiliation may outweigh the process of learning and internalizing.[1]

As discussed in earlier chapters, all clinical discussions − even or especially ones among colleagues at the same level and with similar points of view − tend to veer towards showing the presenting analysts how they *should* have worked; what they have overlooked, what are their mistakes and shortcomings, and how far they did or did not work like me. Examples were given in Chapters 1 and 2 of discussions in journals and conferences. A further one experienced by one of us can be found in the *International Journal of Psychoanalysis* in the 'Analyst at Work' section (Basile, 2006; Frank, 2006; Guimarães Filho, 2006). Among the commentaries on the analyst's technique one encounters expressions like: 'our understanding is exactly the opposite'; 'my view of the material clearly differs'; 'I wonder what may have encouraged Basile to not see this as resulting from . . .'; '[I, the commentator, stress

---

[1] Editorial note added by David Tuckett: At this stage in the book an alert reader may have noticed the many references to Bion's work that are scattered through the various chapters and this, perhaps, deserves comment. One of the author's of Chapter 9, Antonino Ferro, is very well known for his expertise in Bion's work and had made extensive use of Bion's thinking in his own creative elaborations. However, the Step 2 method is not intentionally based on Bion's thinking, just as the Step 1 grid in fact has little to do with Bion's 'grid' (Bion, 1962). Nonetheless, it seems clear that in several respects Bion's thinking (not just on group processes) has clearly provided a facilitating framework for comparative work undertaken by a range of European colleagues, all of whom come from very different traditions. What it is that allows Bion's work to be helpful for a comparative project to colleagues from several different traditions is an interesting but open question.

the] different value I place on the patient's phantasies as well as to a different understanding of the countertransference'; (Frank, 2006: 637). Or again it is said that the presenting analyst (Basile, 2006) relies on the Bionian 'patient as the analyst's best colleague' using in the commentator's words a 'simplified epistemology' (Guimarães Filho, 2006: 641).

In a recent clinical group of colleagues we know some material was presented where the patient told the story of having invited her mother for dinner and having cooked green beans. The mother comments nastily, 'Green beans?!?' 'Yes, why, don't you like them?' asks the daughter. 'Oh no, no . . . I like them,' replies the mother eventually with an embarrassed voice. This passage received a number of comments such as:

- 'I am a Kleinian analyst and I can't refrain from associating the colour green to the idea of envy . . .'
- 'You should have interpreted the patient's inability to tolerate the differences between her and the mother . . .'
- 'You should have interpreted here the sense of disappointment of your patient before the mother's reaction . . .'

Similarly, a colleague who participated in the Athens groups compared the style of discussion in the groups to that of some psychoanalytic societies and commented:

How do we manage the dialogue between us? A discussion in our society – both theoretical discussions as well as clinical material – is often turning to a battle. Very quickly, the various opinions and thoughts turn into a sort of absolute 'Truth'. As if there is a sole, correct way to carry out psychoanalysis. The space for new thought and learning becomes completely closed and the discussion becomes a combat about absolute justice. Primitive thought processes take over the discussion; words are becoming concrete expressions of 'gospel truth' or weapons used to overwhelm the other. There is pressure to impose the one 'correct' way, and a devaluation of different analytic point of view. It is as if a sort of threatening presence hovers about, considerably bullying, a presence that we would call 'Analytical Shared Idealistic Ego', a sort of all knowing deity, thus there is almost no room for simple, probing, partial statements.

We do not mean to imply that no such tendencies exist in the new groups, but they are often more contained.

Again, comparing the two experiences one may say that traditional supervision does allow people to hear interesting new ideas but perhaps it tends to ignore their origins. The comparative groups by contrast are strong on finding the method the participant actually uses and then trying to draw it out to enable the participant to reflect on it and develop areas where there are issues. In this sense these groups seem to us to have an approach that could be described in Bion's language as without 'memory and desire': participants must start with an open mind and don't have anything to demonstrate beforehand, they usually know nothing of their presenter and they have to go in search of the unknown. This can be an extremely attractive and thrilling experience, like travelling in an unknown country. One might object that the groups have a very precise format, but it has to be understood as being like the limits defining a field of play, within which children can play in safety as much as they like and make all the discoveries they can. This searching attitude seems to us to be more reliably evoked using the new methods and this might be a reason for their success.

Synthetically we could say that the supervisee tries to discover not only an understanding but also a whole possible model of working and a possible identification of his own psychoanalytical identity with it. In the usual 'law of supervision' there is more of an asymmetry (at least in that moment) and a request for help, for help to understand, made to someone who is expected to know the answers. The supervisee wants to understand a specific point of difficulty in his or her work, or make an exploration in someone else's model of working.

In the comparative groups the situation is inverted: help is still provided, but only in order to identify the implicit models. The presenter in the groups is like someone who goes to a good painter or photographer for a portrait that may unveil hidden aspects of his or her way of being at work. In these groups there is a stronger emphasis on the analysts, on their model, on the choices they say they are making and on the ones they really do make without a judgement. The personal views of participants interfere minimally, working rather as a stimulus to better understanding. Everybody is invited to dream what the analyst 'dreams' of his or her patient and to work as though with the analyst during those moments. We wonder whether this could not become an ingredient also in more traditional supervisions. Imre Szecsödy (who acknowledges being stimulated by Tuckett, 2004) writes that 'rather than to explain for the candidate, the supervisor should try to explore and help the candidate to discover information he tried to avoid and ward off using different defences to do so' (Imre Szecsödy, personal communication, 2006). He stresses that supervision should turn into 'a learning alliance' with the supervisee. 'Learning alliance' seems to us aptly to describe the experience of working in the groups and much of its surprising appeal. The groups started with the aim of refining our understanding of our clinical models. Unexpectedly we have developed an innovative method of generating new thoughts about psychoanalytic ideas. This method has made us a bit freer than before.

Reflection and comparison
Some final remarks

David Tuckett (UK)

Psychoanalysis is not psychoanalysis just because two people are talking on a regular basis or one is lying on a couch and the other behind. To be psychoanalysis there has to be a setting, a frame. This necessarily implies a theoretical structure defining it, which comes from outside. In other words, as Dana Birksted-Breen wrote in her introductory foreword, the two-person situation has a theory as its 'third object'. This is why the theories underlying how the analyst listens, thinks about the patient and intervenes, which may vary with practitioners but must always be there in at least implicit form, are an inherently necessary feature: defining, so to speak, the model with which the practitioner works.

In the late 1980s, Wallerstein (1988, 1990), after about two decades of what had become known in the United States as theoretical pluralism, began to inquire into the common ground in psychoanalytic practice. He emphasized transference and resistance, only to spark an immediate response that they were understood very differently in different places (Schafer, 1990; see also Abrams, 1989).

In a sense the project described in this book began from Wallerstein's question, but we have attempted to explore the matter more empirically. We also wished to mobilize the psychoanalytic community not only to become more interested in clarifying what each psychoanalyst was doing but also to try to understand and communicate better with each other about it. In Chapter 1, I outlined the many negative consequences for the creative development of psychoanalysis as a credible and specific discipline; if we are unable to define what psychoanalysis is even among ourselves in a world of ever increasing psychotherapeutic approaches and a blurring of boundaries between psychoanalysis and psychotherapy.

The project started in Europe, where psychoanalysis is practised in more than twenty languages and with very different traditions. The method we have described in this book to explore and compare differences in psychoanalytic work evolved as we attempted the task. It was not intended to answer any questions in a definitive way. Rather, we have tried to find a psychoanalytically satisfactory method to draw comparisons that were secure enough to enable a well-informed debate. As a first step we needed a way to discuss among ourselves and then to generate a clear and comparable description of the range of different answers different psychoanalysts might then be considered to give to questions; such as how do we know when what is happening between two people should be called psychoanalysis, what is (and is not) a psychoanalytic process and what is (and is not) a psychoanalytic interpretation?

From the outset we thought that to be meaningful these questions could not be approached only from a theoretical angle (trying to define the specificity of psychoanalysis theoretically by drawing on authoritative texts) or from the angle of the setting (frequency of sessions, etc.) but empirically. In Chapter 2, Paul Denis argued how difficult it is to make any progress in understanding difference unless one is empirical.

We started from the initial assumption, therefore, that those we invited to present would be considered exemplary; what they could describe to us showed what happens in practice when a psychoanalyst is 'doing psychoanalysis'. We then invited experienced colleagues from different traditions to present their work to groups of colleagues from many different traditions, who would try to understand what they did. Through the ensuing discussions we hoped to record and abstract the multiplicity of their ways of working and in doing so to find a way to recognize and describe the underlying models of working which might be expected to lie, usually implicitly, behind the different practices described, eventually identifying the broad outlines of various 'types'. Chapters 3 and 4 have described our early attempts to do this in workshop groups and the often unexpected difficulties we experienced.

Two main problems were encountered early on. First, there was the matter of what might be called overvision – the tendency when discussing someone else's clinical material to introduce competing ideas about what the presenting analyst should have done or not done and largely to override or even deride what the presenter him or herself was doing, however politely. Second, there was the absence of shared meaning for many common terms – for example, transference, resistance, interpretation or even unconscious – and a similar absence of any reliable template against which to make comparisons.

Freud himself modified his theories and did so several times, notably after 1920. As Helmut Hinz discussed in Chapter 5, some of Freud's ideas, such as those concerning the transcription of memory and of multiple determination, multiple function and multiple meaning, make clear that psychoanalytical material is inherently polyvalent in meaning so that it can be responded to in different ways. Even leaving aside the different ways in which Freud is understood when translated into other languages and cultures it does not make sense to talk of one psychoanalytic method. In making the initial assumption that we would treat the presenter's work as exemplary, therefore, we attempted to develop a way of working which would consider differences in understanding and proceeding not as a liability but as an asset.

Paul Denis's argument in Chapter 2 (supplemented by the comments made in Chapter 9) makes the point that clinical discussion has often not respected difference and instead can become a competition between models. To avoid this in the groups it was important to be clear that the presenter's description of what happened in the session constituted the 'facts' and that the task was to explore the presenter's underlying model that generated them. Debate about what might 'really' be happening based on other viewpoints or what is 'really' psychoanalysis is postponed until a later stage of the project when many analysts and discussion groups have reached a sense of understanding about different analysts' models.

One place to start in reviewing the method we evolved is with this crucial decision to ask groups to make the assumption that the psychoanalyst presenting was doing psychoanalysis. The extent of the challenge this essential decision presented within groups has been described – particularly in Chapters 3 and 4 but also in Chapter 8, where it is made clear that although our method may take things forward it by no means eliminates the problem. It seems that emotional factors necessarily intrude in psychoanalytic discussion groups and it is then not easy to accept some differences. Whether emotions are generated by complex aspects of individual group members' responses to the patient's pathology or by the emergence (through an experience of hitherto suppressed differences) of hitherto unconscious implicit ideas about how analysts should treat patients, there is a tendency for the work to be undermined by moral judgements.

The tendency to overvision, the lack of shared terminology or of the conceptual means to make comparisons and the emotional climate that could be generated in the groups, all threatened their capacity to do the comparison work. To help the groups to stay on task we eventually evolved the method (as laid out in Chapter 6) with its three components: the initial assumption that the presenter is a psychoanalyst; attention to the different roles of moderator, presenter and group member; and the sequence of steps (−1, 0, 1, 2). However, even in these circumstances the groups have still sometimes struggled to make the initial assumption. I suspect that this will also have been the case for many readers of this book as they worked through some of the clinical examples.

To judge by the reactions of some colleagues who were kind enough to read early drafts of the manuscript, it is easier to go along with the principle of accepting that the presenter is a psychoanalyst than it is to put it into practice. It seems that it is often tempting to think, 'Yes, but . . . surely not that way of working', perhaps because it is felt to be superficial or implausible; or perhaps because the analyst's response, missing this or that meaning, is felt to be mainly the result of countertransference enactment, or ignores fundamental problems the patient or analyst have with each other, etc. In fact one thoughtful reader wondered if perhaps we had still not learned reliably to select good presenters!

In anticipation of such potential responses I want to emphasize, therefore, that since Helsinki in 2004, every presenter has been not only a respected clinician in his or her own local context but also in most cases also a training or supervising analyst or equivalent. They were asked to present work they thought showed a 'live psychoanalytic process' at work and believe they did so. Thus, like it or not, the work presented by the psychoanalysts in this and the companion volume in which we will present descriptions of the main ways we found people working, is psychoanalysis as it is practised nowadays – in fact 'exemplary' psychoanalysis, which is judged within local groups to be that with which candidates should identify. The starting assumption that the presenters are doing psychoanalysis is essential if we are to have an informed debate about what we actually do and learn to talk to each other about it and discuss it better.

The second key component of our method has been to define and stress the specialist role of moderator. The moderators have worked on evolving the method and have themselves come to articulate the work, gradually learning to be very careful to define their roles and those of presenter and group members as discussed in Chapters 1, 6 and 8.

The third element of the method was the introduction of formal structure, as laid out in detail in Chapter 6. There is an initial period of free discussion but then there are the two steps. Step 1 focuses on the interventions the presenters made and by requiring the group to explore each of them in terms of their function according to six possibilities focuses attention on the detail of the work task: on the way the analysts work rather than on the patient and the clinical problem. Step 1 involves a process of deconstruction. Step 2, on the other hand, involves construction; going deeper by using what has emerged so far to try to tease out the main elements of the analyst's approach. Remembering the idea that the psychoanalytic session involves two people talking to each other and a theory, Step 2 requires the group to try to work out what the analyst's theory is – conceived as the internal template or model which is producing the analyst's way. Each of five linked dimensions are explored to build an overall picture: this is the analyst's explanatory model, the set of theories that make best sense of all the things the analyst says he or she is trying to do.

The term 'explanatory model' could be misunderstood. It is not meant to imply that psychoanalytic practice is mainly conscious, cognitive or explanatory, for instance. As discussed in earlier chapters it is a social anthropological term with a specific intellectual heritage for understanding subtle human activities such as those concerned with religion, illness, managing misfortune or cosmology (Kleinman, 1980; Tuckett, 1993; Tuckett et al., 1985). An explanatory model is a conceptual device to help to explain to an observer underlying but often observable patterns of human activity based on implicit beliefs. It starts from the proposition (perhaps not so foreign to psychoanalysis) that most things that don't make sense from the outside do make sense if understood from the inside. People, especially those from different cultural backgrounds, often have very different ways of understanding many things – for example illness, its consequences, and how best to treat it. They have a different explanatory model. Thus, to understand presenters whose technique is 'foreign', it is necessary to hold one's own ideas in check and to understand their explanatory model – their complex mix of implicit and explicit underlying beliefs and feelings about what is appropriate that cause them to act as they do. A psychoanalyst would include within such beliefs ideas relevant to his or her everyday technique amounting to a theory of language, or development or of what the unconscious is, and so on.

An explanatory model is only a conceptual aid; a way of drawing together diverse elements and constructing them to make sense of one analyst's way of working and compare it to another's. It is important to be clear that the two-step method is not aimed at understanding what the analysts 'really' did. If that element was to be introduced then there would be a return to external judgement from a view external to the analyst. Rather, based on what the analyst says during the presentation and the ensuing discussion, the group tries to construct a way to understand what the analyst has done in his or her own terms; the analyst might not have put it quite like the group does and may even be surprised to realize it. Nonetheless, by the end of the process the analyst should recognize the overall description as one that makes sense, in the context of the evidence of what was said and done, of what the analyst tries to do. The method looks at the preconscious model rather than the dynamically unconscious one.

The question of what analysts might be considered really to know, understood from the framework of their implicit dynamically unconscious theories, is an interesting one. But in this project we want to distinguish and compare various modes of trying to work psychoanalytically and later to debate them; we are not trying to explain why an analyst chooses to use the approach he does.

Many analysts cannot easily actually articulate their theory of how they work – they just do it. The two-step method helps them to become clearer about what they seem to be trying to do and also helps them to see who their analytical relatives are – in other words, into which of the various ways of working they fit and what the potential strengths and weaknesses of each method may be. The assumption throughout the project has been by assuming that presenters are working psychoanalytically and then trying to describe what they are doing, we can begin to see what the differences are and to create the conditions for a better debate.

To try to convey some idea of what we construct as a result of Step 2 and to indicate how we do seem to arrive at a description of several different families of psychoanalytic working, using the comparative method we evolved, I will now try briefly to describe three of the cases we have examined in the last few years and try to bring out some of the systematic differences.

Three psychoanalysts

The three analysts I will discuss (whose patients are named in parentheses along with the number of years they had been in treatment at the time of the first session presented) are Frances (Deidre, 4), Tom (Paul, 9) and Louise (Georgina, 4). I will begin by summarizing the groups' accounts of the analysts' ideas about what was wrong with the patients, and move on to describe what they thought were the psychoanalysts' models of how psychoanalysis would work in these situations. This will lead on to how the analysts were thought to be trying to further a psychoanalytic process and to what the groups thought were their different ideas about the analytic situation itself.

What was wrong?

All three patients were described in some way as depressed but also as somewhat narcissistic in some of their symptom characteristics. They all appeared to suffer from difficult historical circumstances through which the emotional situations they had been exposed to in childhood had left a mark. Their analyst's formulations of the ways these difficulties create problems in their current relationships and with the analysts are interestingly different – perhaps more different than the underlying situations; but this is mere supposition.

Frances: Deidre (age 47) is conceived as narcissistically depressed about her relationships and difficult to reach in the analytic relationship. She is unmarried and without children. She is frightened of and tends to deny her own vulnerability and has tended to laugh at or to reject Frances' work with sarcasm. Frances sees Deidre as traumatized by the way her family handled feelings and its own past (holocaust) history. For Frances, Deidre is entrenched in a defensive structure against severe pain with, perhaps, underlying psychotic anxieties. She thinks Deidre uses intellectualization defences to try to stem being overwhelmed by feelings and threatened by fragmentation – represented by images of worms. Deidre is also the victim of harsh self-accusations and a considerable despair. Frances sees the early somewhat mysterious family experience and the circumstances behind an equally mysterious end of a previous lengthy analysis (with a male analyst about whom Deidre is very critical) as connected but not very approachable; except in the patient's terms.

Tom: Paul (age 50) has been seriously depressed with rivalry and potency problems for many years. By the time of the presentation he is much improved and he and Tom are thinking about termination. Tom sees his depression as a result of classic conflicts of ambivalence arising from a wartime childhood in which his father (towards whom he has much hitherto unconscious hatred and rivalry) was away at war and Paul was left with a somehow problematic mother. In his relationship to Tom, as formerly to business partners, a constantly suppressed rivalry and hatred exists alongside complex feelings of love and submission.

Louise: Georgina (age 50) is seen as a lonely and depressed woman, unmarried and without children and always abandoned by her lovers. Her professional life is unsatisfying and she longs for relationships. She has ideas of suicide. For three years the analysis was a 'deadly' experience that almost led Louise to give up – in fact she might have done so but for a consultation with a senior colleague to whom she was thinking of referring her. Louise found that her interpretations were scorned as 'useless'. Nonetheless, Louise has always felt that somewhere Georgina is alive and this feeling was renewed after Louise had sought consultation. Georgina's feelings cannot be verbalized and Louise believes her problems stem from her very early childhood, about which little was known in the first years. Louise sees Georgina as dominated by a hatred and envy of life (conceived by her as a manifestation of Freud's death instinct) so that relations to objects must be destroyed and unknown. Liveliness is obliterated and aggression is also generally unknown.

How analysis works, listening to the unconscious and furthering the process

The different way the three analysts thought, psychoanalytically, about what was wrong with their patients, is one element that differentiated their explanatory models in terms of the ways that they thought psychoanalysis works for such patients and the ways they construct the process through listening and intervening.

Frances' idea of how psychoanalysis could work for Deidre lays emphasis on providing what can be considered an alternative 'new' experience to what she had in her childhood and in her previous analysis. This means Frances must create a 'safe' space where difficult things can be talked about directly rather than avoided because dangerous and frightening. That in turn requires being able to avoid being experienced as the 'old' and particularly the 'rejecting' object and also being careful to survive Deidre's angry attacks without retaliating. The hope is that over time Deidre will gradually understand but meanwhile there is a constant risk that she may become overwhelmed with her affects; so Frances believes in caution and in sidestepping 'old wounds'; especially from the previous analysis and at least for now.

In terms of the way Frances **listens to the unconscious** issues in the patient's mind, she mainly focuses on possible meanings in Deidre's words in the context of her own feelings; attending in quite a fixed way but attentively listening out for what she senses as shifts in the patient's affect in sessions and trying to be aware of how the patient moves away from being in contact with various feeling states. One session began with Deidre telling a dream and then associating to a range of people. She continued that she had seen two other people with knapsacks on their backs looking homeless and mentally ill. Frances hears this material as expressing feelings about how she neglects Deidre and so makes her feel murderous. When she says this to Deidre, Deidre laughs and says she has been upset about a psychiatrist who was brutally murdered recently and other violent situations. She also thinks of a Jew who was tortured and killed by Arabs. All of this is heard by Frances as continuing the theme. In Frances' mind, Deidre's further associations to university classes and also to Frances' own husband continue to communicate the same meaning so that these sessions exemplify how what Deidre said was regularly transformed into a here and now transference meaning; she feels abandoned by her analyst who goes off in a couple about which she feels murderous.

This appreciation of the unconscious issues brought into the sessions led Frances to try to **further the process** by bringing the emotional focus repeatedly back to the immediacy of Deidre's

251

relationship with her (by gathering the accounts offered by Deidre from the outside and taking them up here and now).

> 'I think I am in the dream as well as all the others, a gay authority figure who leaves the windows open and makes you really murderously annoyed sometimes'; 'The gay person from the dream, not close, not a lover you said . . . or is it us, gay, close . . . like at the end of last session, and homeless next week like the couple you saw'; 'And I would have harmed you.'; 'The pet is you and you think I'm leaving you out, away with my husband.'

Within this approach, she talked to the group about constantly trying to gauge what affects Deidre could bear and trying not to overstep the limits of Deidre's capacity to tolerate disturbance. This was a difficult analysis because Deidre uses intellectual defences and always seemed to 'know' what Frances was going to say; Frances tried to work round this rather than tackling it directly. Frances said she was keen to convey that questions existed rather than answers, as opposed to Deidre's tendency to 'have all the answers'. In this context it was important to try gradually to differentiate between what feelings she felt might be truly unmanageable for Deidre at the moment and what might only appear unmanageable. Her idea was that within these parameters she might help Deidre to be in touch with her feelings about abandonment and other issues; the idea being to make open comments that might initiate a process of reflecting and enquiring, as opposed to closing things down with saturated (explanatory) comments.

Tom thought analysis had already worked significantly for Paul and could continue to do so; insofar as Tom was able to facilitate Paul's affective development by helping him to know about and experience disturbing and hitherto split-off affects. These were to be recovered via verbalization and interpretation of unrecognized feeling derivatives (especially his rivalrous hatred) as they were evident in sessions. An important part of this procedure and so of his whole approach (actually not fully conceptualized by Tom prior to the workshop) was the extent to which he saw it as his task to work through Paul's affective experience as it was provoked in him by Paul.

Tom's way of listening to the unconscious involved quite long periods in which he worked rather subtly in silence to sense what Paul's and his own feelings actually were. This was not exactly a reverie state but neither was it particularly focused. For example, in the first session presented (after a weekend break) Paul gave a lengthy account of a complex social and sexual situation among his relatives which eventually stimulated spontaneous memories of the time, after his mother's death, when his father surrounded himself with young women. Paul then said that he did not want to think of his father like that. There had been a great deal of content which prompted group members to suggest all kinds of hidden symbolic meanings but what caught Tom's attention at that moment was that he sensed Paul trying to ward off *feeling* rivalry and hatred there and then (although not specifically with him). In this way Tom's accounts of sessions suggested a mode of attention very sensitively attuned both to Paul's feelings and his own. He did not take such feeling further – for example by constructing the unconscious phantasies being communicated – although he said he would like to do that if ideas occurred to him and they seemed opportune. Neither did he take the above material about the father surrounding himself with women as, for example, a transference commentary.

Tom's way of furthering the psychoanalytic process – which he saw as trying to develop Paul's affective capacity – took the form of commenting on the affects he sensed that Paul was experiencing – commenting for example that Paul had to turn away from feeling rivalrous because he found it so unbearable. This was an example of the way he tried to verbalize unrecognized affects (especially hate) through his interpretations in the here and now of the sessions. But, as mentioned, Tom also did a lot of work in his own mind, only partly consciously, particularly working over uncomfortable affective experiences which he had; these experiences were quite often provoked by Paul's associations or by small enactments between them. For instance, in describing the first session Tom told the group that he recognized he had had to hold on to an irritated feeling that the patient was being very angry and also about several other past incidents where actually he had not been able to hold on and had in minor ways betrayed his irritation or anxiety to his patient.

Louise appeared to the group who discussed her presentation **to make analysis work** by trying to enable Georgina to re-experience what was happening in her mind at what might be thought of as the deepest (and earliest) levels of experience. She was also concerned with her patient's capacity to tolerate affect but she particularly hoped also to help Georgina to know about and understand how her secret deadliness inhibits all her lively activity. Perhaps her main aim was to help Georgina to know she has feelings (caused by inherently painful internal conflicts and experiences) that can be understood in their detail and tolerated by another human being. Her approach started from observations that caught her attention in the here and now – for example in a session where Georgina actually turned her head to one side at one point. But she then tried to give meaning to and to elaborate her patient's associations; using the images evoked by Georgina in her mind to link ideas and experiences that Georgina did not consciously connect. Louise's emphasis on feelings and deep working through meant she favoured unsaturated interpretation designed to facilitate psychic change through promoting increasingly elaborated psychic representation (linking) but avoiding intellectualization. 'I would like to verbalize what she is denying' and to help her recover projections, said Louise.

In listening to the unconscious Louise adopts what can be called a reverie type position in which she becomes very sensitive to possible verbal links and images. For example at one point Georgina associated to some swirling pots of water – pot holes in a mountain stream. Louise commented to the group:

> A large number of associations took shape within me . . . I saw myself in a number of diverse transference roles and was unclear about the level on which I might interpret. I waited but, I noted, with a feeling of trust and some relief . . . [then] I immediately felt swamped by a collapsing sensation, as if I were falling into one of the pots in the mountain stream . . . I thought . . . Georgina has said '*I couldn't speak*' – perhaps an early preverbal experience, [then] I remembered . . . several weeks ago . . . [various dimensions of] her history.
>
> (words in brackets added)

This condensed example of her thought processes captures many instances of the way in which Louise uses her imagination, her reverie, her own feelings and theories to construct unconscious meaning from the latent text of the patient's associations.

To **further the analytic process** she thinks will work with Georgina, Louise uses brief unsaturated interpretations coming from her sense of internal working over (as just exemplified) and usually aimed at or constructing what she senses to be the here and now phantasy situation:

'Perhaps I am the pot'; 'and you turn your head aside, as a way of telling me about all the sadness and anger you are feeling, and how much I disappoint you . . .'; 'And is there a reason why unconsciously you need to forget your dreams? A reason that has to be discovered?'; 'One would say that you feel as if there is a war between us . . . wouldn't it rather be a war between two voices in yourself?'

The analytic situation

Theories of transference are fundamental to theories of psychoanalysis. However, we learnt in the first workshop meetings described in Chapter 3 that nearly all colleagues thought they understood and used transference as a fundamental property of psychoanalytic work. We also learnt that there was almost no agreement on what was meant by transference. For these reasons we tried to think not about the word transference but the ideas that underlie the potential meanings given to it. Thinking about the way the presenter saw 'the analytic situation' was one of the five topics explored during the Step 2 discussions. In order to explore the different ways transference is used with each presenter, three main elements of the analytic situation were each examined as far as possible – briefly, what is the analytic situation and what is thought to generate it, what is its purpose in relation to the way psychoanalysis is specifically thought to work, and how is experience within a session framed? The three analysts we have been discussing had somewhat different emphases across these elements.

For **Frances** the emphasis is on the analytic situation as an interpersonal setting in which Deidre's actual feelings of insecurity when with her, as with those she knows outside the session, are experienced. This provides Frances with the chance, through her understanding of Deidre's way of experiencing her, to try to be different; to notice her extreme feeling of insecurity as it develops and to try to adapt to it by taking various steps to make things safer. This then seems to be the aim of the setting; to provide a relatively safe haven for Deidre, fairly free of the persecuted anxieties she has and without the experience of retaliation. In this 'safe enough' human environment Deidre can grow to trust her feelings and to alter her relationships to those with her. Finally, the frame for understanding experience in the session is predominantly that of a unidirectional field – Frances focuses on Deidre's transference-induced relations to her and her 'actual' effects on her; she does not emphasize such ideas as that she may be unconsciously enacting a countertransference driven role with Deidre or that any wishes, fears or fantasies might derive from her unconscious response to the patient.

Tom's definition also emphasizes the relational experience he and his patient have with each other − for him the sessions are a real relationship between persons with powerful affective experiences, but underneath there is the notion that they are 'two adults talking together'. Tom sees the sessions as providing the opportunity to experience their relationship and observe it together − albeit that it is Tom who mainly makes such observations explicit but, as we saw above, only when he thought Paul was defending against his experience and he judged him to be ready to hear from him about it. (This judgement is based on Tom's affective experience but also the content of Paul's associations − as when he spoke about the social situation mentioned above or when he came in talking of terrorists.) Like Frances, Tom also sees the frame for understanding experience as mainly unidirectional − his patient's affective relationship to his analyst is based on past (internalized) relationships to mother and father. While Tom is acutely sensitized to his own feelings and can recognize when he has been provoked into an intervention, he does not emphasize or construct such influences in any systematic way. His model does not include such notions as the possibility that he might subtly be enacting aspects of his patient's inner world in the sense of a bi-directional field which can be used to illuminate Paul's transference.

Louise differs from both Frances and Tom in that she not only defines the sessions as an affective relationship but also lays considerable emphasis on identifying precise unconscious phantasies and inner internal processes of representing meaning which give meaning to Georgina's experience and are played out in fragmented forms. Louise 'searches' for complex transference meaning. In fact, for Louise the aim of a psychoanalytic session is that it provides a setting for regression to modes of primary process mental functioning and so has the potential to facilitate Georgina's capacity to develop more elaborate ways of representing the meaning of her experience to herself; making connections never previously made but not necessarily at a conscious level. However, like the other two colleagues the frame in which she seeks meaning is also mainly unidirectional − she considers her thoughts, fantasies, feelings and other experience to be evoked by

Georgina's phantasy representations of her relationships to her analyst; a process facilitated by conceiving of the setting as one of formal regression for both analyst and patient; reverie and free association. In this last respect Louise's explanatory model 'felt' rather different from the other two. At the same time Louise does not emphasize the other possible direction – that her fears, wishes and feelings are subtle constructions of unconscious enactments within the psychoanalytic field.

The comparative method and its surprises

Despite their limitations I hope these brief sketches convey some sense of the differences between the three analysts and also show how we are trying to characterize the differences between them – based on the data coming up in the workshop groups organized by the five axes we selected for Step 2. The axes provoked fruitful group discussion (as described in Chapter 7), but they also do seem to have the potential to provide a template framework against which to make comparisons. The descriptions just offered of the way different psychoanalysts think about what is wrong with their patients, the way they think of the psychoanalytic situation and listen and the way they conceive and try to further the psychoanalytic process, do seem to me, in the language we have been explicating, to reveal that they are enacting somewhat different 'models' of psychoanalysis. We can say they hear different things, say different things and have different ideas about the purpose of what they are doing. The extent of these differences as well as their deviation from traditional ideas about what psychoanalysts do should be apparent and may be rather surprising by the time we have completed the next stage of work.

We can take the listening axis as an example. In this respect we have found there is great variability in how psychoanalysts 'enact' their idea of the analytic approach. While they may all in one way or another think of their attitude when listening as 'free floating' or 'evenly suspended' attention, there is a wide range in what they seem to mean; just as there is a wide range of different understandings of what constitutes free association or resistance on the part of the patient, or of how far, as they listen, unconscious fantasies are recognized and conceived in any detail, as well as of the extent to which analysts treat their patients' material as built up by the detailed primary processes set out by Freud and named as condensation and displacement.

Exploring the differences in the way the three analysts 'listened' across this range of ideas does seem to produce different but comparable models of analytic working. In a further volume we will move on to describe what for us is step three; trying to set out some of the main models of working we have identified and to show how they relate to each other and to traditional psychoanalytic preoccupations, concepts and theories. Insofar as we can achieve that we will be ready to open a debate on the next set of questions: are all these models 'really' and specifically analytic, and if so, how and why?

As I have just been setting out, the main purpose of the comparative methods project and of the two-step method we have evolved was to mobilize efforts to look more rigorously at the different ways psychoanalysts work and to try to create the conditions to enable an informed and constructive debate of those differences. However, as the authors of Chapters 7 and 9 have indicated, the method has proved to have other uses. Presenting analysts, such as Jennifer's analyst (discussed at the end of Chapter 7) or Tom (discussed earlier in this chapter), report that taking part in the group has helped them usefully to understand and clarify what they are doing and so to refine their analytic position. Participants have reported that they find the method useful for supervision and this has been discussed in some detail in Chapter 9. In some ways, therefore, it seems that a method designed for another purpose may mark a possibly radical departure for clinical discussion between psychoanalysts and even for psychoanalytic education.

It is perhaps not surprising that ten hours of attention to one's work is useful and, of course, it is not impossible to gain the kind of insight Jennifer's analyst later reported ('I have realized in the course of the group that unconsciously I have assumed in this analysis that really I am an empty analyst/mother/fridge') from a group supervision organized along conventional lines. The method set out in earlier pages is not claimed as the Via Regia; clearly there are many ways to organize psychoanalytic groups and many of them work. It may be, however, that (as discussed in Chapter 9) there is something specific about the two-step method that it is useful. If so, we should be clear as to what that specificity actually might be.

The particular contribution I think this method might make to supervision comes from the specific way it clarifies the different roles available to presenter, group discussants and moderator and the way it structures discussion to focus on the task of understanding the analyst's explanatory model, *before* attempting to debate it – meaning that the presenter recognizes her reading of material and her model of working as being respected and then debated, which may be more fruitful and more easy to learn from. For me, clarifying roles and focusing on explanatory models are the two features that together protect a two-step discussion group and the presenter from what I have christened *overvision* – the imposition on a clinical account by one person of an alternative 'superior' system of thinking based on entirely different assumptions and ideas held by another. This was the situation described by Paul Denis in Chapter 2 and in my discussion of other presentations and discussions in journals and international conferences in Chapter 1. It is also the concern of Roberto Basile and Antonino Ferro in Chapter 9.

We can think of supervision as providing a set of experiences illuminating the facts of a case in a way in which presenters can feel useful for their further work. If so, then, to the extent it takes the form of *overvision* imposed over the presenter's own way of thinking without detailed investigation of the latter, it does appear likely to have only limited use and may even be dysfunctional – at least insofar as learning is considered to involve a process of internalizing new ideas using an existing internal 'digestive' system. I would say that to internalize new ideas we need to engage in a process of working through in which our current understanding, based on our current explanatory models, becomes modified by ingesting novel ideas. But such new ideas can only have meaning within an explanatory model (i.e. theory), which also functions as a background language of prior assumptions.

My experience of the two-step method has cemented my view that to convey new ideas to a presenter it is useful for a supervisor to try to articulate and share the background assumptions (explanatory models) of all those involved – the presenter, supervisor, other members of a seminar. For example, if I consider, as I do, that to interpret envy and hatred of the analyst's work is essential at some point in most cases but that to make such interpretations work is very difficult; then to put this understanding across at an opportune moment I will need to clarify the presenter's underlying model as well as my own – such as my view about the purpose of verbalization, drive and affect conflict and the role of hate in inhibiting grateful and loving feelings. I will also need to convey my view that if they are to work, such interpretations depend on both depth of exploration and the emotional conviction that the underlying ideas really work. The emotional component is part of what I see as a psychoanalytic model (my explanatory model) and will need to be communicated in many subtle ways. To make interpretations about hatred without such understanding and conviction, based on a supervision where I just demonstrate a patient's envy or hatred, let us say apparently correctly, is useless or worse. Two risks exist: inducing submissive pseudo-interpretation or resistance. For this reason, any supervisors making suggestions along such lines may need to explore not just their own views as to 'what is happening' from their point of view, but also relevant aspects of both explanatory models, including the conviction with which they are held. Once this is done, it may also be very useful to look for implicit theories in the sense of conflicting unconscious theories, as described by Canestri (2006) and his colleagues.

As the project has progressed and we have spent many hours trying to find ways to understand and describe what others are doing, I have also noticed that beginning to have some ideas about the different explanatory models guiding the way different colleagues work has been helpful to me; particularly when I have had to consider how to think about work that is presented to me for discussion. I now find that it is easier to make useful comments if I can reach a point where I feel that I understand something of the presenter's core assumptions. Often this is possible because of all the other ideas prompted in a discussion group – provided the members of the group are disciplined about roles.

I began this chapter by recalling how Dana Birksted-Breen indicated in her introductory foreword that she takes the view that psychoanalysis is necessarily practised with a theory – providing a range of definitions of key processes and procedures – the unconscious, the transference, the nature of psychic conflict, the way the past gets encoded into the present, and so on. All our work to date, along with the brief comparison of three cases I have just attempted, suggests that the combination of pluralism and overvision that have come to characterize our field may have created something of a paralysis of rigorous comparative thinking and perhaps a certain decomposition of clarity. The group discussions reveal that between the participants, every bit as much as between them and the presenters, there are enormous differences and widespread uncertainty over the underlying theories captured through the five Step 2 axes: as, for instance, how analysis is thought to work or how the analytic process is envisaged and furthered. Some theories of practice drawn on by our presenters are relatively close to classical theories of transference, resistance, conflict, and the unconscious as characterized by primary process. But other theories being used have a much less clear heritage, are much more undeveloped and relatively unrelated to mainstream theory; theories are often developed on the job.

For the time being we hope to have contributed a method to investigate these important questions and in the next volume will offer a much more detailed description of how analysts do work and present some ideas to debate.

Helmut Hinz began Chapter 5 with an adaptation from Theodor Adorno, 'Nothing is to be compared, nothing is without comparison', from which, with further adaptation, we took the title for this book. Throughout the book we have been struggling with our conviction that as a discipline for understanding the human mind psychoanalysis is incomparable. It takes feeling and subjectivity as the objects of inquiry as well as using them among the instruments for inquiry; raising many difficulties in terms of meeting the methodological strictures of other successful forms of empirical investigation. The method we have evolved attempts to harness feeling and subjectivity along with cognitive and conceptual rigour, as, I would argue, does psychoanalysis itself. We hope that we have presented sufficient evidence to show that we can retain both the essence of psychoanalysis and the essence of empirical investigation: the comparative method is, therefore, available as a first step for those psychoanalysts who wish to begin more rigorously to compare and debate with each other what they do.

Appendix

The origins of the EPF 'new' scientific policy and the early history of the working party

David Tuckett (UK)

The project described in this book is the first outcome of the EPF Working Party on Comparative Clinical Methods. The working party had its origins in the new scientific policy agreed at the European Psychoanalytic Federation Council in London in April 2000 and the consequent formation of the EPF Working Party on Clinical Issues set up six months later under the chairmanship of Haydée Faimberg. Retrospectively, it is possible to see the 2000 London Council meeting as the initiation of a novel process of evolution leading to new forms of exchange between psychoanalysts, the results of which were only very partially anticipated. As this may be of some interest the early events prior to those discussed in more depth in the book are described in this Appendix.

The London Council meeting (in 2000 comprising a small executive and the presidents of twenty-six psychoanalytical societies with seventeen different mother tongues and based in twenty-one sovereign states) considered and eventually adopted unanimously what was called the new scientific policy. This policy was stimulated by a newly elected president working within the context of a creative and constructive executive who had already begun to create the institutional structure for reform. The opening rubric of the new policy proposal

262

document asserted that in the field of psychoanalysis scientific discussion might be in some trouble:

> Too often we seem to need to return to clarify what ought to be basics. There are some hopeful signs but there is also evidence in the growing pluralism that followed the breakdown of the previous authoritarian orthodoxy that the field may be disintegrating into superficially organised sub-groups with little in common but their aspiration to be called psychoanalysts, creating significant difficulties for clarity within the profession and in the interface with other professions. These difficulties are felt in the complex and rich cultural context of Europe as they are world-wide. But an aspiration we might have in Europe is that we have the clinical and intellectual resources to address them, if we can create the conditions to work rigorously together in depth. The ideas below, which focus on ways to increase the depth and rigor of our scientific activity, are intended to facilitate this potential.

The policy document recognized both the fact and the potential benefit of diversity and argued that there were significant ways in which 'psychoanalysis as a discipline had tended to have . . . difficulty accumulating a deepening core of ideas and techniques about which there was consensus'. It proposed several steps to 'achieve scientific progress', including innovations to increase the possibility to work in depth, to learn from each other, to develop self-sustaining motivation, to increase the amount of work in small groups, to set and monitor objectives and to judge them by their capacity to achieve peer-reviewed publications. Among the institutional innovations was the introduction of an annual rather than biannual conference (creating a greater likelihood of people getting to know each other). Also the new annual conference was to focus as much on small ongoing workshops as on set-piece debates and there was to be an entirely new structure of organization by creating what were at first alternately referred to as 'task forces' or 'steering groups' but became 'working parties' (the terms 'task force' and 'steering group' had unfortunate connotations in one or other of the main EPF languages).

It took their implementation for both the notion and exact functions of working parties to become clearer. At the outset the argument was that

A major purpose of international meetings is to exchange ideas in detail and to learn from each other. It follows that these meetings should be organised to maximise the amount of careful preparation that takes place before meeting and the amount of time actually spent listening to each other discuss matters in depth . . . Original and creative work is unlikely to arise out of an invitation or opportunity to attend a casual conference session or two on a changing theme. Such meetings can stimulate a beginning but originality and creativity requires colleagues willing to worry away at issues and to develop thoughts at depth over sustained periods of time . . . By elaborating and fine-tuning ideas, and coming back to them again and again in a process of internal struggle and external debate, they become refined and deepened. Several colleagues working separately and together on common problems, comparing findings, constitute a self-sustaining workshop or group and have a higher chance of advancing thought and practice . . . in order to move forward it seems likely that it will be necessary to share ideas and findings in such a way that difference can be adequately understood and addressed. A way to do this effectively might be to get small groups of colleagues from different contexts working together so that their understanding and appreciation of each other other's ideas can **grow over time**. Work can be shared at a meeting, further refinement and development can take place over weeks and months and then there can be further sharing, etc.

At first it was supposed that the main function of each EPF working party (for which virtually no budget could at first be found) was to consider how to stimulate deeper understanding in their particular area and to facilitate pan-European groups working in depth. Each group was to hold open meetings at the annual conferences and would also provide a report to the EPF Council on activities and the progress of objectives within twenty-four months. The groups would be responsible for trying to monitor the progress and direction of scientific conferences. Four areas in which ongoing working parties might be useful were then agreed, based on the preoccupations identified by discussions inaugurated by the previous administration (Lisbon, November 1999): clinical issues, educational issues, clarifying theory issues and the 'promotion and protection of psychoanalysis'. In the case of clinical work it was stated that 'there is an urgent need to clarify what are the core features of (a range of) effective psycho-analytic techniques and settings.'

Haydée Faimberg, a distinguished psychoanalytic clinician trained in Argentina, who worked as a training analyst in Paris and had been the 'French' co-chair for many years of the Anglo-French annual colloquium which would meet at Brighton, was appointed chair of the working party which would deal with clinical issues (WPCI). She was and is known for her work on 'listening to listening' (Faimberg, 1996) and from her history and inclination was judged particularly suitable to begin the task. From the outset she wanted to work closely with Jorge Canestri, in fact a second Argentine trained analyst but working in Rome, who had been appointed to chair the Working Party on Theoretical Issues – a parallel group set up to consider and clarify the kind of clinical theory both explicitly and implicitly used in daily practice. At the first meeting of the working party chairs with the Executive of the EPF, several questions were agreed for joint consideration between these two working parties:

- Why do models and theories in psychoanalysis seem to have such emotional implications for the analyst and/or for the psy-choanalytic institutions?
- Are there any psychoanalytical (unconscious) reasons for choos-ing different paradigms (models)?
- What is the influence of language/culture on the creation and/or choice of different models?
- What is the role and meaning of preconscious theories in clinical practice? How can we collect evidence about them? Can we use supervision to produce evidence about their existence? What could the heuristic value be of these preconscious theories if they are recognized?
- How could we improve communication about clinical work using the feedback from these and other researches?

Following this discussion, whereas the Canestri group was asked to examine these questions beginning with theory, the Faimberg group was to examine them beginning with trying to understand in depth how analysts actually work, with a view to building more precise languages for clinical dialogue between European colleagues. Each group was also assigned representatives from the European psy-choanalytic societies by the presidents of the local societies and asked to organize discussion workshops for the first 'new style' EPF conference to be held in Prague in April 2002. Haydée Faimberg subsequently met with the representatives assigned to her group during the EPF and then IPA conferences in Madrid and Nice, respectively, in 2001.

What turned out to be a further crucial starting assumption also became adopted at this time. If we were to develop a method of comparison, it needed to be that each psychoanalyst asked to present was agreed, before the start of each workshop, actually to be doing psychoanalysis. Arguments about what was or was not psychoanalysis would be set aside. The challenge would be to define what doing psychoanalysis in that particular case actually meant: for *that* presenter in *that* case based on *what was actually being described* and demonstrated in *those* sessions. As a way forward to implement this assumption together, Haydée Faimberg identified twenty interested and locally respected clinicians (i.e. felt locally within the twenty or so European societies to be talented psychoanalytic clinicians) willing to present their clinical material. She also found skilled individuals to chair and discuss the groups. Invitations were also sent out to societies to nominate people to take part. The general idea was that ten groups of about twelve people would be organized and that there would be two presenters in each group, which would meet for about six hours in all, over an afternoon and a morning.

Those attending the Prague groups were all to be self-financed but after extensive discussions some finance became available for preparation.[1] To prepare the Prague workshops a WPCI retreat was organized in Brussels at the end of November 2001. It was attended by Haydée Faimberg, Robin Anderson (UK), Paul Denis (France), Antonino Ferro (Italy), Jacqueline Godfrind Haber (Belgium), Helmut Hinz (Germany), Iréne Matthis (Sweden), Lore Schacht (Germany), Paul Williams (UK) and myself. By agreement with Haydée Faimberg, I had written a letter of invitation to one of the presenters for this meeting, as the EPF President. This set out the purpose:

---

[1] Henk Jan Dalewijk, the EPF treasurer, managed to create a small fund within the EPF accounts and after very extensive debate, matched funding for the four working parties was eventually agreed from the IPA, under an inter-regional funding initiative. The high attendance at the 'new style' conferences later enabled the EPF to build up a substantial scientific initiative fund which, after further extensive discussion and lobbying, was matched by a further significant grant from the IPA DPPT funds.

I am trying to create some small groups of highly selected clinicians with the aim of trying to create much more rigorous discussion of what the different ways of doing psychoanalysis actually are. The main immediate requirement is to find some excellent clinicians who are willing to describe their work and then for the group to try to formulate its principles: this is working from the clinical situation to theory and not vice versa. . . . At this stage the idea is to have 4 sessions (on the Friday) in which there is a presentation in each. The following day there might be a further attempt to conceptualise each presentation. The following morning we might try to work out ways to compare. I am strongly of the opinion that until we do this work we cannot really talk to each other properly nor have much understanding of what we mean by standards!

We had twenty hours. Three gifted colleagues presented a summary of his or her work over a period of about a week with two sessions presented in full. Then three equally gifted colleagues took on the task of trying to conceptualize how they thought one of the presenters actually did seem to work. The whole group participated in a lengthy clinical discussion covering many topics. It was one of the most stimulating and interesting experiences I have had discussing psychoanalysis. The discussion was recorded and then transcribed with extensive help from Antoine Corel. This brief excerpt illustrates its content, its diversity, its level and the high degree of participation by all present:

Speaker 1 says her point was not how quick we are to understand, but whether we feel the obligation to understand. Besides, at some points we may observe that Presenter 2 is able to wait for a long time before interpreting (and also to interpret in ways that show he is also sensitive to absence). Thinking of the patient's frame of mind and its oscillations from one moment to the other, we could suppose that the patient attempts to control because he is afraid that the A [analyst] 'will not be fair and impartial' (the A has interpreted this at some moment). We must choose to interpret at the moment when the patient is able to listen. Presenter 2 himself has expressed this, which creates a certain tension with his other aim of putting his discoveries into words.

Speaker 2 says that at times the patient in Case 2 seems not to trust verbal communication.

Speaker 3 remarks that we understand, but not always correctly; or we understand something that does not belong to the core of process. It is difficult to discuss clinical material. For example, Presenter 2 has known the patient for years, he may anticipate how will he react to interpretations, choose another path, and so on. Similarly, he knows the way in which the patient is identified to A's way of functioning and of fathering him. Speaker 3 addresses another point: do we apply rigidly our model of countertransference, to what extent is a model an expression of a kind of Countertransference, or, by the contrary, the model has the purpose of resisting the Countertransference?

Presenter 2 describes the state of mind he was in at the end of the week, perhaps not having entirely grasped the transference, but basically worried about letting the patient go like that: he thinks that he wanted to remain near the little boy, and say something to that aspect.

Speaker 4 says that Presenter 1 and Presenter 2 are engaged with their patients, in different approaches. His experience is that French analysts speak less. He points to one interpretation by Presenter 2, 'packed with information'.

Speaker 3 observes that within the frame of 5× a week, British analysts are able to take difficult patients. He comments that at times he also finds himself giving many words. He recalls the case of a young woman coming in a delusional state to her previous analyst: he had to do a lot of talking to restore in her a favorable disposition.

Speaker 1 says her point was precisely that by listening predominantly to one or another aspect, neurotic or psychotic, we produce more, or less, structured discourses. In a way, we create the patients. Of course, well trained analysts are able to listen to all levels.

Speaker 5 proposes to differentiate two models of the analyst–patient relationship A–P: in one, the conscious reality of both is taken as starting point; in the other, which seems to be preferred by some French analysts, it would not be so important who analyst and patient are: a shared unconscious modality is started that has nothing to do with reality, only with wish, and free association is more easygoing.

Speaker 4 finds this very interesting; the idea is of how to facilitate the unconscious process.

Speaker 6 refers to the underlying criteria allowing us to grasp what is emerging. He quotes a recent presentation by P. Fédida in which it was clear that his model consisted in facilitating the emergence of the story of the past, of repressed memories. The British model, based on the idea that the early ways of dealing with conflict are recreated in the object relationships and in the analytic relationship, attempts to grasp the conflict in the present of the analytic relation. The image is one of pictures constructed in a row. Speaker 6 believes that the effect of both models is in some senses the same, both recover the missing link. In the British model the danger is to get lost in detail without pulling out the fundamental repetitive patterns. While the French model runs the risk of becoming an intellectual exercise that goes over and over memories and avoids transference experience.

Speaker 4 is very happy at the perspective of continuing this way of abstracting models at the meeting in Prague.

Speaker 3 says that in France, Lacan follows a linguistic (non-representational) model; other authors follow representational, pulsional models; and Fairbairn and M. Klein are known as representing the British model described by Speaker 6.

Speaker 1 thinks that not giving precocious transference interpretations could have the advantage of letting the material come, allow for the repetitions to manifest themselves. In particular with a family secret (which was the case in the Fédida example evoked by Speaker 6) it is possible to 'listen' in the repetition to something unspoken.

For Speaker 7, the model used by Presenter 1 requires small stimuli from the analyst to activate the patient, while Presenter 2 thinks he should stimulate the patient. In the first, he says, there are 7 persons in the kitchen and 3 in the restaurant; in the second, the proportion is 5 to 5.

What is common to both, says Speaker 3, is the transmission of the analyst's mental functioning: both models consider that we teach the patient to learn the analyst's way of thinking, analogous to learning a language.

Speaker 8 prefers to think that patient and analyst create a new language, a third language.

Speaker 9 sees that Presenter 2 expands the frame. But if he tries to conceptualize what he thinks he does as analyst in his work, he would say that the patient's learning exists in relation to the analyst's effort to grasp what comes from the patient. The analyst finds himself in an uncomfortable position derived from the attempt to cope, without falling in, as was said before, with the patient in a collusive way. If he used the metaphor of learning, he would say that what for Presenter 2 is transitional, in between, for him occurs inside himself, as an internal work: grappling with what comes from the patient, going back to his good object, and then getting something that can be helpful to the patient; then he is able to teach the patient, and not only with words.

Two features stand out in the transcript when I read it five years later and in my memory. First, the discussion inevitably involved each speaker contributing from their very different models of clinical work; sometimes amounting to a competition between models, although one constructively well modulated here. Second, when it came to comparison (and despite very best efforts) the group had few tools with which to do it. For a start the differences in the analysts' technique might reflect different clinical situations – the diagnostic type of patient and the particular stages of the analysis from which the presentations were taken being particularly confounding variables. But differences were also more fundamental. For instance, different theories about language were present with obvious implications for the kinds of interpretation offered and the kinds of psychoanalytic process envisaged. Interpretations were polysemic, enigmatic and short in one example; or direct, as unambiguous as possible and even lengthy, in another. Behind such differences might be different conceptions of the role of the conscious 'ego' in the psychoanalytic process as well as about what that process actually is. To take another example, some interpretations appeared seductive or evasive to some; while other interpretations seemed intrusive or traumatic to others. Here again differences may reflect differences in underlying theory – for example as to the importance of action and enactment. Finally, we also had difficulties with the meaning of terms we had previously thought shared.

It was, I think, because of these underlying differences that a great deal of the discussion became rather polite competition, with intense efforts then expended to try to draw back and to revert to the task of examining matters in terms of the presenter's own language and approach. My sense was that even when we could overcome the competitive element, we would very soon become bogged down in a maze of detail and idiosyncrasy involving each analysis; unless we could determine an appropriate focus along which to describe differences and recognize them. But what was it to be?

In trying to evaluate the meeting on the final morning the transcript shows that I re-emphasized that the aim of the project was to conceptualize the way in which we work, down to the most detailed levels, avoiding the easy partisan divisions into 'This is analysis, and this is not' albeit that at some level that will remain a very important question. I thought it was the way of posing that question in the past that had been both destructive and confusing – creating enormous difficulties when obviously very different approaches were considered. By contrast the assumption of the meeting we had attended was that the three presenters are psychoanalysts whether different or not. From this standpoint we could observe that there were many effective ways of working in analysis and that great differences among the participants had emerged; differences that correspond to various factors, some of them pertaining to a personal creative style that could not be imitated even if we wanted to. I stressed we must not remain satisfied with being different nor with empty generalizations about how we were the same but needed to arrive at getting a clearer picture of our work beyond the factors of feeling, charisma and narcissism that we all put into it. We were trying to conceptualize with the utmost detail coming from the ground level the way we work and abstract basic information about the models and methods we use. It was at the ground level that we might better understand what we mean. In particular we should learn to recognize 'real' work which is 'psychoanalysis' within the different models, the factors that facilitate the process and favour the P's creativity within the session. The ideal would be to recognize the features of each analyst's way of working, which means abstracting from the basic clinical account the theories and models that the analysts are actually applying in their work, and not the theories they consciously adhere to.

To approach defining the features we might try to recognize and compare I suggested that perhaps one focus could be on listening, that is on what it is the analyst is listening to in the material, a complex question that Haydée Faimberg had studied. A second focus might be on what is privileged in the analyst's interventions: distinguishing perhaps such things as an effort to contain the situation or just to say enough to stimulate the associations, or an effort to describe to the patient what is going on for some purpose, or an effort to present a construction for another purpose. What I had in mind was that the kinds of interventions chosen might reveal a pattern of intention – an implicit or explicit model of the psychoanalytic process and how to further it, in turn suggesting what it is an analyst sees in actual practice as the engine of change in psychoanalysis.

I stated in Brussels that experientially I felt more confident after our discussion than I had before, when I had actually anticipated greater difficulties. At the same time I felt we had taken only a step or two. I suggested to the group that in future it might be particularly useful if we could encourage presenters to tell more about their internal processes of thinking, to try to discover more of what was going on in their minds and not to let them limit themselves to saying, as gifted persons tend to do, 'Well, I just did it'. It seemed to me that although we know perfectly well that we cannot fully or usefully explain what we do in each specific moment, we can discover the main line of the inner processes that disciplined analysts use and, if so, we would know when other analysts sought to work like them when what we observe is the 'real thing' and when it is a pseudo occurrence. I also suggested that thinking after the session and thinking inside it are to be differentiated; what we needed to do and to encourage presenters to do was something that perhaps we did in our everyday work from time to time; review for example the work we have done on a day and discover the constants that appear and thus be able to introduce the necessary adjustments.

Elaborating I said that I did not think it likely a focus would prove effective if we tried to understand in detail why the analysts made the individual interpretations they did – all three analysts, although working very differently, made comments that they could not entirely explain within their approach (and sometimes apparently deviated from its general principles) and whose origins were clearly multi-determined as well as fundamentally uncertain; given that the unconscious should play a major part in the clinical process this was to be expected. Moreover, psychoanalysis is not about single interpretations but a series of them creating a process over time.

Haydée Faimberg, who had also enjoyed the meeting, was understandably unsure how we could go on and make use of the very rich material we had. This caused me to repeat that I thought that to see our way through the detail and to be able to establish patterns of similarity and difference between individual analysts seemed to me to require a theoretical framework; one capable of grasping the essence of very different approaches. A possible level of examination would be one that looked at trends in the detail of what was happening over the course of a number of sessions. Thus, if we focused on their conceptualization of their listening, as colleagues presented and discussed, I wondered if we could think that their clinical theories were in fact all concerned with attention to shifts in some common issues: issues of symbolization and representation on the one hand, and affects and drives on the other. This led me, perhaps rather simplistically, to wonder if we could sum up one of the central propositions of psychoanalysis paraphrasing John Rickman (1937) by saying that *we think only what we want and can bear to feel*, implying that psychoanalytic process aims to provide meaning for previously overwhelming affective experience. I thought this way of thinking was approached differently in each of the presentations but could nonetheless be discerned as an aim in all three. Thus, I wondered if a great deal of analytic work in all schools might be described in terms of the different but precise efforts undertaken to help patients to understand their situation and to be able to metabolize their responses to situations in terms of greater emotional depth. If so, a trend along which an analytic process could be examined would be in terms of the steps taken to increase the emotional depth present in exchanges between patient and analyst and the extent of the analyst's awareness in monitoring it. We did not take comparison much further at that meeting.

After Brussels the transcript of the discussion was prepared and we continued to puzzle over what might be a useful framework for the workshop groups we were organizing for Prague. The presentation by Pierre Fédida (2002) at the EPF Training Colloquium in Budapest in which a patient's history and core fantasy had gradually become elaborated had been mentioned in Brussels. Recalling this, I was reminded of a recent visit to Bulgaria, where I had heard another Parisian colleague, George Lucas, describe an initial assessment interview. In it, through a series of subtle questions, he gradually moved the patient's emotional engagement from an angry dismissal of how all young people of her age had nothing to gain from grown-ups towards reflecting a little about her jealousies and anxieties concerning her parents and so to a deeper internal reflection. Similarly, at the Brussels meeting, one of the presenters had demonstrated how he set out to try to sustain and develop a deepening flow of associations aiming to help his patient represent her unconscious feelings and ideas about a recent abortion and the situation that had brought her to it.

In the UK I thought it was commonplace among some analysts to consider that the analytic process deepened towards greater symbolization of affect and drive – requiring a movement from paranoid-schizoid towards depressive functioning in Kleinian terms, the achievement of object constancy among Anna Freudians or perhaps of object 'use' for Winnicott.

It continued to strike me that some kind of temporal axis of helping a patient to get emotionally deeper (perhaps by exploring how oneself was getting stuck with repetition) and how this was approached might be a possible basis for a descriptive framework to compare efforts different analysts make either to help patients to recognize the unconscious fantasies or repressed memories which drive transference repetition and enactment, or to help the more traumatized patient and less able-to-reflect patient to develop the capacity to represent or think about to what they are responding. It also seemed to me to cover efforts aimed to help patients to see the unconscious wishes that are being satisfied through repetitions or to increase the tolerance of affect.

Still trying to find a more precise focus I thought that perhaps all three Brussels analysts seemed to have at the heart of their work a focus on how they understood and responded to their patient's use of their interventions. If this was so it might greatly simplify exploration. We could focus not on what brought an analysts to make interpretations (so variable I imagined as to be beyond systematic investigation) but on to what extent and in what ways, in practice, the analyst senses, conceives and tracks the patient's *response* to his or her various interventions (including silence or cancelled sessions, etc.) and then how they based interventions on this activity. Freud's own comments on the importance of this activity would be well known.[2] I, therefore,

---

[2] Only the further course of the analysis enables us to decide whether our constructions are correct or unserviceable. We do not pretend that an individual construction is anything more than a conjecture which awaits examination, confirmation or rejection. We claim no authority for it, we require no direct agreement from the patient, nor do we argue with

imagined this might be carried out in the analyst's mind at more or less explicit levels and from this perspective I thought we could ask six questions and then compare approaches according to the different extent to which the questions are relevant to them:

1   How does the analyst understand the patient's response to his or her interventions and how does this understanding get used in the next intervention?

2   In listening to the patient's response, at what levels in the material does the analyst appear sensitive? What guides the analyst (e.g. manifest content, latent content, affects, the analyst's own thoughts and feelings in response to the patient's response, etc.)?

3   Does the analyst actually comment on the patient's response to the interventions and to what extent and in what way – for instance, explicitly by explicating it or more indirectly via allusion or metaphor – and what is the rationale and thinking behind these decisions?

4   In considering whether to comment on the patient's response does the analyst have a concept of titration (for instance, being explicitly careful to match how much affect should be provoked in a patient by a comment according to an assessment of the patient's state) and how is this used and with what rationale?

5   Does the analyst seem to conceive that the patient's response to what the analyst says expresses the patient's unconscious thoughts and feelings about what the analyst is feeling, thinking and wanting from the patient at that moment in the session? (In other words how far is the analyst interested in the possibility that his or her interventions are heard within the transference as expressive of the analyst's desires, feelings and thoughts about the patient and with what consequences?)

6   If so, does the analyst talk to the patient about the patient's response to the analyst and how and why?

We had to make some suggestions for how discussions would go in the Prague workshops but formulating the task as one of trying to ask

him if at first he denies it. In short, we conduct ourselves on the model of a familiar figure in one of Nestroy's farces – the manservant who has a single answer on his lips to every question or objection: 'It will all become clear in the course of future developments.'

(Freud, 1937a: 265)

the same questions in each group immediately produced divergent and quite strong reactions, which has been a theme of several chapters in this book. Some colleagues thought it would help to focus discussion in this way – not taking the questions too seriously – while others felt it was profoundly anti-psychoanalytic to approach clinical discussion with prior conceptualization in mind, that the approach was over-cognitive and that the end result would inevitably exclude the unconscious and so be meaningless. I was very well aware that there could be many other ways to approach the task but that so far they had not emerged. My own experience was that comparative analysis – which is not to be confused with how we work in the session itself – is best done within the framework of specific conjecture trying to make that process as explicit as possible and so explicitly modifiable. Although some colleagues seemed to suspect trying to be clear in the psychoanalytic field, I considered that among Freud's many abilities it was his ability systematically to isolate and conceptualize aspects of his subjective experience, write it down and later amend it as new experience came along, that led him to achieve the kind of paradigm shift in thinking about the human subject that he managed.

I also tried to argue that without categorization it was impossible to think (even in the unconscious if we can conceive of that). We needed some form of common and grounded commensurable framework (Bernardi, 2002) from which to develop comparative ways of working if we were to recognize the available patterns of difference.

In any case, Prague was fast approaching and there was another small meeting in Paris to review what had been achieved in Brussels and much debate. (The meeting was attended by Haydée Faimberg, Antonino Ferro, Iréne Mathis and myself.) Feelings for and against using formal questions or what Antonino Ferro immediately and enthusiastically christened a 'grid' approach were strong and it was clear that a compromise was essential: we decided that while the moderators of the Prague groups might be provided with a modified form of these 'questions' as a possibly helpful guide, they should not be pre-circulated to participants nor pressed too much upon moderators who were not to be given them until we reached Prague. Among the difficulties, probably inevitably, was the fact that the way I formulated the questions was rooted in my tradition and my thinking both of which might be quite at odds with others' thinking and other traditions – if true, the six questions could not provide a commensurable framework. I could see this; although my previous experience suggested to me that in fact any questions of this kind would be likely to be understood in hugely different ways and it would be better to start with something we could reject and modify than no framework at all. Aware how unclear the questions were I found it difficult to imagine they could be understood as a demand for conformity and so did not realize at the time how controversial this idea was or the extent of the feelings which would be stirred up.

Despite these difficulties in arriving at a comparative formulation, Haydée Faimberg and I did feel that the Brussels meeting had been hugely illuminating and wanted somehow to convey the good feeling about what we had been trying to do to the colleagues who would take part in the Prague workshops, which we knew by now had struck some kind of chord because they were very heavily over-subscribed. At this point it turned out that the three Prague pre-senters, discussion of whose material might have formed the basis of a panel, could not take part – either because they had other engagements or the clinical material was too delicate for a wider audience. We resolved that Haydée Faimberg would present some previously published and so safe material and that it would be discussed. It was at the time surprising and horrifying when the morning finally arrived to hear this material not formulated as a way of working by a competent (indeed renowned) psychoanalyst, but rather heavily criticized as overlooking various unconscious communications.

Earlier the same morning I had delivered a plenary address setting out the new scientific policy and what we were trying to do (Tuckett, 2002a). I had suggested that at the heart of our effort to facilitate peer culture for psychoanalysis was the need to find ways to describe and compare the essence of what psychoanalysts do in their consulting room and had introduced the Working Party on Clinical Issues under Haydée Faimberg as one way forward. I suggested that it took pride of place in the first 'new style' conference because better ways to describe precisely and to compare clinical methods was essential in several ways:

- To increase the possibility for all of us to reflect on what we are doing and to learn from each other and to debate with each other much more precisely.
- To identify when we think two colleagues are, or are not, in their

detailed practice, using the same or a different psychoanalytic method.

- To give us the future possibility to recognize when a candidate or a colleague who aspires to use a particular psychoanalytic method, is actually using it competently.
- To recognize a pseudo application of any particular psychoanalytic method (model).

I provided some clinical material from my own practice to try to begin thought and to demonstrate that presenting material to each other was a priority. A presentation of this sort is not really the place for a clinical discussion but I soon had the experience I already described for Haydée Faimberg – the one colleague to address my material felt that I had been cruel to my patient and offered me some supervisory advice.

As is shown in many places earlier in this book, this response to listening to clinical material appears to be widespread. The workshops in Prague exemplified it and were discussed in Chapter 3.

After Prague: two ways forward

It fell to Haydée Faimberg (2002) to report on the Prague experience to the EPF council. She wrote:

> In Prague everybody was meeting for the very first time. Our strong warning, 'not to supervise', arising from our experience in Brussels, was the source of some misunderstanding. Several of the groups in Prague equated 'supervision-clinical seminar' with 'understanding the patient's psychic functioning' (as if the first were the only way to understand the latter). Those groups that because of this misunderstanding felt that they were not encouraged as a first step to understand the patient's psyche, experienced some problems in developing their thinking . . . I now think that had we laid a stronger stress on the objective of building a common language to think psychoanalytically, the group would have felt more encouraged to use their potential creativity.

With general recognition that we did not have a meaningful way of formalizing in a written way either the Brussels or Prague experiences to make use of them to describe to a third party the differences between different psychoanalytic approaches, Faimberg pointed out that she now thought we had been struggling with two different and possibly conflicting approaches. On the one hand, she thought, there was a tendency aimed at formalizing a typology of the technical differences in the actual work of analysts – the approach which has been discussed further in this book. On the other hand, there was a wish (at least first) to explore and articulate the basic assumptions (explicit and implicit) that underlie the particular way of working of any particular analyst with a particular patient and the modalities of this work. Both tendencies had the same starting point and the same aim: to study the actual ways of working of experienced and competent psychoanalysts while understanding their differences and respecting them as such. However, the order in which each tendency would take its next steps would be different. The work discussed in this monograph has at its core the typology discussed in the various chapters. The Faimberg group thought there were other priorities.

Faimberg argued that she wanted to aim first at understanding and articulating basic assumptions and that to do this she would work within a free discussion method where the emphasis was on listening to and explicating the assumptions made by presenter *and listeners* during the course of a clinical discussion. The aim would be for members of the group to clarify their own psychoanalytic constructs and hypotheses and so bring out and share their current way of thinking about psychoanalytical issues. The argument was that individuals in the groups so far conducted had too easily translated other people's ideas into their own, without being aware of the underlying principles involved in doing so.

From her perspective Faimberg suggested it was an illusion to imagine that psychoanalysts

> fully understand the basic assumptions of the presenter (underlying his particular way of working) by translating in our own psycho-analytical language what the presenter is trying to convey . . . I think this to be so because such a translation implies, in my view, that the translators have their own language, in other words that each analyst/translator has his own basic assumptions (with which he translates).
>
> (Faimberg, 2002)

A future group discussion method should be based on the idea that psychoanalysts have trained themselves in listening 'not only to recognize the presenter's clinical assumptions but also to recognize *our* assumptions as well.'

Faimberg proposed to create groups with more time to reflect on the method of understanding each other, the articulation between modes of working and underlying basic assumptions. On the basis of how she saw the discussions in Prague and Brussels developing at their best, groups would focus in detail on the clinical material

> as much as on the way in which this clinical material is actually discussed . . . After a presentation, first, one or several participants would attempt to put into words what they understood of the analyst's presentation. Then the presenter would attempt to put into words how he understood the way the others understood his presentation. The process would then go on being repeated from different points of view (including what the presenter understands of this exchange) because new participants try to express their own understanding in an open hypothetical way. [In this way] it could be said that a language is co-created to discuss differences and understand the presenter's work . . . [and] the aim of this kind of dialogue is to explore from different angles the gap, the inevitable misunderstanding (put into words again and again) produced between the various participants. Of course the presenter's own basic assumptions should also be fully explored in this dialogue. There is no reason to think that while others have their own way of understanding his work, the presenter would 'a priori' be dispossessed of the 'right' to discuss his own perspective. I suggest that it is under these conditions that we can faithfully compare how the presenter believes he works and how his mode of work has finally been understood.
>
> (Faimberg, 2002)

These proposals seemed eminently sensible so that together Haydée Faimberg and I resolved that the best way forward was that she would put them into practice by organizing some groups at the next conference while at the same time I would also attempt to develop the typology approach in earnest. We hoped to benefit from both approaches; the clarification that there were two ways also greatly freed us up to pursue both and to see where it led. How I developed the typology and what happened is described in Chapter 6. Haydée Faimberg's parallel groups have continued very successfully.

References

Abrams, S. (1989) Ambiguity in Excess: An Obstacle to Common Ground. *International Journal of Psychoanalysis*, 70: 3–7.

Ahmed, J. (1994) Meeting of Directors of Training Institutes. *Bulletin of the International Psychoanalytical Association*, 75: 184–185.

Allison, G. H. (2000) The Shortage of Psychoanalytic Patients: An Inquiry into its Causes and Consequences. *Psychoanalytic Inquiry*, 20: 527–540.

Assmann, A. (1998) Stabilisatoren der Erinnerung – Affekt, Symbol, Trauma. In J. Rüsen and J. Straub (eds) *Die dunkle Spur der Vergangenheit: Psychoanalytische Zugänge zum Geschichtsbewusstsein. Erinnerung, Geschichte, Identität 2*. Frankfurt a/M: Suhrkamp Taschenbuch Wissenschaft.

Baraldi, C., Corsi, G. and Esposito, E. (1998) *GLU Glossar zu Niklas Luhmanns Theorie sozialer Systeme*. Frankfurt a/M: Suhrkamp Taschenbuch Wissenschaft.

Basile, R. (2006) Flaming Red: A Session with Agnese. *International Journal of Psychoanalysis*, 87: 629–635.

Beland, H. (1998) Am Ende des Vergleichs. In *Talismane: Klaus Heinrich zum 70. Geburtstag*. Basel: Stroemfeld.

Bergmann, M.S. (ed.) (2004) *Understanding Dissidence and Controversy in the History of Psychoanalysis*. New York. Other Press.

Bernard, C. (1999) *Experimental Medicine*. Trans. H. Copley Greene, introd. S. Wolf. New Brunswick, NJ: Transaction.

Bernardi, R. (2002) The Need for True Controversies in Psychoanalysis. *International Journal of Psychoanalysis*, 83: 851–873.

Bion, W. R. (1952) Group Dynamics: A Re-View. *International Journal of Psychoanalysis*, 33: 235–247.

Bion, W. R. (1961) *Experiences in Groups, and Other Papers*. London: Tavistock.

Bion, W. R. (1962) *Learning from Experience*. London: Karnac.

282

Bion, W. R. (1970) *Attention and Interpretation: A Scientific Approach to Insight in Psycho-Analysis and Groups*. London: Tavistock.

Britton, R. (2003) *Sex, Death and the Superego: Experiences in Psychoanalysis*. London: Karnac.

Canestri, J. (2002) Projective Identification: The Fate of the Concept in Italy and Spain. *European Psychoanalytic Federation Bulletin*, 56: 130–139.

Canestri, J. (ed.) (2006) *Psychoanalysis: From Practice to Theory*. London: Karnac.

Canestri, J., Bohleber, W., Denis, P. and Fonagy, P. (2006) The Map of Private (Implicit, Unconscious) Theories in Clinical Practice. In J. Canestri (ed.) *Psychoanalysis: From Practice to Theory*. Whurr Series in Psychoanalysis. Chichester: Wiley.

Chianese, D. (2007) *Constructions and the Analytic Field: History, Scenes and Fate*. New Library of Psychoanalysis. London: Institute of Psychoanalysis and Routledge.

Cooper, A. (1988) Review of *How Does Analysis Cure* by Heinz Kohut. Edited by Arnold Goldberg with collaboration of Paul Stepansky. Chicago: Univ. Chicago Press, 1984, 240 pp., $27.50. *Journal of the American Psychoanalytic Association*, 36: 175–179.

Cooper, A. (2003) Commentary on 'Psychoanalytic Discourse at the Turn of our Century: A Plea for a Measure of Humility'. *Journal of the American Psychoanalytic Association*, 51: 108–114.

Dahl, H., Kaechele, H. and Thomae, H. (eds) (1988) *Psychoanalytic Process Research Strategies*. Heidelberg: Springer.

Dantlgraber, J. (2002) Wolfgang Loch: Die Kunst der Deutung. *Zeitschrift für psychoanalytische Theorie und Praxis / Journal for Psychoanalytical Theory and Practice*, 17, 4. Frankfurt a/M: Stoemfeld.

Donnet, J. (2001) From the Fundamental Rule to the Analysing Situation. *International Journal of Psychoanalysis*, 82: 129–140.

Doolittle, H. (1976) Huldigung an Freud. Rückblick auf eine Analyse. Mit den Briefen von Sigmund Freud an H.D. Berlin: Ullstein. Also in English (1956) *Tribute to Freud*. Edited by N. Holmes Pearson. New York: Pantheon.

Duncan, D. (1993) Theory in Vivo. *International Journal of Psychoanalysis*, 74: 25–32.

Eickhoff, F-W. (1996) Über den Konstruktivismus im Werk Wolfgang Lochs. In H. Henseler (ed.) '. . . da hat mich die Psychoanalyse verschluckt.' In Memoriam Wolfgang Loch. Tübingen: Attempto.

Erikson, E. H. (1956) The Problem of Ego Identity. In *Identity and the Life Cycle*. New York: International University Press.

Faimberg, H. (1996) Listening to Listening. *International Journal of Psychoanalysis*, 77: 667–677.

Faimberg, H. (2002) Working Party on Clinical Issues: Report for the EPF Oslo Joint Meeting, October 2002.

Faimberg, H. (2005) Après Coup. *International Journal of Psychoanalysis*, 86: 1–6.

Fédida, P. (2002) Constructing Place: The Supervision of a Psychoanalytic Cure. Psychoanalysis and Psychotherapy. *European Psychoanalytic Federation Bulletin*, 56.

Feldman, M. (1997) Projective Identification: The Analyst's Involvement. *International Journal of Psychoanalysis*, 78: 227–241.

Feldman, M. (2005) Die Ausleuchtung der Geschichte. *European Psychoanalytic Federation Bulletin*, 59. Jahreshauptkonferenz, Vilamoura, Portugal, 17–20 March.

Ferro, A. (2002) *In the Analyst's Consulting Room*. Hove: Brunner Routledge. Originally published in Italian (1996) *Nella stanza d'analisi: emozioni, racconti, trasformazioni*. Milan: Raffaello Cortina Editore.

Foresti, G. (2005) Playing with Undisciplined Realities. Osservazioni sull'esperienza dei gruppi clinico-teorici della FEP. *Rivista di Psicoanalisi*, 51: 1089–1115.

Frank, C. (2006) Serious Things to be Faced. *International Journal of Psychoanalysis*, 87: 637–639.

Freud, S. (1887–1904) *The Complete Letters of Sigmund Freud to Wilhelm Fliess*. Trans. and edited by J. Moussaieff Masson. Cambridge, MA: Belknap Press of Harvard University Press.

Freud, S. (1900) *The Interpretation of Dreams*. GW 2–3; SE 4–5.

Freud, S. (1907) Delusions and Dreams in Jensen's *Gradiva*. GW 7: 31–125; SE 9: 1–96.

Freud, S. (1909) Analyse der Phobie eines Fünfjährigen Knaben / Analysis of a Phobia in a Five-Year-Old Boy ('Little Hans'). GW 7: 241–377; SE 10: 5–147.

Freud, S. (1911) Formulierungen über die Zwei Prinzipien des Psychischen Geschehens / Formulations on the Two Principles of Mental Functioning. GW 8: 230–238; SE 12: 218–226.

Freud, S. (1912) Recommendations to Physicians Practising Psycho-Analysis; The Case of Schreber, Papers on Technique and Other Works. GW 8: 376–387; SE 12: 109–120.

Freud, S. (1915) Das Unbewußte / The Unconscious. GW 10: 264–303; SE 14: 159–215.

Freud, S. (1918 [1914]) Aus der Geschichte einer infantilen Neurose ('Der Wolfsmann') / From the History of an Infantile Neurosis ('The Wolf-Man'). GW 12: 27–157; SE 17: 1–122.

Freud, S. (1926) *Inhibitions, Symptoms and Anxiety*. SE 20.

Freud, S. (1930) *Civilization and its Discontents*. SE 21.

Freud, S. (1937a) Constructions in Analysis. *GW* 16: 43–56; *SE* 23: 255–270.

Freud, S. (1937b) Konstruktionen in der Analyse. *GW* 16: 43–56; *SE* 23: 255–270.

Freud, S. (1939) *Moses and Monotheism. SE* 23.

Garfinkel, H. (1967) *Studies in Ethnomethodology.* Malden, MA: Polity.

Gattig, E. (2000) Models for Training in Psychotherapy and Psychoanalysis. *European Psychoanalytic Federation Bulletin,* 54.

Glaser, B. and Strauss, A. (1967) *The Discovery of Grounded Theory: Strategies for Qualitative Research.* London: Weidenfeld & Nicolson.

Goldberg, A. (2003) Commentary 1: On How One Sees Catherine. *International Journal of Psychoanalysis,* 84: 1422–1424.

Green, A. (1993) Two Discussions of 'The Inner Experiences of the Analyst' and a Response from Theodore Jacobs. *International Journal of Psychoanalysis,* 74: 1131–1136.

Green, A. (2000) *Le Temps éclaté* [*Time in Psychoanalysis*]. Paris: Presses Universitaires de France.

Guimarães Filho, P. D. (2006) Commentary on the Agnese Case. *International Journal of Psychoanalysis,* 87: 641–644.

Haas, J-P. (2006) Buch-Essay. Spur und Umschrift – Die konstitutive Bedeutung von Erinnerung in der Psychoanalyse. In *Jahrbuch der Psychoanalyse: Beiträge zur Theorie, Praxis und Geschichte,* vol. 52. Stuttgart: Frommann-Holzboog. Also in Haas, J-P. (2006) [Book review] Spur und Umschrift: Die konstitutive Bedeutung von Erinnerung in der Psychoanalyse [Trace and Transcription: The Constitutive Meaning of Remembrance in Psychoanalysis] by Ilka Quindeau. Munich: Fink. 2004. 238 pp. *International Journal of Psychoanalysis,* 87: 1399–1403.

Hanly, C. (2007) The Unconscious: Further Reflections. In J.C. Calich and H. Hinz (eds) *Psychoanalytic Ideas and Applications 5.* London: International Psychoanalytic Association.

Hinz, H. (1991) Gleichschwebende Aufmerksamkeit und die Logik der Abduktion. *Jahrbuch der Psychoanalyse,* 27: 146–175.

Hinz, H. (2001) Zur klinischen Leichtgewichtigkeit des Diskurs-Diskurses. Was Sie schon immer über 'sex and life' wussten und doch nicht glaubten. In *Psyche: Zeitschrift für Psychoanalyse und ihre Anwendungen.* Stuttgart: Klett-Cotta.

Hinz, H. (2002) Projective Identification: The Fate of the Concept in Germany. *European Psychoanalytic Federation Bulletin,* 56: 118–129.

Ilahi, N. (2006) Putting on the Green with Winnicott: Some Reflections on Communicating and Not Communicating across Psychoanalytic Cultures. Unpublished paper presented at the UCL Psychoanalysis Unit Conference, Winnicott Today, 10 June.

Jacobs, T. J. (1993a) The Inner Experiences of the Analyst: Their Contribution to the Analytic Process. *International Journal of Psychoanalysis*, 74: 7–14.

Jacobs, T. J. (1993b) Response. *International Journal of Psychoanalysis*, 74: 1140–1145.

Jaffe, D. S. and Pulver, S. E. (1978) Survey of Psychoanalytic Practice 1976: Some Trends and Implications. *Journal of the American Psychoanalytic Association*, 26: 615–631.

Kernberg, O. F. (1986) Institutional Problems of Psychoanalytic Education. *Journal of the American Psychoanalytic Association*, 34: 799–834.

Kernberg, O. F. (1993) The Current Status of Psychoanalysis. *Journal of the American Psychoanalytic Association*, 41: 45–62.

Kernberg, O. F. (2006) The Coming Changes in Psychoanalytic Education: Part I. *International Journal of Psychoanalysis*, 87: 1649–1673.

Kernberg, O. F. (2007) The Coming Changes in Psychoanalytic Education: Part II. *International Journal of Psychoanalysis*, 88: 183–202.

King, P. and Steiner, R. (eds) (1991) *The Freud–Klein Controversies 1941–1945*. London: Routledge.

Kleinman, A. (1980) *Patients and Healers in the Context of Culture*. Berkeley, CA: University of California Press.

Loch, W. (1972 [1964]) Psychotherapeutische Behandlung psychosomatischer Erkrankungen. In *Zur Theorie, Technik und Therapie der Psychoanalyse. Conditio humana. Ergebnisse aus den Wissenschaften vom Menschen.* Frankfurt a/M: Fischer.

Loch, W. (1976) Psychoanalyse und Wahrheit. In *Psyche: Zeitschrift für Psychoanalyse und ihre Anwendungen.* Stuttgart: Klett-Cotta.

Loch, W. (1988) Rekonstruktionen, Konstruktionen, Interpretationen: Vom 'Selbst-Ich' zum 'Ich-Selbst'. In *Jahrbuch der Psychoanalyse.* Stuttgart: Frommann-Holzboog.

Loch, W. (1991) Variable und invariante Objektbeziehungen im psychoanalytischen Prozeß. In *Jahrbuch der Psychoanalyse: Beiträge zur Theorie und Praxis*, vol. 28. Stuttgart: Frommann-Holzboog.

Loch, W. (2001) *'Mit Freud über Freud hinaus'. Ausgewählte Vorlesungen zur Psychoanalyse.* Compiled and edited by J. Dantlgraber & W. Damson. Tübingen: Edition Diskord.

Loch, W. (2006) *The Art of Interpretation: Deconstruction and New Beginning in the Psychoanalytic Process.* Edited and introd. P. Wegner, trans. H. Hasenclever with G. Jappe. London: International Psychoanalytical Association.

Luhmann, N. (1995) *Soziologische Aufklärung 6. Die Soziologie und der Mensch.* Opladen: Westdeutscher.

McCall, G. G. and Simmons, J. L. (1966) *Identities and Interactions.* New York: Free Press.

McGuinness, T. (2006) Discussion. *International Journal of Psychoanalysis*, 87: 1443–1446.

Malinowski, B. (1922) *Argonauts of the Western Pacific: An Account of Native Enterprise and Adventure in the Archipelagos of Melanesian New Guinea*. London: Routledge & Kegan Paul.

Matte-Blanco, I. (1988) *Thinking, Feeling and Being: Clinical Reflections on the Fundamental Antinomy of Human Beings and World*. New Library of Psychoanalysis. London: Institute of Psychoanalysis and Routledge.

Matthis, I. (2003) To Play or Not to Play with a Grid. Unpublished report on the Sorrento workshops.

Mead, G.H. (1934) *Mind, Self, and Society*. Chicago, IL: University of Chicago Press.

Miller, N., Luborsky, L., Barber, J. and Docherty, J. (eds) (1993) *Handbook of Dynamic Psychotherapy Research and Practice*. New York: Basic Books.

Money-Kyrle, R.E. (1968) Cognitive Development. *International Journal of Psychoanalysis*, 49: 691–698.

Money-Kyrle, R.E. (1971) The Aim of Psychoanalysis. *International Journal of Psychoanalysis*, 52: 103–106.

Parsons, T. (1951) *The Social System*. New York: Free Press.

Peirce, C.S. (1958) *Collected Papers of Charles Sanders Peirce*. Volumes I–VI edited by C. Hartshorne and P. Weiss, 1931–1935; Volumes VII–VIII edited by A.W. Burke 1931–1958. Cambridge, MA: Harvard University Press.

Quindeau, I. (2004) *Spur und Umschrift: Die konstitutive Bedeutung von Erinnerung in der Psychoanalyse* [*Trace and Transcription: The Constitutive Meaning of Remembrance in Psychoanalysis*]. Munich: Wilhelm Fink.

Reiche, R. (1999) Subjekt, Patient, Außenwelt. (Subject, Patient, Outside World.) In *Psyche: Zeitschrift für Psychoanalyse und ihre Anwendungen*, vol. 53. Stuttgart: Klett-Cotta.

Richards, A.D. (2003) Psychoanalytic Discourse at the Turn of our Century: A Plea for a Measure of Humility. *Journal of the American Psychoanalytic Association*, 51: 73–89.

Rickman, J. (ed.) (1937) On 'Unbearable' Ideas and Impulses. *American Journal of Psychology*, 50: 248–253. Also in J. Rickman (1957) *Selected Contributions to Psycho-Analysis*. London: Hogarth Press.

Rolland, J. (2006) A Young Woman's Distress. *International Journal of Psychoanalysis*, 87: 1433–1442.

Rothstein, A. (1992) Observations on the Utility of Couples Therapy Conducted by a Psychoanalyst: Transference and Countertransference in Resistance to Analysis. *Psychoanalytic Quarterly*, 61: 519–541.

Roussillon, R. (2003) Commentary 2. *International Journal of Psychoanalysis*, 84: 1424–1429.

Sandler, J. J. (1983) Reflections on Some Relations between Psychoanalytic Concepts and Psychoanalytic Practice. *International Journal of Psychoanalysis*, 64: 35–45.

Schafer, R. (1990) The Search for Common Ground. *International Journal of Psychoanalysis*, 71: 49–52.

Schneider, G. (2003) Fokalität und Afokalität in der (psychoanalytischen) Tiefenpsychologisch Fundierten Psychotherapie und Psychoanalyse. In A. Gerlach, A.-M. Schlösser u. A. Springer (eds) *Psychoanalyse mit und ohne Couch*. Haltung und Methode. Gießen (Psychosozial-VerB.), 108–127.

Schutz, A. (1953) Translated from the German (1973) The Problem of Social Reality. In *Collected Papers Volume 1*. The Hague: Martinus Nijhoff.

Séchaud, E. (2000) Discussion of Ekkehard Gattig's Paper. *European Psychoanalytic Federation Bulletin*, 54.

Spillius, E. (2002) A Brief Introduction to the Concept of Projective Identification. *Bulletin of the European Psychoanalytic Federation*, 56: 115–118.

Stein, R. (2006) Commentary. *International Journal of Psychoanalysis*, 87: 1447–1451.

Tuckett, D. (1993) Some Thoughts on the Presentation and Discussion of the Clinical Material of Psychoanalysis. *International Journal of Psychoanalysis*, 74: 1175–1189.

Tuckett, D. (1994) Developing a Grounded Hypothesis to Understand a Clinical Process. *International Journal of Psychoanalysis*, 75: 1159–1180.

Tuckett, D. (2000) Theoretical Pluralism and the Construction of Psychoanalytic Knowledge. In J. Sandler, R. Michels and P. Fonagy (eds) *Changing Ideas in a Changing World: The Revolution in Psychoanalysis. Essays in Honour of Arnold M. Cooper*. London: Karnac.

Tuckett, D. (2002a) The New Style Conference and Developing a Peer Culture in European Psychoanalysis: Presidential Address, Prague. *European Psychoanalytic Federation Bulletin*, 56.

Tuckett, D. (2002b) Subsidiary Report of the Working Party on Clinical Issues: Towards a Comparative Typology (Track 1) Presented to EPF Joint Meeting, Oslo, October.

Tuckett, D. (2003) How Did 18 Different Psychoanalyst Work? Some Reflections on the Track 1 Working Party on Clinical Issues (WPCI) Reports from Sorrento. Unpublished report to the EPF Council, available on the EPF website.

Tuckett, D. (2004) A Ten Year European Scientific Initiative. EPF Presidential Address. *European Psychoanalytic Federation Bulletin*, 58.

Tuckett, D. (2005) Does Anything Go? *International Journal of Psychoanalysis*, 86: 31–49.

Tuckett, D. (2007) Civilization and its Discontents Today. In L. Braddock and M. Lacewing (eds) *The Academic Face of Psychoanalysis*. London: Routledge.

Tuckett, D., Boulton, M., Olson, C. and Williams, A. (1985) *Meetings between Experts: An Approach to Sharing Ideas in Medical Consultations*. London: Tavistock.

Uexküll, T.v. and Wesiack, W. (1988) *Theorie der Humanmedizin. Grundlagen ärztlichen Denkens und Handelns*. Munich: Urban & Schwarzenberg.

Vermote, R. (2003) Two Sessions with Catherine. *International Journal of Psychoanalysis*, 84: 1415–1422.

Waelder, R. (1980) Das Prinzip der mehrfachen Funktion. Bemerkungen zur Überdeterminierung. In *Ansichten der Psychoanalyse. Eine Bestandsaufnahme*. Stuttgart: Klett-Cotta. Zuerst erschienen (1930) *Internationale Zeitschrift für Psychoanalyse*, 16: 3–4.

Wallerstein, R. (1988) One Psychoanalysis or Many? *International Journal of Psychoanalysis*, 69: 5–21.

Wallerstein, R. (1990) Psychoanalysis: The Common Ground. *International Journal of Psychoanalysis*, 71: 3–20.

Weber, M. (1920) Wirtschaft und Gesellschaft. Trans. from the German as *Economy and Society*. Volume 1: *Conceptual Exposition*. New York: Bedminster Press.

Wurmser, L. (1989) Vom Handwerk Des Psychoanalytikers: Das Werkzug Der Psychoanalytischen Technik: By Johannes Cremerius. Stuttgart-Cannstadt: Frommann-Holzboog, 1984, 2 vol., 448 pp. *Journal of the American Psychoanalytic Association*, 37: 233–239.

Wurmser, L. (1994) A Time of Questioning: The Severely Disturbed Patient within Classical Analysis. *Annual of Psychoanalysis*, 22: 173–207.

Index

abductive conclusions 124
action vector 160
activity balance 225–6; group members 225–6; moderator's role 225–6; presenter's role 225–6
affects 273–4
anal modalities 121
analyst orientation 213
analytic process 187
analytic situation 184–5, 197
analytic space 102
Analytical Shared Idealistic Ego 240
annual conference 1, 263
anxiety 13–15, 57–8, 102, 109, 126
Athens workshops (2006) xix, 12, 68–9, 85, 234–5; dialogue 240
authority 6, 8–9

Babelization 62–3
Balint, Michael 116
Barcelona workshops (2007) 12
basic assumption organization 19, 29, 62; evaluation 19; regression 34; Step 0 171
being vs doing dichotomy 60
Beland, Hermann, comparison 10, 106, 108
Berlin Institute 163
Bion, W. R.: basic assumption organization 19, 29, 62, 171; beta and alpha elements 120; caesura 130; Grid

73, 171, 239; inherited expectation 113; K (knowledge) 236, 239; models 94; paranoid-schizoid and depressive position 119; realization 89, 91; selected fact 124; without memory and desire 79, 241; work group 235
boundaries, problems 19
Bowlby, J. 56–7
British model 91–3, 95, 154, 235, 269
British Psychoanalytical Society 42
Brown, George Spender 97
Brussels meeting (2001) xix, 11–12, 95, 132, 266–77; supervision 26

Canestri, Jorge: Working Party on Theoretical Issues (WPTI) 265
case discussion 234–42; Analytical Shared Idealistic Ego 240; culture 235; emotionality 235; grid 236; language 235; moderator's role 236; presenters' experience 237; rights to citizenship 237–8; supervision group 235–6; supervision and new method 238–42; technique 235; timeframe 235–6; without memory and desire 241
categorization 101–2
characters 196–7
clinical discussion 195–207, 245; evolving understanding 197–203; free discussion 200–3; new method of

291

treatment of unconscious phenomena 42–3

two-step method 21, 33–7, 85, 104, 132–66, 248–9; basic assumption regression 34; clinical discussion 195–207; discussion method 134–5; framework 134; grid as instrument 33; grid used instrumentally 33; internal template construction 147–9; introduction 172–3; moderator role 34–5, 134; preliminary testing 145–9; presenter task 134; questionnaire 35; six intervention categories 135–7; Step 0 34, 134; Step 1 34–5, 101, 109, 135–6, 138–44; Step 1 revision 154–7; Step 1 testing 145–9; Step 2 34–5, 101, 108–9, 135–6, 144–5; Step 2 development 133, 157–66; Step −1 34, 135; supervision 36; trial case 149–54; work group 34

two-step method use 167–207; clinical discussion 195–207; method introduction 172–3; Step 0 170–2; Step 1 173–8; Step 2 179–82; Step 2 group discussion 182–95; Step −1 167–8; Step −2 167–8

typology *see* grid

unanimity and disagreement 229–31
unconscious processes 8, 36, 46, 117–22
understanding other's perspective: Prague 59–60

verbalization 24
Vermote, Rudi: presentation 22, 25–8; supervision 25–6

Vilamoura workshops (2005) xix, 12, 85; presenter 209

Waelder, Robert 122–3; interpretation 125; multiple functions 123; multiple meanings 123; repetition compulsion 122–3
Wallerstein, R. 243–4; theoretical pluralism 243
warming up 56
Weber, Max: ideal type form of analysis 146; social organization 30
Winnicott, D. W. 57–8, 98, 204–5; New York Psychoanalytic Society (1967) 26; object use 274
without memory and desire 241
work groups 29, 34; performance 19
working from the surface 54
working methods 14–15
working parties 263–5; areas 264–5; function 20–1
Working Party on Clinical Issues (WPCI) 50, 70, 262, 277; Brussels meeting (2001) 266–77; Haydée Faimberg 262; questions for consideration 265
Working Party on Comparative Clinical Methods (WPCCM) 21, 70–1, 96, 99, 234
Working Party on Education (WPE) 20
Working Party on Interface (WPI) 20
Working Party on Theoretical Issues (WPTI) 149, 159; Jorge Canestri 21, 265; questions for consideration 265
workshops: languages 12, 50, 54; problems 13; response 12–13; structure 12